Advance Praise for *Investing in a Sustainable World*
by Matthew J. Kiernan, Ph.D.

"Matthew Kiernan has redefined global thinking around sustainable finance and responsible investment. Without Kiernan's work since the late 1980s, the battle to drag institutional investors to the sustainability table would have been immeasurably harder. Kiernan's magic, as this book gives witness to, is based on a deep intellect, the confidence to continually challenge the investment status quo and the ability to see fundamental changes in the markets well in advance of the mainstream."

—Paul Clemants Hunt
Head, United Nations Environmental
Program Finance Initiative (UNEP FI),
Member of the Board
Principles for Responsible
Investment (PRI)

"If you're a long-term investor, you have to care about sustainability, because it also equates to the ultimate sustainability of corporate earnings. As a fund that invests across multiple generations, we believe that seeking short term gains at the expense of our planet and mankind will ultimately prove too costly to long-term corporate earnings and therefore reduce our overall return. We at CalSTRS therefore take this book's messages very much to heart."

—Christopher Ailman, Chief Investment Officer CalSTRS

"In an age where financial risks are prowling "the street," where complex instruments defy evaluation, where profits are privatized and losses are nationalized, Matthew Kiernan argues passionately—and convincingly—that the financial markets can, and should, become an engine for improving environmental and social conditions rather than for undermining them!"

—James L. Goodfellow F.C.A., Vice Chairman,
Deloitte & Touche (Canada)

"Matthew Kiernan has successfully scaled the Green Wall that often separates those working in the financial and sustainability domains. His latest book demystifies the concept of sustainable investment and provides a compelling rationale for Wall Street to consider environmental and social criteria, not as afterthoughts but rather as core considerations in our investment decision-making framework."

—Abyd Karmali, Managing Director,
Merrill Lynch/Bank of America

"Why should savers watch passively as their nest eggs shrink? Matthew Kiernan's sparkling, breakthrough book explains why they don't have to—and how they can protect—and even expand—their investments."
—Dr. Stephen Davis, Project Director and Fellow
Millstein Center for Corporate Governance & Performance
Yale School of Management

"Matthew Kiernan has turned his considerable experience and energy on the ES themes into this lucid but sophisticated narrative. This is perfectly timed to inform investors of the early mover advantage that is achievable in this field."
—Roger Urwin, Watson Wyatt Worldwide

"A colorful and personal analysis examining why the financial sector, for the most part, has not understood that increasingly business success will be shaped by both social and environmental challenges. Highly recommended."
—Bjorn Stigson, President,
World Business Council for Sustainable Development

"*Investing in a Sustainable World* explains the new sustainability paradigm driving the way investors, companies, and indeed society must now think about value creation. Kiernan masterfully dissects the forces that are transforming the landscape of capitalism, and he highlights trends that investors must take into account and that corporate leaders simply cannot afford to ignore."
—Dr. James C. Murphy, Director,
International Institute for Strategic Studies

"Climate change has the potential to be the dominant investment theme of the 21st century. There are people who know about climate and change and there are those who know about investing. In Matthew you have someone who is passionately and effectively involved in both. That's why this should be at the top of your reading pile."
—Alan Brown, Group Chief Investment Officer,
Schroders Investment Management

"Never boring, always provocative and challenging . . . mainstream investment professionals who ignore Matthew Kiernan's messages here will do so at their peril."
—Tim Gardener, Global Head of Investment Strategy,
Mercer Investment Consulting

"True to form, this book is both provocative and opinionated. In a field where much that is put to paper is either mind-numbingly technical or just bland, this book is a refreshing change!"
—Dr. Raj Thamotheram, Head of Responsible Investments,
AXA Investment Management

"Investors can enhance their own competitiveness through innovations that take closer account of environmental risks and rewards, recognizing the growing nexus between finance and sustainable development. In this important, timely, and compelling book, Kiernan shows how this can be done, and why it is essential if we are to forge an economy the earth can sustain indefinitely."
—William L. Thomas, Counsel
Skadden, Arps, Slate, Meagher & Flom LLP

"Financial investment and sustainable development are allies, not adversaries. With Matthew Kiernan's expertise, talent, persuasion, and sense of humor in *Investing in a Sustainable World*, you'll see that it's a simple but powerful idea."
—Antoine de Salins, Member of the Board,
French Pensions Reserve Fund (FRR)

Praise for Matthew Kiernan's previous book, *The 11 Commandments of 21st Century Management*:

"A brilliant and prescient analysis by one of the most original and visionary thinkers—and doers—I know. We ignore its messages at our peril."
—Maurice F. Strong, 7-time Under-Secretary General of the
United Nations Senior Advisor to the President of the World Bank

INVESTING
IN A
SUSTAINABLE
WORLD

INVESTING
IN A
SUSTAINABLE
WORLD

Why GREEN Is the New Color of
Money on Wall Street

MATTHEW J. KIERNAN, PH.D.

AMACOM

New York • Atlanta • Brussels • Chicago • Mexico City • San Francisco
Shanghai • Tokyo • Toronto • Washington, D. C.

This publication is designed to provide accurate and authoritative information in regard to the subject matter covered. It is sold with the understanding that the publisher is not engaged in rendering
legal, accounting, or other professional service. If legal advice or other expert assistance is required, the services of a competent professional person should be sought. Although this book does
not specifically identify trademarked names, AMACOM uses them for editorial purposes only, with
no intention of trademark violation.

Library of Congress Cataloging-in-Publication Data

Kiernan, Matthew J.
   Investing in a sustainable world : why GREEN is the new color of money on Wall Street /
Matthew J. Kiernan.
      p.   cm.
   Includes index.
   ISBN 978-0-8144-1092-9
   1. Investments—Enviornmental aspects.   2. Investments—Social aspects.   3. Green
movement.   4. Social responsibility of business.   5. Investment analysis.   I. Title.   II. Title:
GREEN is the new color of money on Wall Street.
   HF451.K54   2009
   332.6—dc22   2008030023

This title is printed on 60# Thor Plus D56 Antique, which is (ECF) Elemental Chlorine Free, meeting the requirements of American National Standard for Information Sciences-Permanence of Paper
(ANSI) Z39.48-1992, is Sustainable Forestry Initiative (SFI), and has 15% PCW (post-consumer
waste) content.

Printing number
10 9 8 7 6 5 4 3 2 1

Contents

Changing Finance and Financing Change: The Genesis of This Book

In one sense, this book has taken more than 20 years to write; it is the product of three different sets of experiences, dating back at least until 1987. At that time, I was a senior partner in the strategy consulting practice of KPMG, the global accounting and consulting firm. I was part of a team working on a billion-dollar privatization project in the forest products sector. (This was *so* long ago that a billion dollars was actually a reasonably significant amount of money!) The transaction came very, very close to collapsing, primarily because of community and governmental concerns about the project's potentially adverse environmental and social impacts. Although I had completed a Master's degree in environmental studies 15 years previously, this was actually my first practical, real-world indication that environmental and social issues could readily become critical *business* and financial issues as well.

The second set of experiences that directly catalyzed this book occurred several years later. I had left KPMG and had the unique opportunity to become a director with what is now the World Business Council for Sustainable Development (WBCSD) in Geneva, Switzerland. Founded in 1989 and led by Swiss industrialist and billionaire Stephan Schmidheiny, the WBCSD had been given the somewhat daunting task of representing "the private sector" and advising the Secretary General of the UN Earth Summit in Rio de Janeiro in 1992. In short order, Schmidheiny had managed to assemble a "dream team" of global industry titans:

the chairmen or CEOs of leading companies, such as DuPont, Royal Dutch/Shell, Mitsubishi, Volkswagen, and Dow Chemical.

Despite having this "who's who" of global business luminaries in tow, however, Schmidheiny could *not* in the early days recruit a single banker or financier to join the group! Normally, in my limited experience, invitations from multibillionaires are reasonably well received by bank chairmen. This is particularly true when the invitation *also* includes an 18-month opportunity to rub shoulders with more than two dozen heads of the world's leading industrial companies (i.e., mouth-wateringly attractive potential banking clients!) Notwithstanding these commercial inducements—not to mention a fascinating, worthwhile, and totally unprecedented group challenge—Schmidheiny was turned down by the chairmen of several of the largest banks in the world. The reason? At that point, the bankers literally could not see the connection between what they did for a living and the future of the planet. As one bank chairman put it at the time: "But we don't cut down *any* trees here at the bank; your mission has nothing to do with us." Well, there you have it, then! Silly us for even asking!

Lacking a proper global bank chairman, it initially fell to me to coordinate the work of the WBCSD's task force on capital markets. It was a galvanizing, breakthrough experience for me. For the first time, I began to understand the truly transformational potential of the global financial markets. They were, after all, the providers of the financial "oxygen supply" for most of the world's largest companies.

I reasoned that even if major corporations had not in fact created 75 percent of the world's environmental and social *problems,* they certainly represented at least 75 percent of the potential *solutions.* But in order for this to happen, their behavior simply *had* to change. I know of only two sure-fire ways to turn an industrial CEO into a sustainability advocate and practitioner. One is to ensure that his 16-year-old daughter consistently hectors him at breakfast about the deplorable environmental and social track record of his company. This is highly effective, but very difficult to pull off on any kind of a large scale!

The *other* way would be to send him a clear message through the financial markets. If his company's share price suffered or desired bank loans became more expensive or even unavailable altogether because of significant environmentally or socially driven risks or poor performance, that *would* get his attention—and quickly! Now that *could* achieve a large-scale systematic impact!

First, however, there were two major obstacles to overcome:

- Investors first needed to be convinced that environmental and social (ES) risk, performance, and strategic positioning could actually be financially and competitively *material;* and
- Investors would need access to credible, financially oriented company *research,* so that they could begin to distinguish corporate leaders from laggards and then act on that information.

If the tepid response to Schmidheiny's overtures to the global bank chairmen was anything to go by, it promised to be a long, uphill struggle indeed! Neither key precondition could be achieved quickly or easily, but someone had to start somewhere. I decided that the "somebody" might as well be me and that the "somewhere" needed to be the creation of a totally different kind of investment research company.

That new research vehicle turned out to be Innovest Strategic Value Advisors, about which we will hear more in Chapter 10.[1] The 15-plus years that my colleagues and I have spent since then helping build Innovest's global business have provided the third set of experiences that directly catalyzed this book. Over that time, my colleagues and I researched both the sustainability *and* financial performance of thousands of companies from all over the world. In some cases, we tracked them for a full decade; in virtually all cases, it was for a period of at least 5 years. The results of that research were unequivocal: *companies with superior performance and positioning on "sustainability" (i.e., environmental and social) issues achieved, on average, superior financial returns.* In the course of that 15-year period, I have personally "pitched" the sustainable investment thesis to hundreds of trustees at pension funds and foundations, to chief investment officers and senior investment bankers, and to pension fund consultants all over the world. The results of all of these interactions have convinced me of six fundamental "truths":

1. Environmental and social issues and problems are not "just" problems on those levels alone; they are also absolutely—and increasingly—critical to the competitiveness and financial performance of both individual companies and the broader economies and societies in which they operate.
2. Any serious attempt to make a *systematic* impact on global environmental and social problems will absolutely *require* the fundamental

reengineering of the very "DNA" of the capital markets. Those issues must be brought from the periphery of the investment decision-making process—at best—into its very center. Nothing less comprehensive could possibly suffice.

3.   At present, most of the major players in the financial markets remain blissfully, if not determinedly, unaware of the close connection between companies' ES performances and their financial results.[2] And the vast majority of those few who *have* even considered such a connection are highly skeptical about it.

4.   This lack of awareness—or even hostility—could be costing a lot of people a lot of money. Contrary to widespread belief among "professional" investors, the failure to systematically consider ES risks and opportunities in investment decisions is very likely *impoverishing*, not improving, their financial results.

5.   This, in turn, means that ordinary investors and savers are essentially being short changed. There is a better than even chance that the managers of their pension plans and mutual funds are *not* performing as well as they could be. In brief, people's money is being left on the table.

6.   For this situation to improve significantly, *all* of the key actors in the investment "food chain" will need to be convinced of the potential materiality of ES factors to companies' financial performances. This includes the asset owners and their trustees and fiduciaries, the asset managers, and the researchers, analysts, and consultants who advise them all.

Providing the arguments and evidence necessary to do that convincing is the primary purpose of this book. It is designed to accomplish at least four major objectives:

*   To provide a compelling *investment* case—not necessarily an ethical one—for integrating environmental and social considerations directly into the investment process;
*   To attempt to explain why, despite the powerful logic for doing so, this practice remains overwhelmingly the exception rather than the rule;
*   To provide concrete examples of some leading-edge organizations that are pioneering new approaches—and several that should be but are *not;* and

- To provide both the conceptual and practical tools necessary to equip investors—both institutional and individual—to "future-proof" their portfolios by integrating environmental and social factors.

It will, of course, be for the reader to decide how well or poorly those objectives have been met. I, for one, have become absolutely convinced of at least one thing, however: that the systematic integration—or at least consideration—of ES factors has now become an absolute imperative. Both financial returns and the fate of the planet depend on it.

The book's intended audience is necessarily a broad one: ordinary savers and investors ("Main Street"), professional money managers and investment banks ("Wall Street"), the trustees, fiduciaries, and investment consultants for pension funds, endowments, and foundations, and their professional staffs. It is also hoped that the book will be of interest and value to the executives, boards, and staffs of the *companies* that investors are evaluating and considering. At this stage of the game, the corporations are, on the whole, far ahead of their investors in this regard, but I hope that even they will find some new insights and ideas in this book that will help them do their jobs even better.

There is one additional—and powerful—motivation for writing this book. I hope that it will help to fill a critically important void that I believe still exists in the burgeoning literature about sustainability. In addition to a constant barrage of information in the daily media and popular press, a number of excellent books have been written on the subject over the past few years. At least two of them are being published virtually contemporaneously with this one. They are by world-class writers and thinkers Tom Friedman and Peter Senge.[3] Those books focus on a number of the key elements in the "value chain of change"—government, private sector corporations, nongovernmental organizations, and civil society. While each of these sets of actors undeniably has a major role to play in the Sustainability Revolution, none, in my view, has anything *close* to the overwhelming, transformational power of investors and the capital markets. The financial markets constitute the "financial oxygen supply" for the major corporations that determine so many of the actual sustainability impacts and outcomes on the ground. Despite this, however, the sustainability literature has remained curiously silent on both the current and potential role of finance and *investors.* Since I firmly believe them to be *the* single most critical variable in the equation, this book is intended to focus attention there, where I believe it is long overdue.

A "Road Map" to the Book

Chapter 1 introduces the reader to the brave new world of investing in the first decade of the twenty-first century. As we shall see, it is a world increasingly being shaped by an unprecedented confluence of powerful global megatrends. Those trends pose fundamental challenges to a number of deeply embedded orthodoxies in investment thinking and practice. Among the most fundamental and transformational of those emerging trends is the inexorable increase in the importance of ES factors. Investors who fail or refuse to come to grips with them are likely to be increasingly marginalized—and financially unsuccessful.

Chapter 2 explores the reasons *why,* despite their growing importance, ES factors have historically received such short shrift from investment experts. A series of powerful myths and misconceptions has effectively blinded them to both the risks *and* the opportunities that ES factors can present. It is hoped that a better understanding of both the genesis and the anatomy of that mythology will help to accelerate its repudiation and disappearance.

Chapter 3 looks at some of the rather bizarre real-world *results* of those cognitive blinders. It is a litany of both perverse behavior and significant lost opportunities, and it will surprise even sustainability "experts" who will, logically enough, have presumed such things to be impossible in this day and age.

Chapter 4 then takes a look at what the evidence *actually* says about the impact of including sustainability factors. Setting the record straight is vitally important here. For far too long—indeed, for decades now—investment professionals have solemnly reassured their clients that ES factors were at best irrelevant and at worst actively injurious to their financial returns. On those rare occasions where their clients might dare to push back, they were almost invariably assured that there is a vast body of financial performance "evidence" to support the advisor's or money manager's contention. (This is often accomplished by the additional, patronizing implication that this evidence is so abstruse and difficult to comprehend that only a trained investment professional could possibly fathom it. "Just trust me.") Well, it turns out that while there *is* indeed a large and growing body of both academic and empirical evidence on the subject, most of it points to a *positive,* rather than a negative, impact from considering ES factors. It is, we believe, vitally important to put the *real* evidence on the table, to counter the widespread misconceptions to the contrary. And what is even *more* important is that *regardless* of what the historical evidence says, the major megatrends currently reshaping the global investment environment make it virtually certain that this positive impact will become even *greater* as we go forward.

Chapter 5 attempts to outline the conceptual underpinnings of a new "theory" or approach to "sustainable investing"—that is, investing as if environmental and social factors actually *matter*. At this point the reader might object: "but isn't there already an entire, well-established school of 'socially responsible' investing (SRI), for which ES issues are absolutely *central?*" Quite true, but they remain a relatively peripheral, statistically small segment of the market, and anyway, those investors already "get it" and need no convincing from us about the saliency of ES factors.

Instead, this book is primarily directed at the *other* 95 percent of the investment world—those whose primary concerns are good *financial* returns, a college education for their kids, and a secure retirement. They likely fall into one of two categories: those who have never even *heard of* or considered the notion of integrating ES factors in their investment strategies, and those who have considered it and rejected it, often on the advice of "expert" advisors. It is primarily for *them* that this book is written. Chapter 5 provides a conceptual and theoretical foundation for sustainable investing and places it in the broader context of overall investment theory. We present here a new, *post*modern theory of investing.

Chapter 6 is intended to take a step back and remind us why all of this matters in the first place. It provides a quick "crash course" tutorial on where we actually stand today—and are likely to stand tomorrow—with respect to the major environmental and social challenges of our time. We examine briefly critical sustainability issues, such as climate change, air and water pollution, human and labor rights, access to affordable medicines in emerging markets, and global poverty and income inequality. This chapter argues that we simply cannot afford—environmentally, socially, *or* financially—to continue along our current investment trajectories.

Chapter 7 shifts gears and perspectives somewhat and focuses on the kinds of *companies* that sustainability investors will want to consider. It demonstrates how and *why* ES issues have become increasingly critical to companies' competitive success. It also highlights the opportunity/ upside part of the ES equation for companies. Too many boards and executive teams, like their investors, have tended to view ES issues as primarily—if not exclusively—sources of downside risk. Chapter 7 uses real-world examples from a wide variety of both countries and industry sectors of innovative companies that have both recognized and seized some of the myriad new business *opportunities* being created by the "Sustainable

Investment Revolution." These examples should be illuminating for both company leaders *and* investors alike, and, for the latter, should point them toward the sorts of twenty-first century companies for which they and their investment advisors should be searching constantly. This chapter is intended to put to rest the widely held belief that it is possible to choose to invest *either* in more "sustainable" companies *or* financial outperformers, but not both. It provides proof that this is possible and reinforces some of the aggregated statistical findings of Chapter 4.

The next three chapters (8–10) focus on the "Game-Changers"— the cutting-edge organizations and individuals who are currently leading the Sustainable Investment Revolution. They are all from different perspectives, but with dizzying speed, building the organizational and conceptual infrastructure of this emerging new investment universe. Chapter 8 focuses on a number of examples of unprecedented collaborations among large and diverse groups of investors and other stakeholders. Chapter 9 profiles *individual* asset owners—pension funds, endowments, and foundations—that are pioneering new ways of integrating environmental and social factors into their investment strategies and decisions. Chapter 10 looks at the service providers—the consultants, advisors, researchers, and money managers—who are helping redefine both leading-edge thinking and practice in this emerging new investment field. Chapters 8, 9, and 10 together are meant to provide positive proof that sustainability investment *can* indeed be done, and done successfully and profitability.

Chapter 11 proceeds from the optimistic assumption that the reader will by that point be convinced that environmental and social factors *must*—and can—in fact be systematically considered in any successful, forward-looking investment strategy. It is intended as a bit of a "how-to" manual; once convinced of the merits of sustainable investing, the reader will still need some new tools to actually get it done. It is hoped that Chapter 11 can help provide at least some of them. For some specific investment decisions, upon closer examination, it may turn out that ES factors simply do *not* in fact loom large. If so, fair enough; the important point is that they should at least be seriously *considered* before they are rejected out of hand as immaterial. At present this is emphatically *not* the case, but it should be and it *can* be.

Chapter 12 provides some concluding thoughts and a reminder that "sustainability"—and therefore sustainability investment—is a dynamic, moving target, with the "bar" being raised constantly. Complacency has no place in the vocabulary of the sustainability investor.

At the end of the day, though, this book is really all about awareness and *empowerment*. It is intended to provide readers with both the conceptual and practical tools to make a real difference with their investment assets. Most investors and their advisors are not yet fully aware of the potential that they have to combine environmental, social, *and* financial objectives at the same time. Once this realization emerges, the potential for wholesale global transformation will truly have arrived. The financial markets will have become an engine for *improving* environmental and social conditions rather than for undermining them!

So, welcome to the Sustainable Investment Revolution! Investors of the world unite! You have nothing to lose but your philosophical and intellectual chains.

Acknowledgments

This book was written in a somewhat unconventional fashion, with direct implications for the Acknowledgments. *No one* reviewed draft chapters and gave helpful suggestions; in fairness, they were never asked to. Indeed, no one saw so much as a single paragraph until this book was completed. For better or worse, this approach gives new meaning to the classic bromide that "any errors or mistakes are the responsibility of the author." *That's* for sure! As a result, the usual acknowledgments to the kind souls who enriched the book by commenting on it cannot truthfully be made here. That is *not*, however, to imply that I am without intellectual debts; far from it. Individuals far too numerous to mention (some of them perhaps unknowingly) have contributed to my ongoing and sometimes painful education over the past 15 years—roughly the gestation period of this book.

Chief among them are my colleagues and friends at Innovest Strategic Value Advisors. First among equals are Hewson Baltzell, Andy White, and Pierre Trevet, as well as my former Innovest colleague Martin Whittaker. I also owe a huge debt to my talented research assistants: Priti Shokeen, Nick Brown, Simon Gargonne, and Darwin Fletcher. Their work on the dozens of case studies was literally indispensable.

I am also indebted to my literary agent Cynthia Zigmund, who engineered what was for me a match made in heaven with my publisher, AMACOM. At AMACOM, I am particularly grateful to American Management Association CEO Ed Reilly and AMACOM President Hank Kennedy for their vision, enthusiasm, and consistent support throughout the project. My editor, Bob Shuman, was unfailingly both accessible and helpful, and both I and the reader are the beneficiaries of his many contributions. Barbara Chernow and Andy Ambraziejus also made major contributions to both the quality and the timely emergence of the book; my thanks to both of them!

Finally, I will always be in the debt of my family: my wife Catherine Harris and our children—now young adults—Susannah and Patrick. All three are a constant inspiration. And, for Susannah, additional special thanks for the expert and patient shepherding of the manuscript.

Chapter 1

Welcome to the Sustainable Investment Revolution!

It is becoming increasingly clear that sustainable development will be one of the major drivers of industrial change over the next 50 years, and that there is a growing demand from both companies and institutional investors to understand its financial impacts.

—COLIN MONKS, HEAD OF EUROPEAN EQUITY RESEARCH, HSBC

The Imperative—and the Opportunity— for Twenty-First Century Investors

The world of international investment is now on the cusp of a revolution more profound than anything it has witnessed in literally decades. Hard-nosed Wall Street investment bankers, not a species previously noted for excessive hand wringing about environmental quality, social justice, or the fate of the planet, are suddenly writing reports about climate change, water scarcity, human rights in China, and a host of other topics that they have been studiously avoiding for most of their careers. Large pension funds from Sacramento to Bangkok, under strict fiduciary obligations to focus only on issues directly material to investment performance, are now beginning to pay close attention to these same issues and to allocate money to "sustainability" funds for the first time.

In less than 18 months, the United Nations Principles for Responsible Investment have already attracted more than 380 signatories, with combined assets under management of over *$14 trillion.* Investment banks, such as Goldman Sachs and JP Morgan, are pouring billions of dollars into clean technology companies, carbon trading, and other investment opportunities driven by the Sustainable Investment Revolution. A global investor coalition focused on climate change, the Carbon Disclosure Project, has now attracted supporters with over 55 trillion dollars worth of assets in only its sixth year of existence. This represents well over half of all of the professionally managed financial assets in the world. What is more, over 20 major institutional investors from seven countries, with more than $2 trillion in combined assets under management, are already redirecting some of their research budgets toward sustainability issues through a collaborative initiative called the Enhanced Analytics Initiative. What on *earth* is going on here? What's going on here is, quite simply, the Sustainable Investment Revolution. I firmly believe that over time, this Revolution will have as great an economic impact and be viewed as being at least as transformational as the development of the Internet or, before that, the advent of the railroads and electricity.

Like its predecessors, the Sustainable Investment Revolution is driving a worldwide industrial restructuring, radically changing the very basis of competitive advantage for companies and, therefore, for their investors. Like any other global restructuring, this new one will create both new winners and new losers. This book is predicated on the premise that it will strongly behoove twenty-first century investors to try to figure out which companies are which!

But why are investors acting this way—at least *some* of them? Because it is now increasingly evident that the "tried-and-tested" approaches that have dominated the investment field for the past 20 years are simply inadequate to cope with the complexities, subtleties, and competitive turbulence of the early twenty-first century. Contrary to the popular and deeply held belief among investment "experts," sustainability or ES issues such as climate change, air and water pollution, and affordable access to medicines in emerging markets *do* indeed matter to companies. They are *already* directly affecting companies' competitiveness, profitability, and ultimately their share price performance. Think, for example, of the runaway commercial and reputational success of the Toyota Prius hybrid car and the frantic if fatally belated efforts of Detroit's "Big 3" automakers to catch up. Think too about GE's multibillion dollar Ecomagination initiative and its galvanizing impact on that industrial giant. Consider the worldwide attempt by Walmart's leadership to make quantum improvements in environmental efficiency—both within the company itself and across its enormous, worldwide supply chain. In the process, they are slowly but surely turning Walmart from global pariah into an exemplar of environmental leadership.

While sustainability is far from being a magic bullet or panacea for corporate competitiveness, for a growing number of top performers, it *has* allowed them to gain market share, create attractive new products and services, create and enhance customer loyalty, recruit, retain, and motivate top talent, reduce energy costs, and reduce the risk of both customer backlash and litigation.[1]

All of these attributes are the hallmarks of better managed, more farsighted, agile, and adaptable companies. Today's—and especially *tomorrow's* —investors will increasingly need to learn how to find them, and the traditional investment tools and approaches, on which they have relied for decades, are becoming less and less helpful in doing so.

What may be even more remarkable than the velocity and extent of this revolution, however, is the fact that it has been so long in coming, despite all of the warning signs. Indeed, notwithstanding the pioneering efforts of a few brave "heretics" willing to challenge Wall Street and City of London orthodoxy, a surprisingly—and disturbingly—large percentage of major investors continue even now to act as if this investment revolution had still not begun. But this is all beginning to change.

Global hypercompetition, accelerated by a "perfect storm" convergence of a number of powerful global megatrends, is creating both challenges and opportunities for investors that are quite literally without precedent. To confront those challenges and seize the opportunities, investors will need both a radically different mindset and an entirely new arsenal of analytical tools. This book is intended to contribute to both.

To date, however, the majority of large institutional investors have for the most part been sleepwalking through the early part of the twenty-first century—having already dozed through the latter part of the previous one as well. Hobbled by grossly obsolete mental models and a set of "conventional wisdoms" that turns out to be anything but, they have until very recently missed out almost entirely on what is arguably the most extraordinary economic and sociopolitical transformation of the past 30 years—the Sustainability Revolution.[2]

The logic of "sustainability investment" is, in fact, disarmingly straightforward. Indeed, it should be obvious to any reasonably literate 10-year-old child: companies capable of managing ES challenges better than their competitors are quite likely to be better-managed companies, period. It therefore follows logically that they are likely to be superior *financial* performers as well. (The real tragedy here, of course —with due acknowledgment to Marx—Groucho, that is—is that we rarely if ever have the luxury of *having* a 10-year-old child *with* us in JP Morgan's or Goldman Sachs's boardroom when we desperately need one!).

Let me be clear from the outset: this book is emphatically *not* about traditional "ethical" or "socially responsible" investment (SRI). That approach, driven largely by investors' personal values, will always and deservedly have its place, and it has enjoyed a long and largely successful run, particularly in the retail (individual investor) marketplace, and especially in the United States and Britain. But traditional SRI's ability to penetrate the *mainstream,* institutional marketplace, where the *really* big money is, will always remain severely limited, in my view. Very few major institutional investors wish to step onto the rather slippery conceptual slope of values-based investing. Should they support—or oppose —contraception, genetically modified foods, animal testing, investing in Sudan, or any of the myriad value judgments that a traditional SRI not only demands but actually thrives on? Traditional SRI holds very little appeal for those unwilling or unable to make those kinds of value judgments, and since that describes well over 95 percent of the USD 60 trillion in professionally managed assets worldwide, I fear that traditional or "neoclassical" SRI will always be confined to a somewhat marginal role.

Since definitions of what is truly "ethical" or "socially responsible" behavior—and therefore investing—vary widely, getting a handle on the actual size of the conventional SRI market is a highly difficult and controversial task. While SRI partisans regularly advance much larger numbers, my own back-of-the-envelope calculations would put it at well under 5 percent of the total managed assets worldwide—at the very most. The focus of this book, by contrast, is on the *other* 95 percent of investors: those whose primary concern is maximizing their risk-adjusted financial returns and finding the best managed, most agile, and far-sighted companies they can lay their hands on in which to invest their retirement savings.

The potential benefits of sustainable investing are both considerable and growing:

• It allows investors to gain a much fuller understanding of companies' true risk and opportunity profiles.
• As a result, it allows them to identify better managed, more agile, "future-proof" companies.
• As a direct result of *that*, it gives them superior odds of achieving better medium and long-term *financial* performance.
• For some organizations (endowments, foundations, public sector and labor pension funds), it also allows investors to reinforce their program objectives and activities by better aligning their investment choices with their program priorities.
• In virtually all cases, it will build "reputational capital" for the investors and their organizations.
• Increasingly, fiduciary best-practice simply demands it.

What's Driving This Sustainable Investment Revolution Anyway?

The phenomenon that lies at the center of this book is the embryonic but rapidly accelerating penetration of the *mainstream* investment market by ES issues—in short, the Sustainable Investment Revolution.

A number of secular global megatrends are converging rapidly to create and accelerate that revolution, thereby giving birth to a radically changed and far more challenging environment for investors. As we shall see repeatedly throughout this book, however, that does *not* mean that the sustainability revolution is already fully formed and well established. Far from it; enormous obstacles and barriers remain. Having said that, however, I believe that the combined power of the secular trends and forces listed below, among others, will make that revolution both inevitable and irreversible:

• Accelerating natural resource degradation, scarcity, and constraints, driven to a significant extent by the explosive pace of industrial development, population growth, and urbanization, especially in emerging market economies, such as those in Brazil, Russia, India, and China (the so-called "BRIC" countries);

- Dramatically increased levels of public and consumer concern and expectations for companies' ES performances, turbocharged by unprecedented levels of information transparency with which to assess it;
- Tightening national, regional, and global regulatory requirements for stronger company performance and disclosure of "nontraditional" business and investment risks;
- Accelerating economic interdependence internationally, so that economic, social, and political shocks occurring in any single region are more likely to reverberate globally;
- Major demographic and economic shifts, concentrating the most rapid population *and* economic growth in emerging markets, particularly the BRIC countries;
- The expansion and intensification of both industrial competition and institutional investment into emerging markets, where ES risks tend to be most acute;
- The growing economic, sociopolitical, and competitive impact of major public health issues, such as HIV/AIDS, malaria, and tuberculosis;
- The ongoing revolution in information and communications technologies (the Internet, YouTube, Facebook, Web casts, bloggers, et al.), which has enabled and accelerated the emergence of a stakeholder-driven competitive environment for companies with unprecedented transparency and, therefore, business risk;
- The growing pressures from international nongovernmental organizations (NGOs), armed with unprecedented financial and technical resources, credibility, access to company information, and global communications capabilities with which to disseminate their analyses and viewpoints;
- "The retreat of government"—the erosion of national governments' financial, political, and managerial ability to solve major, global ES problems, with a concomitant *increase* in the burden (and the opportunities) for private sector corporations;
- A substantial reinterpretation and broadening of the purview of legitimate fiduciary responsibility to include companies' performance on ES matters;
- An institutional investor base that is increasingly sensitized to ES issues, newly equipped with better information, and both willing and able to act on its concerns;
- A growing appreciation by senior corporate executives of the competitive and financial risks and benefits of ES factors; and
- A growing body of both academic and empirical evidence illuminating the tightening nexus between companies' performance on

ES issues and their competitiveness, profitability, and share price performance.

Any one of these 14 megatrends should be powerful enough to attract attention from investors. Taken together, and mutually reinforcing, they create a set of virtually irresistible, tectonic forces that seem certain to transform the competitive and investment landscape for decades to come. Collectively, the megatrends are driving what amounts to a thorough-going, global industrial restructuring. Indeed, they have already begun to transform the very basis of international competitive advantage for both corporations and investors. Any corporate executive or investor myopic or complacent enough to disregard this radically changed competitive environment will do so at his or her peril.

The "Universal Owner" and the Rise of Fiduciary Capitalism

One of the most subtle but powerful drivers of the Sustainable Investment Revolution has been the recent emergence of the concept of the "universal owner" and the concomitant rise of "fiduciary capitalism." The universal owner construct was first advanced by Robert Monks and Nell Minow, two innovative and insightful advocates of active share ownership and seminal figures in the corporate governance field. The concepts were later taken up and elaborated by two California academics, Jim Hawley and Andy Williams.[3]

Briefly, the universal owner thesis is as follows: major institutional investors (notably pension funds, insurance companies, and some of the larger endowments and foundations) have now become so large and so broadly invested that they in essence collectively "own" a slice of the entire global economy. They hold investments in virtually every asset class, every industry sector, and every national and regional market in the world. The universal owner's interests therefore transcend those of any single country, industrial sector, or company; they have a vested economic interest in virtually *all* of them. As Hawley and Williams have aptly put it:

> For a universal owner, and thus for its beneficiaries, the whole may well be greater than the sum of its parts, since long-term profit maximization for the portfolio of a universal owner involves enhancing not just returns on a firm-by-firm basis, but enhancing productivity in the economy as a whole.[4]

This is clearly true in aggregate. The world's 300 largest pension funds have combined assets under management of some $30 *trillion*.[5] The very largest individual funds, including ABP (Netherlands), CalPERS (USA), and the Japanese, Norwegian, Korean, Canadian, Australian, and New Zealand national funds, own at least a nontrivial piece of the global economy all by themselves. Perhaps equally important, many of them are growing exponentially. The Norwegian, Canadian, and Australian funds, for example, are three of the most rapidly growing in the world and will be at multiples of their current size in a relatively short time. The so-called "sovereign wealth funds" in China, Russia, and the Persian Gulf have similar size, impact, and growth prospects. Both individually and collectively, all of these major investors share a common interest in improving the macrolevel global economic, social, and environmental conditions that both affect and are affected by the investment choices they make. And all of those choices have consequences.

Let's take a concrete example. Making an investment in a company operating a poorly run nickel smelter in Russia whose emissions cause downstream acid rain and other environmental problems in North America may conceivably generate some short-term excess returns from avoiding the necessary expenditures on pollution-abatement equipment. Those gains, however, are likely to be more than offset by the impact of dealing with those same "externalities" in North America. In some jurisdictions, the extra remediation costs may be borne by other companies in which the universal owner may also have a financial interest. In other cases, where the externalities are instead shouldered entirely by the public sector and civil society, the universal owner will likely suffer from either increased taxes or cutbacks in the quality of public services, such as education, health, infrastructure. One way or another, in today's increasingly transparent and interconnected global society, the piper must—and will—be paid.

As we shall see in greater detail in the next chapter, however, institutional investors and universal owners face some prodigious and deeply entrenched obstacles in any attempt to use their economic power and investment strategies to raise all corporate boats with a rising tide of improved environmental and social conditions overall. There is simply far too much inertia "hard wired" into the current system. A toxic cocktail of overly timorous, deferential pension fund trustees and fiduciaries, egregiously bad, uninformed advice from spuriously self-confident investment consultants and equally smug and myopic money managers, hopelessly archaic interpretations of what fiduciary responsibility really constitutes, and serious agency problems have created an enormously uphill battle for those who seek to mitigate the modern-day Tragedy of the Commons.[6]

Investment Mythologies Abound

The combined and pernicious effect of these factors has been to create a mindset among large institutional investors, the "logic" of which could be summarized as follows:

1. We "know" (but please don't ask us *how* we know!) that ES factors are, on a good day, simply immaterial and irrelevant to the financial performance of our investee companies and therefore a waste of an investor's time. On *most* days, however, it is much worse than that: taking ES factors into account would actually *harm* our financial returns, since weeding out the "bad apples" simply reduces the investment opportunity set for reasons that have nothing to do with financial performance.
2. As an investor and/or fiduciary, I am legally obligated to focus *only* on generating the best financial returns for my clients and/or beneficiaries. Any other considerations, such as social or "political" objectives, are directly incompatible with my fiduciary responsibilities and could therefore expose me to legal liabilities—to say nothing of ridicule from my investor peers.
3. Ergo, ES factors have no relevance or place in any "professional" investment process and should be avoided like the plague.

We will examine both the nature and the impact of this mythology more fully in Chapters 2 and 3, but it may be useful to provide at least one concrete illustration, even at this early juncture. The United Nations had been busily crafting and promoting its much-touted Principles for Responsible Investment for nearly two years. The Principles were officially unveiled amid great fanfare at the New York Stock Exchange in mid-2006, with UN Secretary General Kofi Annan himself ringing the bell to open the New York market. Major pension fund representatives from the United States, the United Kingdom, Canada, Norway, France, the Netherlands, and as far away as Thailand had traveled to New York to demonstrate their commitment and sign the Principles. So far, so good. But guess what? Unbeknownst to almost all of the attendees, the UN's *own* $37 billion staff pension fund representatives had doggedly refused to sign the Principles for months, relenting less than 24 hours before the signing ceremony!

Sadly, as we shall see, this resistance is far more the rule than the exception today. Indeed, I am reminded of a recent personal conversation

I had with the chief investment officer of another major North American pension fund that had signed the UN Principles. Indeed, not only had their representatives signed them, but the executive waxed positively lyrical about his organization's fanatical devotion to them. When I innocently asked him what steps his organization had taken over the past year to actually *implement* the principles that it had signed, he burst out laughing and said with a dismissive wave: "oh, we don't do any of *that!*" And that attitude and behavior unfortunately sum up the majority view today.

Readers at this point could be forgiven for objecting incredulously: "but such a response is so manifestly misguided, hypocritical, and indefensible in this day and age that it could not possibly be occurring." Sadly, however, this mindset and world view are not only not unusual, but they have been *dominant* in mainstream investment thinking for decades. And for the most part, they remain conventional "wisdom." This book is all about proposing what we believe to be a superior, more robust, and forward-looking approach and providing examples of some leading-edge practitioners who have already begun to apply it.

So What Are the Key Sustainability Issues, Anyway?

"Sustainability" is a term that is at least as ambiguous as it is now becoming popular. But what does it actually *mean?* Well, the classic definition of sustainable development can be found in the book *Our Common Future,* also known as the Brundtland Report, after its lead author, Gro Harlem Brundtland, the former Norwegian Prime Minister who chaired a major UN Commission that reported in 1987. The report famously stated:

> Sustainable development is development that meets the needs of
> the present without compromising the ability of future genera-
> tions to meet their own needs.[7]

This is profound and even inspirational stuff, but perhaps a bit too abstract and ethereal for your average investor. For the purposes of this book, "sustainability" issues are simply a shorthand for ES issues, *both* of which typically also have profound *economic* impacts and implications. But even that definition is still a trifle vague. So, in the interests of greater clarity, *these* are the sorts of issues we're typically referring to in this book:

Some Key Environmental Issues
- Climate change
- Water quality and scarcity
- Air pollution
- Waste management
- Deforestation
- Chemical and toxic emissions
- Land contamination
- Biodiversity loss
- Depletion of the ozone layer
- Quality of fisheries and oceans

Some Key Social Issues
- Poverty and income disparity
- Public health
- Human rights
- Labor rights
- Affordable housing
- Human resource management
- Racial and gender diversity
- Access to affordable medicines in both the developing *and* developed worlds

Reengineering the "DNA" of the Capital Markets

As we near the end of the first decade of the twenty-first century, traditional, accounting-driven investment analysis appears to have reached the limits of its usefulness. As recently as the mid-1980s, financial statements were arguably capable of capturing 90 percent or more of the true risk profile and value potential of major corporations.[8] According to New York University Stern Business School accounting guru and business professor Baruch Lev, however, by the beginning of the current century that figure had dropped to less than 20 percent on average.[9] Wallison and Litan summarize the situation nicely:

> Conventional financial statements do not provide sufficient information concerning a company's prospects to be of great value to investors. Increasingly, these reports are becoming irrelevant to an accurate valuation of knowledge companies and others.[10]

This tectonic shift reflects the inexorable transformation of developed economies to the point at which wealth is now being created primarily by knowledge capital, organizational relationships, and other intangible assets, rather than by land, factories, physical labor, or even finance capital. Intellectual capital has become the single most important factor in creating wealth; ergo, identifying and managing it has become the single most important driver of competitive advantage and sustainable value creation. Yet accounting statements have almost no light to shed on these "nontraditional" value—and investment risk—drivers. ES factors are increasingly conspicuous examples of these nontraditional risks and value drivers, and they have been almost entirely ignored by both accounting regulation and its practice.

The "Iceberg Balance Sheet" and the "Four Pillars" of Corporate Sustainability

What is required today is an "iceberg balance sheet" approach[11] that focuses priority attention where it belongs: on those investment risks and value drivers that lie hidden, largely impervious to traditional financial analysis. Increasingly, it is this unseen part of the "corporate value iceberg," that much larger portion *below* the surface, which contains the primary drivers of the company's future risks, unique comparative advantages, and value-creation capabilities (Figure 1.1). Among the most potent of these intangible value drivers are four of the key pillars of sustainability, or ES, analysis:

- Environment;
- Human Capital;
- Stakeholder Capital; and
- Strategic Governance

The "Environment" category is probably the most self-explanatory of the Four Pillars. By minimizing and managing their adverse impact on the natural environment, companies can achieve many of the competitive advantages referenced earlier in this chapter—a "social license to do business," improved brand value and differentiation, cost efficiencies, the ability to attract top talent, and others.

In our typology, the category of Human Capital includes the ability of companies to identify, recruit, train, motivate, and retain the best people, their ability to build and disseminate new knowledge throughout the company, and their innovation capacity, among other attributes.

Stakeholder Capital addresses the ability of companies to interact with their myriad of important stakeholders *outside* the company, including local communities, regulators, suppliers, customers, alliance partners, and even competitors.

Strategic Governance may be the least intuitive of the Four Pillars. Here we refer to the ability of companies to direct and govern themselves strategically *on sustainability issues.* In other words, it addresses the capacity of companies to scan the competitive horizon constantly and effectively

Financial Capital

Stakeholder Capital
- Regulators &
  Policymakers
- Local communities/NGOs
- Customer relationships
- Alliance partners

Strategic Governance
- Strategic scanning capability
- Agility/adaptation
- Performance indicators/
  monitoring
- Traditional governance
  concerns
- International "best practice"

Intangible Value

Human Capital
- Labor relations
- Recruitment/retention
  strategies
- Employee motivation
- Innovation capacity
- Knowledge development &
  dissemination
- Health & Safety
- Progressive workplace practices

Environment
- Brand equity
- Cost/risk reduction
- Market share growth
- Process efficiencies
- Customer loyalty
- Innovation effect

FIGURE I.I The "iceberg balance sheet." Source: Courtesy of the author

in order to identify and manage both current *and* potential sustainability driven issues, risks, and opportunities. In this sense, it is a more specific and somewhat esoteric (and rarely practiced) subset of the more familiar category of "corporate governance." Usually, but not always, Strategic Governance is the province of the senior executive team and its board of directors.

The Sustainable Investment Thesis

The sustainable investment hypothesis (which lies at the very heart of this book) is born directly out of a recognition of the inadequacy of traditional, accounting-based financial analysis to cope with the radically changed competitive and investment environment of the twenty-first century, where the ES factors cited above (and other "nontraditional" ones like them) have assumed unprecedented competitive significance. The basic logic of the sustainable investment thesis is as follows:

- Traditional financial analysis cannot possibly provide a complete picture of the true competitive risks, value potential, and future performance of companies. Typically, at least 80 percent of a company's value is now driven by "intangibles" that cannot be adequately captured in financial statements.[12]

- "Management quality" is arguably the number one intangible— the factor most critical to the competitiveness, profitability, and— ultimately—the share price performance of companies. Assessing it accurately is, therefore, the "Holy Grail" of twenty-first century investing.

- ES issues are and will remain among the toughest, most complex management challenges of the next 20 years. They are, therefore, a potent, forward-looking proxy and litmus test for a company's management quality and execution capabilities overall.

- Companies with superior positioning and performance on ES factors tend to be

  - More forward looking and strategic
  - More agile and adaptable
  - Better managed in general

  Therefore, they are likely to be *financial* outperformers as well.

- ES factors will become even more important to companies'—and investors'—competitive and financial success over the next 3–5 years.

- Despite this, they are currently grossly underrecognized and underresearched by mainstream investors. Those prepared to do the necessary research and analysis on sustainability factors, therefore, will be rewarded with a significant information advantage.

- The most compelling investment solutions will be those that *combine* institutional-quality ES research with best-in-class fundamental and quantitative research, portfolio construction, and asset management capabilities. ES analysis should *not* be regarded as a substitute for traditional investment analysis, but rather as a powerful enhancement to it.

Taking It to the Next Level: Confronting Some Inconvenient Truths

From where I sit, however, all of the preceding arguments are merely prologue: if investors *really* want to maximize financial returns and value creation—not to mention help create the kinds of environmental and social conditions in which they would actually want to *spend* those returns and savings—they *must* raise their games to the next level. What *is* the next level? Simple. It requires putting at least some of their money where their mouths have been for quite some time now. *This* is where the rubber truly meets the road. ES issues need to be consciously, visibly, and *systematically* integrated into the nuts and bolts of investing: asset allocation, stock selection, and portfolio construction. And in order to do that effectively, a *sine qua non* is access to company-specific ES research and analysis, whether conducted by in-house staff or purchased from external specialist providers. Judged by these criteria, as we shall see in Chapter 3, institutional investors' performance to date has generally been abysmal.

What could possibly explain this parlous state of affairs? In a nutshell, I believe that the root cause can be found in the two most abundant and, apparently, infinitely renewable resources that we seem to possess as a species: personal intellectual inertia and collective organizational inertia. To my mind, any other explanations are simply disingenuous at best. What is worse, this inertia has been exacerbated by three additional, profoundly injurious trends:

- The distressing tendency of most investment professionals to treat all ES investment strategies as one homogeneous, undifferentiated—and generally unhelpful—mass.
- The "silent conspiracy of passive resistance" by most pension fund consultants, key gatekeepers who have until quite recently been virtually unanimous in their ignorance of and, therefore, indifference or even hostility to ES factors. Unfortunately, few if any of the many critics of sustainability investing have taken the trouble to test the veracity of their assertions, either through their own original research or by consulting the growing financial literature in this area.[13]
- The extraordinary deference of pension fund trustees and fiduciaries themselves, who tend to be unduly intimidated by their professional advisors and sometimes forget that the advisors and money managers work for *them* and not the other way around. In essence, the investment manager and financial advisor tail has been wagging the fiduciary dog here, and in a *big* way. This simply has to stop.

Escaping the Hypocrisy Trap: Toward a New Hierarchy of Organizational Self-Actualization

As a direct result of these powerful forces of inertia, many large institutional investors have, to date, chosen to confuse form with substance with respect to ES issues. They point proudly to the ringing declarations that they have signed, such as the recently promulgated UN Principles for Responsible Investment or the Carbon Disclosure Project, as if signing a piece of paper were tantamount to taking real action. To be fair, such efforts are *not* entirely useless. Even if the "commitments" themselves are initially purely cosmetic and even disingenuous, they *do* have the considerable virtue of setting the "accountability clock" ticking. Stakeholders, both external and internal, can tolerate an extreme rhetoric/reality gap for only so long; at some point the signatories and rhetoricians will in fact be compelled to deliver *something*.

And so, with due apologies to Abraham Maslow and his celebrated "hierarchy of needs," I would like to propose here a new "hierarchy of self-actualization" for major institutional investors (Figure 1.2). The first and most primitive stage is one that I would label "wanton ignorance of the materiality of ES factors." As a rough and totally unscientific guess, I would venture that at least 20 percent of the world's major institutional owners of capital currently fall into this category. The next level might be called the stage of "denial"; investors have now become aware of the *potential* materiality of ES issues, but completely dismiss it. That cohort is likely the largest of all, accounting for roughly another 50 percent. This stage is often followed—in some cases literally decades later—by the third stage—"embryonic understanding." Let's say this group represents roughly 10 percent. This third group usually graduates fairly quickly to what might be termed the stage of "hollow, pious, empty rhetoric," where the newfound awareness triggers outpourings of professed enthusiasm, commitment, and the signing of various ringing international declarations. This group may represent another 15 percent. Make no mistake, though. This still represents a considerable advance over the previous stages. As noted earlier, at the very least it provides a basis for subsequent accountability from stakeholders.

At the very zenith of the new hierarchy, however, lies the fifth stage: true organizational self-actualization—real action. In this case, self-actualization comprises the actual, systematic incorporation of ES factors into investors' securities selection and portfolio construction processes. I'd guess that this group comprises at most 5 percent today, but its numbers are growing rapidly.

The very best, most far-sighted institutions often skip level 2 (denial) and level 4 (hollow rhetoric) and move quickly from understanding to action. At present, I would guess that they currently account for less than half of the top 5 percent, and we shall profile a number of this elite

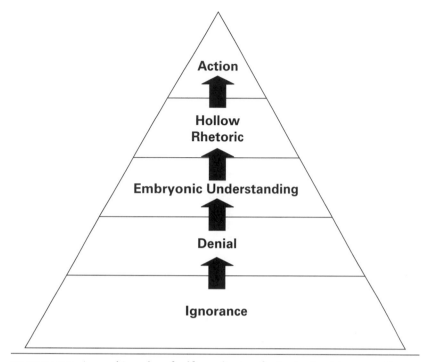

FIGURE I.2 A new hierarchy of self-actualization for institutional investors. Source: Courtesy of the author

group in Chapter 9. The worst and most laggardly, by contrast, find themselves stuck at either the "denial" or the "hollow rhetoric" stage. We shall meet a number of the members of that "rogues's gallery" in Chapter 3. The careful reader may note that the three *largest* categories, in descending order of size, are "denial," "wanton ignorance," and "hollow rhetoric." Enough said.

There are actually two pieces of *good* news about all of this, however. The first is that these guesstimated percentages are extremely fluid and dynamic; they are absolutely *not* cast in stone. The second is that the overwhelming trend toward "groupthink" in the institutional investment community remains every bit as strong as ever. Until quite recently, this "lemming instinct" served as an extraordinarily powerful impediment to action on the ES front. Today, however, there is reason to believe that now that a handful of brave institutions is beginning to step forward (as we shall see in Chapters 8, 9, and 10), mass inertia will convert to mass momentum, and the next 30,000 "converts" to the sustainability investment thesis should be a piece of cake!

In the next chapter, we turn to a deeper examination of how and why the seemingly common-sensical tenets of the sustainable investment hypothesis have proven to be so deeply counterintuitive and even offensive to the vast majority of professional investors and their advisors. We must understand why the Sustainable Investment Revolution has encountered so many obstacles if we are to have any hope of surmounting them. As George Santayana wrote, those who cannot remember the past are condemed to repeat it.

Chapter 2

What's *Taken* Us So Long?
The Power of Intellectual and Organizational Inertia

We believe that a sustainable investment approach, taking account of a wide range of environmental, social and governance issues alongside more traditional financial factors in the investment process, can help active managers to gain a better understanding of the risks and opportunities within their investment universe.

This in turn should enable them to construct portfolios with superior long-term risk and reward profiles.

—WATSON WYATT INVESTMENT CONSULTANTS

The sustainable investment thesis is nicely and succinctly captured in the quotation above.[1] Its central proposition is—or at least *ought* to be—beguilingly simple and straightforward: managing the risks and exploiting the opportunities generated by the constantly shifting kaleidoscope of multistakeholder environmental and social pressures is one of the most complex management and leadership challenges confronting twenty-first century corporate executives and boards of directors. Those companies capable of navigating those shoals better than their competitors are quite likely to be better-managed companies, period. Better-managed companies in turn, *ceteris paribus,* are likely to be *financial* outperformers as well, at least in the medium and longer term. Thus, increasingly, investors should be looking at the sustainability performance and strategic positioning of companies as robust proxies and leading indicators for their *overall* management quality. And, since Wall Street is constantly telling us that "management quality" is the number one determinant of the ultimate financial performance of companies, sustainability analysis *should* be able to give investors a significant leg up. Indeed, as we shall see later, it already *has*.

That's it. It is emphatically *not* rocket science. So if the logic is so simple and compelling, why has it taken so long for mainstream investors and fiduciaries to accept it? The answer, I believe, can be found in two of the most powerful cognitive forces of nature: individual intellectual inertia and collective organizational inertia. We seem, as a species, to have virtually inexhaustible and constantly renewable supplies of both.

At the risk of some hyperbole, I liken the situation to the mind-set of the Flat Earth Society. If you have been brought up and trained to believe that the earth is flat, and all of your training and all of your peers continually reinforce that view, then ways *will* be found to denigrate and dismiss all evidence to the contrary, no matter how apparently persuasive. Shown a photograph of the planet earth taken from outer space, a devout Flat Earther will dismiss its apparently spherical shape as a visual distortion, likely caused by an errant speck of dust on the space camera's lens. Simple. End of discussion.

And thus it has been with the sustainable investment thesis. The mounting body of both academic and empirical evidence concerning the alpha-generation (outperformance) potential of environmental, social, and other "nontraditional" investment factors has largely been either ignored, dismissed as the product of faulty, self-serving analysis, or both. We shall return to this growing body of evidence in Chapter 4.

This myopia, sadly, has afflicted each of the three key sets of actors in the investment "food" chain. We provide a simplified, schematic illustration of that food chain in Figure 2.1.

The first and most important link in the chain *ought* to be the asset owners, as represented by the beneficiaries, trustees, executives, and investment staffs of pension funds, endowments, and foundations. The second is their investment consultant advisors, and the third is the external money management firms to which are entrusted literally trillions of dollars of *other* people's money. Unfortunately, individual intellectual inertia and collective organizational inertia have dominated all but a very few of the players in each category. Equally worrying, it is astonishing how frequently both the owners and their money managers and advisors forget whose money it actually is, and who should therefore be calling the shots!

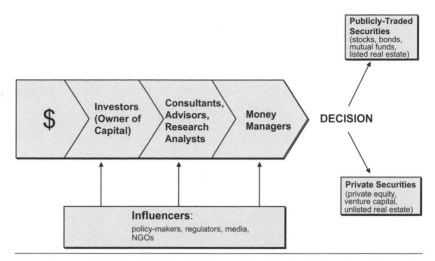

FIGURE 2.1 The investment value chain. Source: Courtesy of the author

Further exacerbating this problem has been a highly unfortunate ten-dency to confuse and conflate contemporary, sophisticated sustainability in-vestment approaches with traditional "socially responsible" investment, or SRI. The differences between the two approaches are, in fact, quite stark and fundamental. Traditional SRI is primarily driven by *values.* Investors view companies through the prisms of their own personal values: for or against contraception, alcohol, genetically modified foods, pornography, animal testing, company involvement in Sudan or Myanmar, and so on. Historically, financial returns have been only a secondary consideration; expressing one's personal values through investment practices has been paramount. As a direct result, despite its commercial success among re-tail (individual) investors, SRI has engendered considerable skepticism and rejection from *mainstream* investors, for at least four reasons:

- Values-based company exclusions narrow investors' opportunity sets for nonfinancial reasons. In some cases, entire industry sectors, such as mining and oil and gas, are prohibited as having unacceptably high environmental or social impacts. Modern portfolio theory[2] teaches us that this must inevitably lower the financial returns of the port-folio, increase the risks, or possibly both.
- The research methodologies supporting SRI analysis, most of them heavily reliant on company responses to questionnaires and gener-ally devoid of serious competitive industry analysis and company-level

financial analysis, are nowhere near sufficiently robust for returns-seeking investors and other fiduciaries.

- Few public institutions are eager to set foot on the slippery slope of ethical exclusions. Drawing the line on what is and is not "ethical" company behavior can be a highly contentious, no-win situation when, as is almost always the case, the beneficiaries are a heterogeneous group with widely diverging views. Moreover, many if not most of the ethical issues confronting investors are of a distinctly *gray* hue; the real world seems to contain an inconveniently small number of purely black-and-white situations.

- There is a widespread (but largely erroneous) belief that traditional SRI funds have had outstandingly poor performance records.

Sustainability investing, on the other hand, is a different kettle of fish entirely. As we have seen, it is *all* about investment risk and return and simply uses the analysis of the performance and positioning of companies on ES and other "nontraditional" issues as proxies to help identify better-managed, more nimble companies. Instead of expressing personal values, sustainability investing seeks to generate *financial* value through the application of a more robust, comprehensive, and forward-looking analytical framework.

Unfortunately, the penetration of mainstream investment thought and practice by sustainability considerations has been *severely* retarded by widespread confusion between these two fundamentally different philosophies and approaches. Of the two, SRI has a much longer pedigree, and SI has had enormous difficulty escaping the suspicion and even opprobrium created in the mainstream by traditional SRI. This has been unfortunate in the extreme, because both styles do share a common concern over issues, such as climate change, labor practices along supply chains, water quality and availability, and access to medicines in emerging markets. What has separated the two camps has been their objectives, methodologies, and investment results. I can confirm from direct personal experience that at the mere mention of the word "environment" or "social," 99 percent of chief investment officers default to the presumption that traditional (and therefore presumably underperforming) SRI funds are about to be discussed. Their eyes then promptly either glaze over or actually roll back in their heads.

One unfortunate byproduct of this SI/SRI conflation and confusion has been a vigorous and long-lasting but entirely spurious debate over the question "does SRI outperform, or not?" Sadly, this debate has generated far more heat than light, and it too has retarded the advance and mainstream penetration of common sense, sustainability driven investment.

The ongoing debate over whether SRI outperforms traditional investment approaches has been, in many respects, sterile and unhelpful. By its very nature, SRI is values driven, and there will never be a universal consensus on which—and whose—values are most important and legitimate. There are, therefore, almost as many flavors of SRI as there are SRI investment products. Since SRI is not even remotely homogeneous, posing the question "Does SRI outperform?" is no more helpful than asking "Does equity investing outperform? Or how about fixed income? Real estate? Private equity? How about infrastructure funds?" The answer in all cases must be a resounding, unequivocal, "that depends." It depends on the investment style, the quality of the underlying company research, the stock selection and portfolio construction skills of the money manager, and the specific time period and market conditions under consideration.

Indeed, sweeping generalizations in all of these cases are not only completely useless, they can be actively misleading and dangerous. That's one reason why investment managers and advisors are normally at such pains to characterize each of their offerings as precisely as possible—e.g., "a U.S. domestic, large-cap equity fund, actively managed, with a 'growth' bias/philosophy." Just for the record, by the way, despite the disdain with which most mainstream money managers have treated sustainability investing, each year over *three-quarters* of the active stock-pickers routinely *under*perform their benchmarks! To date, this inconvenient fact seems to have done little to temper the egos and sense of omniscience of the profession generally.

Studying the performance of companies on ES issues can provide important insights about their likely financial performance in the medium and long term by shedding new light and an additional perspective on the overall quality of their management. As we shall see later, for example, sustainability analysis enabled one research house to alert its clients to the impending subprime mortgage debacle literally months before mainstream Wall Street did.

The ability of companies to manage the complex, ever-changing constellation of ES issues provides an increasingly robust—but heretofore largely neglected—proxy for their *overall* management quality. As mainstream financial analysts from New York to Tokyo will confirm, management quality is viewed as the single most important determinant of the ultimate competitiveness and financial performance of companies. Strangely enough, however, those same analysts almost never articulate precisely what a well-managed company in any given sector would actually *look* like, nor do they explain convincingly just what it is that makes any particular company well or poorly managed.

By contrast, the best ES and "extrafinancial" analysts actually do both, often with a level of analytical rigor and specificity that would put their mainstream counterparts to shame. Despite this, ES analysis is almost universally dismissed by traditional financial analysts as vague and wooly-minded—an intellectual double standard if ever there was one!

Just How Bad Is It, Anyway?

Hard data on precisely what factors analysts and investors actually utilize in their daily work are hard to come by, but several recent studies certainly make for sobering reading. A study undertaken for the Swedish Foundation for Strategic Environmental Research (MISTRA) in 2006 examined nearly 250 investment research reports and discovered that fully 65 percent of them contained no environmental sustainability information or analysis whatsoever.[3] Two things make these findings particularly worrisome: first, all of the reports were about companies in either the oil and gas or chemicals sectors, two sectors widely acknowledged as having particularly significant environmental impact. Second, the study focused on Europe, where sustainability awareness remains light years ahead of that in North America. If the majority of analysts covering two of the highest-impact industry sectors in the most sustainability-aware region on earth are largely ignoring ES issues, what are the prospects for analysts and portfolio managers in *less* obvious sectors or geographies? Or for other, less blatantly obvious sustainability issues?

Similar conclusions were reached in a much larger study by the European Centre for Corporate Engagement (ECCE) in the Netherlands, led by Dutch finance professor Dr. Rob Bauer. The ECCE study analyzed survey responses from over 850 finance professionals in Europe, from over 320 institutions. The researchers' overall conclusion was that "ES issues remain a niche market and are incorporated into mainstream investments to only a limited extent."[4]

Innovest Strategic Value Advisors also conducted a similar but much smaller-scale study of analysts and portfolio managers in North America, which intuitively should be an even less commodious environment for sustainability investing. Roughly 100 investment professionals from the United States, Canada, and Mexico were contacted and interviewed. That study explored three major questions:

- To what extent does the mainstream financial community currently incorporate environmental sustainability information into stock assessments?
- To the extent that they do, how is it done?
- To the extent that they do not, what are the principal barriers?

Not unexpectedly, the survey results revealed that the systematic integration of ES factors was virtually nonexistent among North American investors and analysts.[5] The reasons for this are numerous and complex, but the most fundamental barriers by far were clearly the cognitive ones.

Cognitive Barriers against Sustainable Investment

Change is predicated on altering conventional wisdom. There are at least six persistent misconceptions at the root of the pervasive resistance to the inclusion of sustainability factors in the investment process by mainstream investors.

Six Enduring Myths about Sustainable Investment

1. **Addressing sustainability factors is irrelevant or even injurious to risk-adjusted financial returns.** Conventional investment "wisdom" has long held that the performance of companies on ES issues is either immaterial to their financial performance or may even impose costs that add no financial value and therefore impede the competitiveness and profitability of companies as well as those of their investors.
2. **It is very likely a breach of fiduciary duty to incorporate sustainability factors into investment strategy.** This myth follows directly from the first one. On a good day, analyst time spent assessing the ES performance of companies is alleged to be simply a waste of time; on a bad day, including them in the construction of clients' portfolios may actually harm the financial performance of both companies and investors by arbitrarily narrowing the available investment opportunity set. Some traditional SRI managers, for example,

will simply not invest in *any* mining, oil and gas, or forestry stocks on principle, notwithstanding any financial (or, for that matter, environmental) virtues they may have.

3. **There is no academically credible evidence to support the sustainable investment thesis.** This is at once the most central and the most misguided of the six investment myths. The fact that it is blatantly untrue has done little to prevent some of the most respected and influential investment analysts and consultants in the world from parroting it from the highest mountain tops. The problem is not a lack of evidence, it is the fact that the skeptics are either blithely dismissive of it or, more frequently, both unaware of its existence and disinclined to look for it.[6]

4. **Sustainability and other "extrafinancial" analyses are inevitably less rigorous and more arbitrary than traditional investment analysis.** My earlier comment on management quality as the number one determinant of company performance according to mainstream analysts is only the beginning of a rebuttal on this point. Sadly, this particular myth is not simply intellectually inaccurate, it is actively preventing otherwise progressive institutional investors —particularly in the United States—from even considering sustainability strategies that could improve their risk-adjusted returns substantially. In many cases, they have thrown the sustainable investment "baby" out with the SRI "bath water."

5. **All SRI/sustainability research and investment approaches are essentially the same.** While it is true that some SRI analysis and investment products are of inferior quality and generate poor returns, precisely the same can be said for much of the analysis and many of the products on offer from the mainstream. In neither case should investors abandon the entire genre because of the failings of the worst.

6. **Unlike any *other* single set of investment factors, sustainability factors have to add value *all* of the time;** otherwise they clearly must be intellectually bankrupt, worthless, or even harmful. The "logical" corollary of this view is that the underperformance of any ES/sustainability fund or, even worse, several of them, invalidates the entire investment approach. By contrast, every year, according to respected Princeton finance professor Burton Malkiel, roughly *80 percent* of all active, large-cap *mainstream* asset managers underperform their benchmarks.[7] This, however, is apparently no reason to call into question the entire discipline of active management. In the world of sustainable investment, however, this "shortcoming" is, ap-

parently, fatal. We shall return to this strange double standard later in this chapter.

Here's how this constellation of myths actually plays out in practice. Let us imagine a hypothetical but typical meeting of the board of trustees or investment committee of a large pension fund or endowment. During a discussion on global asset allocation, one of the "lay" people on the board raises the issue of climate change. She notes that the institution's international portfolios seem to have a relatively heavy exposure to industry sectors and regions likely to be most directly affected. She goes on to quote some alarming statistics about climate change and asks what analysis the board's in-house investment staff or outside money managers have done to assess the potential investment risks involved for the fund's portfolios.

At this point, the institution's investment consultant clears his throat and begins a patient—or otherwise—explanation of why such considerations have no place in the board/committee's deliberations. First, "everyone knows" that climate change, *if* it is in fact occurring at all, is such a long-term, amorphous issue that it will not affect the institution's investments, certainly not during the lifetime of anyone in the room. Second, climate change is "just" an environmental issue, and "studies have shown" that if they have any impact whatsoever on investment results, it is a deleterious one and is likely to compromise financial returns. Any time spent on analyzing such issues would therefore be wasted at best, and potentially much worse. Third, the consultant sternly reminds the board member that she has a fiduciary *duty* to attempt to maximize the risk-adjusted financial performance of the investment portfolios for the institution's beneficiaries. That must be her only concern, *not* anything as frivolous as, say, saving the planet. Introducing "extraneous," "nonfinancial" considerations would constitute a clear abrogation of her fiduciary obligations and could potentially expose her to lawsuits and even jail time.

At that point, the chairman of the investment committee himself weighs in—and it *is* invariably a "he"! A retired partner of one of Wall Street's leading investment banks, he has chaired the committee for a decade. He is, self-evidently, an investment *expert*. He concurs with the consultant 100 percent, adding for good measure that "all the evidence" and investment performance history support their joint view. The institution's CEO and chief investment officer nod sagely in agreement.

And that's it. End of discussion of an issue that the World Economic Forum in Davos (not heretofore known for extreme anticapitalist,

Marxist views) has described as "the business issue of the millennium." The poor trustee, completely intimidated by the phalanx of "experts," retreats apologetically and is not heard from at a meeting for the next 18 months. Any other like-minded trustees, witnessing the intellectual carnage, keep their thoughts to themselves.

Oh, and one more thing: the chairman of the investment committee is about to step down, after a distinguished, 10-year period of service to the board. Fortunately, though, he has found a replacement for himself: yet *another* retired partner from his former investment bank. The "new boy," in his late sixties, not surprisingly views the world in precisely the same way as his predecessor. And so the cycle continues; the "circle of ignorance and inertia" remains unbroken.

These six investor myths lie at the heart of the persistent resistance to sustainable investment, and have produced a myriad of perverse and sometimes startling consequences that we will explore in Chapter 3.

The Tyranny of the Double Standard

Over the past 15 years, I have been subjected to literally hundreds of withering "cross-examinations" by skeptics of the sustainable investment hypothesis, including the chairmen of major investment banks, chief investment officers of major pension funds, fund trustees, money managers, and investment consultants. What is most striking about these interrogations—other than their sheer ferocity and negativity—is the glaring intellectual double standard that often underpins them.

Now, I am happy to accept that the burden of proof on any intellectual "insurgent" (in this case, proponents of the sustainable investment thesis) will inevitably be more onerous than that placed upon the "incumbents" (supporters of investment orthodoxy, and therefore highly skeptical of virtually any new approaches). But in my experience, when it comes to the mainstream investment world, there *is* no burden of proof on the incumbents. Zero. *Their* investment beliefs seem to have acquired a kind of secular theological status—they are taken to be so self-evident as to require neither explanation nor proof, not unlike the existence of gravity.

For example, it is widely accepted on Wall Street that "management quality" is the number one determinant of the financial performance of companies. Fair enough; I would concur. Wall Street analysts are frequently quoted in the business press commenting that a particular company is "well managed"—or that it isn't. Precisely what *constitutes* "good management" in a given industry sector at a particular point in time is rarely, if ever, explicitly articulated. As near as I can make out, the most compelling evidence of "good management" to most Wall Street analysts is that the company "made its numbers" for the most recent year, quarter, or 15 minutes. Period. The question of whether or not those numbers are remotely accurate indicators of the true competitive risks and future financial potential of a company or rather merely accounting artifacts does not seem to be a particular concern. Whether or not the historical trends that produced those numbers are likely to persist into the future receives similarly short shrift. (To take but one contemporary example, historical or even current financial returns can tell us *nothing* about an electric utility's potential financial and competitive exposure to taxes on carbon dioxide emissions that might well be in effect in the United States in 2 years or less.) Under some entirely plausible scenarios about the cost of carbon, such taxes could consume as much as 50 percent or more of a company's earnings.[8] With risk exposures in the very same industry sectors varying by a factor of *30* or more, ignoring such risks would seem both reckless and irresponsible.

Despite this, however, future cash flows are blithely projected years forward (and then discounted back to a notional present value) using heroic assumptions that are only rarely defended or even explicitly articulated. Those assumptions only occasionally include any systematic recognition of climate risk. The result is a series of numbers with the patina of precision, authenticity, and six-sigma accuracy, but that often belies a potential margin for error of 300 to 400 percent or even more.

None of this would be particularly vexing were it not the case that many of these very analysts and investors are the same ones accusing advocates of sustainable investment as being imprecise! If anything, I would argue that quite the opposite is true.

For starters, let's revisit "management quality," supposedly the primary determinant of the financial performance of a company. In my experience, the better sustainable finance analysts attempt to define it with a level of precision that would actually *shame* most Wall Street analysts. While they steadfastly proclaim the critical importance of management quality, the latter tend to do next to nothing to actually define it.[9] By contrast, a good sustainability analyst would consider a global integrated oil and gas company to be "well managed" on ES issues if it exhibited, *inter alia,* positive characteristics, including those listed below, for each of the "four pillars" of sustainability:

Environmental Performance
- The existence and difficulty of environmental performance targets, such as a 30 percent reduction in greenhouse gas emissions by 2012
- The adequacy of the organizational architecture for risk management, including the appointment of a board level locus of responsibility
- The absolute, relative, and trending levels of toxic emissions, spills, and accidents
- A high percentage of global facilities receiving an environmental audit, their frequency, and the percentage of those audits vetted by independent third parties
- The quality of supply chain risk management systems, whereby a company routinely screens the environmental and social performance of its subcontractors
- The adequacy of annual reserves for potential environmental liability and litigation costs
- The absolute and relative energy efficiency of key refineries
- The level of phase-out risk for strategic products, such as the additive MTBE in gasoline
- Current and historical CO_2 emissions in each jurisdiction of operations
- Organizational structures and capability for identifying environmentally driven profit opportunities—e.g., renewable energy

Human Capital
- The quality of programs for recruitment, retention, and motivation of staff
- The frequency and severity of any health and safety problems
- The quantity and quality of training and development resources and programs
- The level of employee turnover, relative to competitors
- The quality of labor relations
- The presence and efficacy of any "high-performance" workforce practices, including flex-time, job-sharing, telecommuting, geographic and functional transfer opportunities
- The frequency and comprehensiveness of employee opinion surveys and management responsiveness to the results
- Access to management—level of engagement and dialog

Strategic Governance
- The level of executive and board-level level of responsibility and oversight for sustainability issues
- The adequacy of board and executive-level capability to identify sustainability-driven business risks and profit opportunities
- The adaptability and responsiveness to a changing competitive environment
- The level of integration of sustainability factors with core business processes
- The level of coordination among relevant functions and departments
- The ability to achieve high sustainability standards in all jurisdictions of operation
- The existence and quality of mechanisms for monitoring and evaluating progress toward articulated ES goals
- The degree of fit between sustainability policies and objectives and performance "on the ground"

Stakeholder Capital
- The quality of relationships with regulators, local communities, and key external constituencies
- The existence and quality of strategic alliances with nongovernmental organizations (NGOs), academe, etc.
- The existence and quality of external advisory boards
- The quality of supply chain management: adequacy of screening, training, and monitoring mechanisms
- The level of community investment and development in emerging markets
- Responsiveness to stakeholder concerns
- The quality and strength of "social license to operate"

It should be stressed that these are only a smattering of the more than 100 factors and indicators that a top-notch sustainability analyst would examine. The more sophisticated research houses will also have developed an explicit, sector-specific (although sometimes proprietary) factor weighting system that recognizes the differential impacts of ES factors in different industry sectors and at different points in the market cycle.

The matrix shown in Figure 2.2, for example, was developed and is used by my own firm, Innovest Strategic Value Advisors. It reflects the varying financial and competitive significance of different environmental, human capital, and other sustainability factors in the global integrated

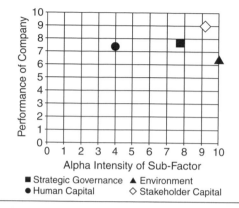

FIGURE 2.2 Royal Dutch Shell and the "Four Pillars" of sustainability.
This matrix situates the four key intangible value drivers along 2 dimensions:
1. How well or poorly the company performs on each of the 4 key factors.
2. How much impact that particular factor has on financial performance in that industry sector; its "alpha intensity."
Source: Innovest Strategic Value Advisors

oil and gas sector. In this matrix, the horizontal axis describes the relative financial and competitive significance of each of four individual factors, with 10 as the maximum score. The vertical axis reflects this particular company's relative performance on each major set of factors relative to its industry competitors. In sum, what this snapshot tells investors is that in this sector, environmental performance is the most significant sustainability factor and differentiator, followed by stakeholder capital. Royal Dutch Shell has been judged to be strong on the former, but even stronger on the latter factor. Of the four sustainability metafactors, human capital is seen as a less critical differentiator in this sector. Each of these judgments and assessments is, of course, open to legitimate dispute and debate, but at least they are all *explicit*.

At the end of this analytical process, the myriad of individual factor judgments are rolled up into an overall, synthesized score or rating, relative to same-sector industry peers. Some sustainability analysts will even derive those weightings by analyzing and decomposing historical stock returns. I don't know about you, and I acknowledge a personal conflict of interest in commenting on this particular analytical tool, but this analysis does not strike me as particularly vague, or arbitrary, as the sustainable investment critics imply. Indeed, I have rarely if ever seen "management quality" defined as precisely or systematically on Wall Street, despite its ostensible importance to the analysts there.

Now, admittedly, evaluating and making judgments about elusive, ethereal issues like these is inevitably a subjective matter, defying six sigma quantitative precision. (It *is,* after all, *management quality* that we're trying to get a handle on here!) Conclusions are, therefore, always going to be open to legitimate debate. The point, however, is this: at least the better sustainability analysts actually *attempt* the exercise in the first place, and they do so in a systematic, organized, and repeatable way that allows meaningful "apples-to-apples" comparisons to be made among companies. And the evaluation frameworks are generally *explicit.*

Most Wall Street analysts, in my experience, could not meet those very same tests. I may have led an overly sheltered existence, but I for one have never encountered a traditional Wall Street analyst with an approach that was remotely as well structured and systematic. When was the last time *you* saw a Wall Street analyst specify which 20—or 100— operational proxies were being used to identify a "well-managed" company in any particular industry sector? Despite this, of course, it is the sustainable investment analyst who is generally dismissed as imprecise and wooly minded. Most of this dismissal, I believe, is caused by the persistent confusion between traditional SRI approaches and the much newer and more sophisticated, returns-oriented sustainability approaches. While the two approaches, investment objectives, and research methodologies are wildly different, as we have seen, mainstream analysts too often throw the sustainability "baby" out with the SRI "bathwater" and dismiss both.

Similarly, while sweeping (and usually unquestioned) assumptions seem to be perfectly acceptable on Wall Street, they are treated as evidence of intellectual bankruptcy when found in the sustainable investment field. I distinctly recall a recent conversation with the chief investment officer of a leading global asset management firm, with several hundred billion dollars under management. I tried to provide a concrete example of how sustainability analysis might be integrated into a traditional investment process. I said "for example, *if* you believed in the financial materiality of ES analysis, you might alter the discount rate assumption in one of your discounted cash flow models from 0.8 to 0.7 for a top ES performer, or increase it to 0.9 for a bottom quintile performer." His response: "Gee, moving from 0.8 to 0.7 or 0.9 sounds pretty arbitrary to *me!*" Maybe so, but one wonders about the scientific rigor underpinning *his* initial assumption of 0.8 in the first place! I very much doubt that the figure emerged from a carefully controlled experiment in a Princeton physics laboratory!

This same sort of double standard can be found in the interpretation of performance results. As we have seen, and as noted above in the Six Enduring Myths about Sustainable Investment, year in and year out, roughly 80 percent of traditional active money managers can be counted on to *under*perform their investment benchmarks. (Luckily for their investors, it tends not to be the *same* 80 percent every year!) While these statistics have certainly provided ample ammunition for advocates of index funds like the legendary Jack Bogle, they are rarely if ever used to argue that the entire enterprise of active management should therefore be discredited and abandoned. Yet, despite *superior* statistics on the sustainable investment side, any underperformance there is gleefully seized upon as positive proof that sustainable investment "doesn't work."

I was recently challenged by a senior investment consultant to demonstrate and *document* a direct, cause-and-effect relationship between a company's performance on an individual ES factor (the frequency of their environmental audits, as I recall) and its financial outperformance. I was challenged to demonstrate precisely how much of the 300 basis points (3 percent) of outperformance a particular environmental performance factor was responsible for, and to *prove* it. The clear implication was that if I could not, the sustainable investment hypothesis could then be safely banished to the intellectual scrap heap where it presumably belonged.

My response was two-fold: first, no I could not demonstrate a precise, quantified, cause-and-effect link, and any attempt to do so would be both disingenuous and dangerously simplistic and reductionist; and two, could he kindly provide any similar proof of the precise impact—and causality—of any of the *traditional* investment factors in which *he* placed such unwavering faith? Needless to say, he could not, but it didn't really matter; as a defender of the status quo, he didn't need to. The fact that no single factor or sets of factors "works" all the time, in all industry sectors, and under all market conditions in the traditional investment world either is apparently neither here nor there.

Allow me to provide just one concrete example. The price/earnings ratio (p/e) has acquired an almost iconic status among mainstream investors as a virtually indispensable part of their analytical toolkit. Indeed, it is a ubiquitous and largely unquestioned factor in nearly every investment decision regarding publicly traded securities. Analysts routinely screen companies on the basis of their p/e ratios, thereby producing precisely the same narrowing of the potential investment opportunity set that they reflexively decry and dismiss when their sustainability counterparts do likewise. Despite this, however, there is compelling academic evidence that p/e ratios are badly flawed as analytical tools and virtually *useless* as predictors of companies' subsequent financial performance. Michael Mauboussin, Chief Strategist for the giant investment firm Legg Mason, makes the point starkly:

> Research shows that there has been no statistically significant relationship between a price-earnings ratio at the beginning of a year and the subsequent twelve and twenty-four month returns over the past 125 years.[10]

One cardinal weakness of earnings per share (EPS) calculations is that they are notoriously open to varying accounting conventions, not to mention "earnings management" by firm executives. A second serious weakness is that EPS ignores one hugely critical question: what was the cost of capital required to generate those earnings in the first place? Is the company actually *creating* net economic value for its shareholders, or destroying it?

Getting the "p" part is pretty straightforward; it's getting the *other* 50 percent of the ratio right, the "e" bit, that borders on the impossible. Just how accurate *are* the reported earnings anyway? Between their abject dependency on fundamental—and varying—accounting assumptions, the routine appearance of multibillion dollar "extraordinary items" on profit and loss statements 5 years in a row, "restructuring charges" from mergers and acquisitions, "in process research and development costs," and selective earnings management, reliance on stated earnings figures requires a rather prodigious leap of faith. But it is one that is made on Wall Street every business day when analysts use p/e calculations to assess companies.

But where are the banshee-like cries denouncing advocates of p/e ratios as intellectual frauds and snake-oil salesmen if they cannot convincingly demonstrate their effectiveness? Apart from a few contrarians such as Mauboussin, such critics are both invisible and inaudible. Why? Because whether or not the factor actually "*works,*" those who use p/e ratios have three huge advantages denied to sustainable investing advocates: they're dead simple, they've been in general use for a long time, and everybody *else* uses them too. In Chapter 4, we shall return to the themes of both accounting distortions and sheep-like herd behavior.

And, while we're at it, let's look at the actual *results* of traditional Wall Street analysis. (And remember, there is very little tolerance within the mainstream financial community for anything short of perfection from sustainability analysts and portfolio managers.) Every year, the venerable and iconic *Wall Street Journal* assesses the accuracy of the investment recommendations of both individual analysts and entire brokerage houses, all of whom are given "batting averages" reflecting the 12-month subsequent performance of their recommendations. The results? Well, they aren't pretty. The *top*-performing Wall Street firm in the 2008 survey was Morgan Stanley, with a batting average of 0.273. It was closely followed by Goldman Sachs, with 0.269. The other big names were UBS, 0.149; Citigroup, 0.115; and JP Morgan Chase, 0.068.[11]

Now, I don't know about the baseball players and teams that *you* follow, but where I come from, those batting averages would be categorized as tepid at best and atrocious at worst. The two leaders' averages would not usually qualify either of them for the All Star game, and players with averages at the UBS/Citigroup/JP Morgan levels would be on the next bus to the minor leagues. And yet *this* is the cream of the crop of almost 2000 Wall Street analysts? *These* are the demigods who routinely dismiss sustainability analysis as wooly minded, imprecise, and ineffective? Let's get *serious!*

My point here is simply this: if mainstream investment analysts and portfolio managers were ever forced to meet even 10 percent of the burden of either proof or performance demanded of proponents of the sustainable investment hypothesis, they would almost certainly fail miserably. Unfortunately, however, as guardians and champions of the status quo, they are almost never required to do so. But they would do well to remember that fact, demonstrate a bit more intellectual humility (or at least curiosity), and temper the vehemence of their critiques accordingly.

Thus we can see that whether at the level of the individual or an entire investment organization, intellectual inertia has displayed both unimaginable potency and staying power in resisting sustainable investment approaches. And it has led to consequences that are both perverse and profoundly unhelpful—in both financial *and* sustainability terms. It is to these perverse consequences that we now turn in Chapter 3.

Chapter 3

Perverse Outcomes
and Lost Opportunities

*The greatest hindrance in bettering our understanding of the world
is our natural tendency to cling to outdated ideas.*

—THE ASTROPHYSICS SPECTATOR, MAY 2006

The mythologies, ideological and cognitive barriers, and double standards, which we have examined in Chapter 2, have had a very real, powerful, and pernicious impact on the behavior of real-world investors. We describe some of the most egregious examples in this chapter, not out of some perverse sense of sadomasochistic pleasure, but because, in the absence of concrete evidence such as this, most reasonable people would have a very hard time believing that the current situation could possibly be as it is. And, before things can be dramatically changed for the better, people generally need to understand what's wrong with them *now*.

In this chapter, we have selected examples from five of the most important subsets of the world of institutional asset owners and investors: multilateral financial institutions, such as the United Nations and the

World Bank, public pension funds, endowments and foundations, not-for-profit groups, and organized labor funds. In all five cases, the organizations are doing valuable and praiseworthy work in their day-to-day operations and program activities. Indeed, it is precisely the excellence and nature of their work in their primary areas of focus that makes their inactivity and resistance to sustainability considerations on the *investment* side so striking and incongruent.

The six investment myths that we reviewed in Chapter 2 will be on full display in the examples that follow. At bottom, however, they ultimately manifest themselves in a single, curious phenomenon: a seemingly inexplicable psychological separation between the *operating* side of the organizations on the one hand and their *investment/fiduciary* side on the other. It is as if there were a thick concrete barrier separating the two "hemispheres" of the organizational brain. The synapses between them seem to have been completely severed—or perhaps they never existed in the first place.

And remember, each of the examples cited here is typical of literally hundreds if not thousands of similar organizations around the world. Indeed, it is almost unfair to single them out; in most cases, they are absolutely no worse than their peers. They do, however, make for arresting —and sobering—reading.

The Multilateral Financial Institutions

Multilateral financial institutions, as the name implies, are organizations whose membership and funding come from a large number of countries. The United Nations and World Bank may be the two highest profile examples; others include the Asian Development Bank and the Inter-American Development Bank in Latin America. The United Nations, as we shall see, provides a particularly striking example of the perverse outcomes and lost opportunities resulting from the ideological orthodoxies that we examined in Chapter 2.

The UN Joint Staff Pension Fund

There is perhaps no more blatant demonstration of the disconnect between the operating side of a major global organization and its investment activities than the United Nations Joint Staff Pension Fund (UNJSPF). The Fund manages the retirement assets of not only UN employees, but also those of over 20 related organizations, including the WHO (World Health Organization), the ILO (International Labour Organization), and the WTO (World Trade Organization). As of early 2008, the Fund had investable assets of over $40 billion.

The UN Fund has fiduciary responsibility for investing the retirement savings of over 100,000 people. We can fairly presume at the very least, I think, that most of these folks have no strong *objection* to the concept of improving the economic, social, and environmental circumstances of the world's underprivileged. Indeed, they may even be in *favor* of doing so! So how, exactly, have these sentiments and concerns been translated into investment strategies and concrete investment choices on their collective behalf?

Well, at the level of announced policy and rhetoric, all would appear to be well. The Fund has produced a stand-alone document called "Sustainable Development Agenda 21," which reads in part as follows:

> The UNJSPF must participate and take the appropriate measures to protect the environment, motivate its staff, secure its long term viability, and align its practices with the principles of the Global Compact.[1]

These noble but somewhat general aspirations are given greater specificity in a series of policy documents fleshing out the Fund's Management Charter and published since 2001. The following points are from the environmental section of the document on sustainable development:

- *Paper:* limit the negative impact of paper production on the ecosystem, e.g., forest destruction; use of chemical products.
- *Energy:* limit the negative impact on the ecosystem of energy production, e.g., exhausting natural petrol resources; radioactive waste produced out of nuclear energy.
- *Waste:* limit the negative impact on the ecosystem of waste production, e.g., unattended waste stocking area; toxic smoke generated by unsorted waste.
- *Transport:* limit the negative impact on the ecosystem of car pollution; limit the use of nonrenewable resources; improve health conditions.[2]

So how does the UNJSPF actually go about "participating and taking the appropriate measures" to align its investment practices with the noble ES goals of the UN Global Compact? Despite considerable prodding from both internal and external critics stretching back at least a decade, the answer to this question is, to put it delicately, not entirely obvious. True, the UN's own pension fund *did* in fact sign on—albeit reluctantly—to the UN Principles for Responsible Investment (PRI) in 2006. (That would be the *same* UN in both cases.) Those Principles are as follows:

> As institutional investors, we have a duty to act in the best long-term interests of our beneficiaries. In this fiduciary role, we believe that environmental, social, and corporate governance (ESG) issues can affect the performance of investment portfolios (to varying degrees across companies, sectors, regions, asset classes and through time). We also recognise that applying these Principles may better align investors with broader objectives of society. Therefore, where consistent with our fiduciary responsibilities, we commit to the following:
>
> 1. We will incorporate ESG issues into investment analysis and decision-making processes.
> 2. We will be active owners and incorporate ES issues into our ownership policies and practices.
> 3. We will seek appropriate disclosure on ESG issues by the entities in which we invest.
> 4. We will promote acceptance and implementation of the Principles within the investment industry.
> 5. We will work together to enhance our effectiveness in implementing the Principles.
> 6. We will each report on our activities and progress towards implementing the Principles.

This is not exactly breathtakingly radical stuff and is certainly congruent with all of the high-minded principles of the UN's own Management Charter and the Global Compact.

Perhaps surprisingly, though, even the relatively modest gesture of *signing* the document was agreed to only at the eleventh hour (literally!), and only through the personal intervention of then Secretary General Kofi Annan, overriding the objections of the Fund's professional investment staff. As for actually *implementing* the Principles, well, that's another story entirely.

At present, the UNJSPF still has no dedicated sustainable investment strategy or asset allocation, and indeed has declined repeatedly to avail itself of any specialized externally provided ES research to help enrich its day-to-day investment decisions. To put it starkly, the Fund's investment staff currently has *no way whatsoever* of systematically assessing the environmental, social, and governance risks in its $40 billion investment portfolio. To do so would, clearly, require access to company-specific research, and there is no evidence that the Fund has either generated any internally or chosen to use any of the widely available external sources of such research.[3] And similarly, with respect to the UN's own Global Compact, the Fund currently has no systematic means of ascertaining how many, if any, of its investee companies were violating, say, three or more of the 10 Global Compact Principles.[4]

But how can that possibly be? All that would be required—at least to get started in implementing *either* the UN Global Compact or the UN Principles for Responsible Investment—would be to do what hundreds of other investment organizations (none of which has the words "United Nations" in its organizational title) have already done: access some of the company, industry sector, and thematic research that is available from at least 20 independent research providers.[5] So why hasn't that obvious and modest step been taken?

For an explanation, I fear that we must revert to what I have previously described as the two most powerful forces of nature: individual intellectual inertia and collective organizational inertia. The Fund appears to have an abundance of both. Numerous private conversations that I have had personally with senior Fund officials over the past 10 years have persuaded me that the organization is firmly in the thrall of most if not all of the investment myths that we examined in Chapter 2. More specifically, there seems to be a pervasive (if unexamined) belief that ES factors are at best immaterial and, more probably, injurious to the Fund's (or anyone else's) financial returns. It would therefore clearly be incompatible with the Fund's fiduciary obligations to consider ES factors systematically. It is a mantra that we have heard repeated literally hundreds of times; unfortunately it just resonates a bit more loudly because of who actually owns the money being managed here and the principles espoused by the organization for which they work.

One last thing. Since rejecting sustainable investing is usually based on (unjustifiable) fears of hurting financial performance, how *has* the UN staff pension fund actually done? Well, the professional investment staff has managed to *lose* $1.1 billion over the past year—a return of *minus* 2.7%.

In fairness to the poor old UN, however, things are little better at that other prominent global institution and sustainability rejectionist—the World Bank.

The World Bank

The World Bank Group, headquartered in Washington, D.C., has 185 member countries and since its inception in 1944 has made loans of over $430 billion to low-income countries, all ostensibly to reduce poverty, promote economic and social development, and/or improve the environment.

As might be expected, "sustainability" has become an increasingly central program theme and objective for the World Bank, particularly over the past decade. To quote the Vice President of Sustainable Development Katharine Sierra:

> By promoting economic growth strategies based on environmental responsibility and social acceptability, we are bringing a sustainable future closer to today's reality.[6]

In a document entitled "World Bank Socially Responsible Investments," the Bank emphasizes the importance it places on ES factors in each of the projects, grants, and loans that it undertakes. Indeed, in 2006 alone, it gave out more than $1.6 *billion* in ES-related grants through its Global Environment Facility, a nearly 10 percent increase over the previous year. In the most recent 5-year period, a rough tally of the Bank's ES-related lending easily tops $10 billion. Additionally, the Bank goes to great lengths to measure and monitor its own direct environmental footprint from staff activities and travel as well as buildings. The Bank also aggressively promotes the use of environmentally sound and energy-efficient products and services in its own buying and procurement activities and has active recycling and composting programs for its staff. The Bank's world headquarters in Washington D.C. is an environmental showcase, and has already achieved "carbon neutrality" through both energy efficiency initiatives and the purchase of renewable energy.[7]

The Bank's private sector arm IFC (International Finance Corporation) has published dozens of reports emphasizing the critical significance of sustainability in the emerging markets, which are its sole programmatic focus. IFC has even committed program funds to an innovative emerging markets sustainability fund, managed by Rexiter Capital Management. IFC's 2007 Annual Report reassures readers that "ensuring environmental and social sustainability" is one of its five main strategic pillars.[8] In 2007, IFC's investment in development projects exceeded $8 billion, with renewable energy and energy efficiency investments alone estimated at over $450 million.

While the Bank's many critics can and do dispute the true "sustainability" of many of these program activities and expenditures (for example, its funding support of major hydroelectric projects, such as China's massive Three Gorges dam), there can be little doubt that the Bank is sincere in at least its intentions in this regard. And it has invested billions of dollars in pursuit of those same, laudable objectives.

The unwary might be tempted to think, therefore, that the impact of those investments of public money on the program side would be reinforced or at least safeguarded by investing the Bank staff's *own* retirement savings in a manner congruent with its program objectives. Sadly, however, it exhibits precisely the same institutional schizophrenia on the subject as so many other multilateral institutions, governments, endowments and foundations, NGOs, and labor funds. Briefly put, there is simply *no connection whatsoever* between the World Bank's activities on the program side and what it actually does on the *investment* side of the organization.

This dichotomy is at its most apparent in two areas: the investment of the Bank's $60 billion core liquidity portfolio (the revenues that finance all of its program activity) and its own staff pension fund, with current assets of some $12 billion. The former funds the World Bank's program work and the latter represents the retirement savings of nearly 20,000 people who have in many cases dedicated their entire careers to the Bank's professed objectives of alleviation of poverty, economic and social development, and improved environmental conditions in emerging markets. So how exactly is the $70 billion+ being invested by the Bank's Investment Management Department?

In brief, it is invested precisely the same way it would be if no one at the Bank had ever *heard* the words "environment," "social development," or sustainability! There is *no* evidence that ES considerations play any role in the day-to-day investment practices of the Bank's pension fund. There are no published investment principles or policies of *any* kind, never mind any with specific regard to sustainability.[9] The Bank is even conspicuous by its absence from the list of signatories to the UN Principles for Responsible Investment. (Come to think of it, though, I'm not quite sure which behavior displays the greater cognitive dissonance: the World Bank's refusal to sign them at all or the United Nations' *creation* and promotion of the Principles, very reluctant signature, and then subsequent refusal or inability to implement them!)

What about the World Bank Investment Management Department's actual financial performance track record? Well, we wish we could tell you, but the most recent publicly available performance information is from 2005, so we simply don't know. This is somewhat odd for an organization so passionately concerned about openness and transparency in *others*, but perhaps we quibble.

Just to review our contentions:

- It is arguably a fundamental breach of the Bank's basic fiduciary responsibility to have no specific strategies or resources with which to assess the environmental and social risks and impacts of its investment activities;
- Based on both the academic and practical evidence that we shall review in Chapter 4, the Bank's financial performance could have been even *better* had ES factors been considered systematically—or even at all; and
- At worst, the World Bank's investment activities could well be actively *undermining* many of the environmental, social, and governance objectives that its program expenditures have been designed to accomplish. At the very least, the Bank is foregoing any opportunity to use its investment muscle to advance and *enhance* its positive program impact in those areas. Perhaps the most troubling thing of all is that we'll never know any of the answers to either of these questions: from a sustainability perspective, the Bank simply has no idea *what* it has invested in!

The Public Sector Pension Funds

The next broad category of asset owner that we shall examine here is the public sector pension funds. There are over 2700 public sector pension funds in the United States alone, and they represent over $2.5 *trillion* worth of the retirement savings of public servants, teachers, police and firefighters, and others. They are a critical component of the capital markets and, as we have seen in our earlier "universal owner" discussion, they *should* be the ultimate long-term investors, with an overarching interest in improving the environmental and social quality of the overall global economy as a whole. Nine of the 10 largest pension funds in the United States are typically "State" funds—investing the retirement savings of state employees. We shall look at one of the State funds here and two more in Chapter 9.

The State of Connecticut

If ever there were a "poster child" for an institutional investor well positioned to implement an ES integration strategy it is the $26 billion pension fund of the State of Connecticut. To begin with, it is the only state in the United States with enabling legislation specifically allowing its pension fund to consider environmental factors in its investment strategies. So much for the "fiduciary responsibility" bogeyman that we discussed in Chapter 2 and that has proved to be such an impediment elsewhere! Second, State Treasurer Denise Nappier is the *sole* trustee for the funds—there is no tiresome need to engineer and mobilize a consensus on a fractious nine-person board, as is the case with other state funds such as CalPERS and CalSTRS in California. Best of all, Treasurer Nappier has been a real leader in the ES integration crusade. She has co-chaired two major, pioneering UN conferences on climate change. For the first of them, in November 2003, her co-chair was no less a luminary than then-Secretary General Kofi Annan. She co-chaired a second "climate summit" in New York at UN headquarters in May 2005 and was also a co-convener of the third major Investor Summit on Climate Risk in February 2008. She has also testified before the U.S. Senate on the critical importance of climate change to large institutional investors and fiduciaries. The State of Connecticut was one of the founding signatories of the breakthrough Carbon Disclosure Project back in 2002. Ms. Nappier was also one of the founding signatories of the UN Principles for Responsible Investment, standing right beside Dr. Annan when he rang the opening bell at the New York Stock Exchange (NYSE). In short, in the world of institutional investors, it simply doesn't get much better than this for sustainability.

We would, therefore, logically expect the State of Connecticut to be leveraging all of those contextual advantages into an aggressive, leading-edge ES integration program, right? Wrong! To date, the sum total of the State's action on this front has been voting its proxies on a long list of ES issues, including global warming, air pollution, human rights, and labor rights.

Now, don't get me wrong: voting proxies is an important tool in the active shareholder's toolkit, and Connecticut has been doing it better and longer than most. But at the end of the day (as the UN PRI themselves make clear), ES integration should manifest itself in actual investment *decisions* and choices; assets *must* be allocated at least somewhat differently than would otherwise have been the case had the institutions never heard of or signed the Principles in the first place!

Unlike several other U.S. states, Connecticut has no dedicated "sustainability" fund allocation, and neither its internal nor external money managers have systematic access to sustainability research and analysis, so that it could even potentially be integrated into their investment decision making. On climate change, for example, with same-sector risk exposures varying by *30* times or more among companies, Connecticut's money managers have no systematic way of distinguishing the most risky companies from the least.

To its credit, the State *does* attempt to use its economic muscle for social objectives by encouraging minority groups and local economic development through its procurement practices. But, relative to its enormous *potential* for much broader action and impact, Connecticut is actually doing very little. It has no formal investment policy of ES integration, and, as we have seen, no explicit allocation of assets to any sustainability-enhanced public equities strategies. Unlike other public funds with much less favorable decision-making environments, it conspicuously does not insist that its external money managers acquire the necessary research and integrate ES factors on its behalf. In short, the story is one of significantly underutilized potential. Based on the performance research that we will discuss in Chapter 4, the State of Connecticut is leaving *both* financial returns *and* positive ES impact on the table.

So what's been the impediment? Basically, it's been the constellation of misconceptions we catalogued in Chapter 2, the most important of which is the automatic but erroneous assumption that ES integration would inevitably hurt returns. And, as ever, there's "maverick risk." As Lord Keynes observed many years ago, it is apparently preferable to fail conventionally, staying with the herd, than to succeed unconventionally.

Oh, and one last thing: as of April 2008, the State fund overall had achieved a 12-month return of only 0.61%. This was about 30 percent *below* the median performance of its peers.[10]

Foundations and Endowments

Another critical group of asset owners for whom sustainable investment *should* be both logical and beneficial is the major foundations and university endowments. One recent estimate suggested that worldwide, foundations alone invest over USD 600 billion per year.[11] Typically, they spend only a small fraction of that (usually 5 percent) on grants and programs consistent with their particular mission—education, health, environment, poverty alleviation, etc. What is of primary concern to us here, however, is the *other* 95 percent of their assets—the so-called corpus, which is intended to generate sufficient investment returns to enable the organization to continue to fund its program activities in perpetuity. Unfortunately, as we have seen with other major investors, the two sides of the endowment and foundation "house" not only rarely work in concert, they very frequently work at *cross-purposes!* We need look no further than the largest private foundation in the world for a striking example.

The Gates Foundation

The Bill & Melinda Gates Foundation has current assets of nearly $40 billion and the virtually certain prospect of growing to at least $65 billion due to the multiyear generosity of legendary investor and multibillionaire Warren Buffett. The Foundation focuses on improving people's health and giving people in underdeveloped and developing countries the chance to lift themselves out of hunger and extreme poverty. In the United States, it seeks to ensure that all people, especially those with the fewest resources, have access to the opportunities they need to succeed in school and in life. Based in Seattle, the foundation is led by CEO and former Microsoft executive Patty Stonesifer and co-chair William H. Gates Sr. (Bill's father), under the direction of Bill and Melinda Gates. It is worth recalling here that as a *private* foundation, the Gates Foundation's investment policies can be a direct and unmitigated reflection of the founder's wishes. In this case, the decision-making chain is an exceptionally short one indeed.

According to its annual report, the Foundation is focused on three broad areas:

- Global Development (biodiversity preservation, growth industries in Africa, technology for the poor, banks for Africa's poor);
- Global Health (HIV—awareness, vaccine, delivery; tuberculosis, and other forgotten diseases that kill the poor); and
- USA (reconnecting communities, education, housing).

In addition to grant making, the Foundation also partners with for-profit organizations, such as Merck and MTV, on issues such as HIV/AIDS.

Underlining the commitment of the Gateses to maximize the impact of all their resources by focusing on a comparatively narrow set of
major global issues, the Foundation is set up to spend all of its resources
within 50 years after Bill's and Melinda's deaths.[12] Considering that both
Bill and Melinda are in seemingly good health, the responsibility of the
investment trust runs at least 70 years in the future, making the Foundation a long-term investor and another "universal owner" par excellence.

The trust is not governed under any strict investment guidelines
and discloses no investment policies apart from a preference of Bill and
Melinda not to invest in tobacco stocks. Any ES perspective or awareness
is conspicuous by its absence from the discussion on the Foundation's
website on the trust's investments.

In January 2007, the *Los Angeles Times* published a series of highly
critical articles about the Gates Endowment's investments. Titled "Dark
Clouds Over Good Work of Gates Foundation,"[13] the initial article
highlighted the apparent dichotomy between the Foundation's excellent
efforts on global health issues (including HIV, tuberculosis, and other
"neglected diseases") and its endowment's investment in industrial pol-
luters, such as oil companies. The article contended that the investments
of the world's largest endowment were contradicting and undermining
its core mission. The article identified a number of geographic areas in
which the Foundation is providing immunization from diseases and
health services to underprivileged populations, but in which the very
same populations are at health risk from companies that are polluting the
environment. The article also documented that the Gates Foundation
has holdings in many companies that have failed tests of social responsibility because of environmental lapses, employment discrimination, disregard for worker rights, or unethical practices.

The supreme irony here, of course, is that the Foundation *gives* away
nearly 3 *billion* dollars every year toward efforts to attack sustainability
problems, not to exacerbate them. And, just to be clear, we are *not* recommending the wholesale divestment of companies simply because they
are in high-impact sectors, such as oil and gas; that is the approach of
traditional SRI, which we categorically reject. Like them or loathe them,
the hard reality is that (1) oil and gas companies currently comprise a
large and critically important component of the global economy, can be
expected to do so for the foreseeable future; (2) several oil and gas companies (notably Royal Dutch/Shell and BP) are making substantial strategic investments in "sustainability-friendly" energy technologies, such as
solar, wind, and biomass; and (3) some oil and gas companies are demon-

strably better than others at managing sustainability issues. To reject entire industry sectors as "unsustainable" is, in our view, both simplistic *and* an abrogation of the ability to have any leverage with companies, to engage with them, and to try to *change* their practices. For all of these reasons, I believe that many of the article's criticisms were in fact unsound and unfair. At the same time, however, it does seem difficult to dispute the argument that fiduciary responsibility alone should require that the Foundation's money managers at least be *aware* of any significant ES risks in the portfolio. At the moment, there is virtually no possibility that they could be.

After an initial reaction to the article suggesting that it would indeed review its investment policies and practices, the Gates Foundation quickly recanted and stood by its existing investment process. Bill Gates himself made it very clear publicly the same week that the *L.A. Times* article appeared that ES considerations had no place in the endowment's investment strategy. Reasons given for inaction were summarized in statements from Chief Operating Officer Cheryl Scott:

- . . . there are dozens of factors that could be considered, almost all of which are outside the foundation's areas of expertise, and questions such as "should a company get a failing score if 1 percent of its output is used in cigarette packaging, or if 1 percent of its stores' sales are in tobacco? How far back in time do you evaluate behavior? If a company disagrees with your assessment, what appeals process is available? Which social and political issues should be on the list?"
- Bill and Melinda have prioritized our program work over ranking companies and issues because it allows us to have the greatest impact for the most people. They also believe there would be much room for error and confusion in such judgments, and that divesting from these companies would not have an effect commensurate with the resources we would divert to this activity. The Foundation's not owning a tiny percentage of a company or selling it to another investor would often go unnoticed, and Bill and Melinda would not be comfortable delegating this kind of judgment.

Statements such as these—and similar comments from Mr. Gates himself —reflect a strikingly dated, ill-informed, and unsophisticated understanding of what contemporary sustainable investment actually comprises. They betray a total confusion between that approach and traditional, exclusions-based SRI.

As I hope we have already made clear, the brand of investment being advocated here has nothing to do with the often arbitrary, reductionist "SRI" approach described and apparently understood by the Gates Foundation and its founder. It is impossible for any outsider to pinpoint the precise locus of the obstructionism, but there is no shortage of candidates, and they are all the usual suspects: the actual owners of the capital (Bill and Melinda), their new partner and co-benefactor Warren Buffett, the executives of the Foundation and endowment, their investment managers, and their outside advisors and consultants. The fact that an individual with the allegedly insatiable intellectual curiosity of a Bill Gates would refuse to even *consider* the possibility is ample testimony to the persistence and power of the conceptual resistance to the sustainable investment paradigm.

In a nutshell, then, despite the enormous brainpower of the Gates Foundation's principals, professional employees, and advisors, it may very well be leaving *both* program impact and money on the table. They simply do not know. And, in sheer dollar terms at least, the Gates Foundation represents the single greatest lost opportunity in the foundation world. Like many of its peers, its dogged refusal to even *consider* what sustainable investing might offer is particularly striking and regrettable, given both its mandate and its high visibility. The Foundation *could* have a truly electrifying and galvanizing effect on foundations and endowments worldwide. To date, regrettably, it has consciously and conspicuously elected not to do so.

There are at least four compelling arguments in favor of incorporating ES research into the investment process at the Gates Foundation—or any other:

- From a program impact viewpoint, opportunities are being lost to reinforce the Foundation's positive impact, or *at least* to avoid actively undermining it;
- From a financial perspective, there is considerable evidence that risk-adjusted returns could be enhanced;
- Significant and additional reputational capital could be built for the Foundation, with both internal and external stakeholders; and
- Global fiduciary best practice now demands it.

Not that the Gates Foundation is noticeably worse than its peers; very, very few of them are doing any better. The Ford Foundation, for example, *gives* away over $550 million each year to promote the improvement of environmental and social conditions, yet has steadfastly refused to even consider assessing the ES risks in its $12 billion investment portfolio. The Rockefeller Foundation is in a similar situation, albeit with smaller numbers: grants that could fairly be characterized as "sustainability-oriented" amount to at *least* $100 million each year, yet the potential investment power of the $4 billion endowment itself is entirely untapped for this purpose. Indeed, the extent to which its investments may be actively *undermining* its program objectives is entirely unknown; from a sustainability perspective, the foundations currently have no way of knowing *what* they're investing in!

What is truly ironic here is that major U.S. foundations such as Ford, MacArthur, Rockefeller, and Hewlett Packard, all *do* recognize—to a point—the positive programmatic impact that their investment dollars can generate; all of them make so-called "program-related investments." These are investments—not outright grants—that are expected to further the mission and objectives of the foundations, but from which market-rate financial returns are not expected. The problem is that such investments are statistically miniscule; the persuasive logic of maximizing program impact via investment strategy is typically confined to less than 1 percent of the foundations' investment portfolios. One recent estimate identified USD 600 *billion* in foundation assets worldwide, virtually *none* of which is currently invested in a manner reinforcing their program objectives.[14]

And by the way, investment returns for the Gates Foundation for the year 2007 were approximately 12.67 percent, trailing their "heavyweight" peers, such as the Ford Foundation (16.5 percent) and the Rockefeller Foundation (14.8 percent).[15] So it is not as if the Foundation's money managers have already attained earthly perfection and have no need to consider any new investment insights or approaches!

Oh, and there's one final irony: at the 2008 World Economic Forum in Davos, Switzerland, Bill Gates gave a major and widely publicized speech with the provocative title "A New Approach to Capitalism in the 21st Century." The speech was an impassioned plea for a new business paradigm he called "creative capitalism." According to Gates, businesses could and should be using their economic power, creativity, and management skills to tackle social problems—and, indeed, make a profit while they're at it. (Does this theme sound at all familiar?) The tragedy is that he and his advisors have apparently yet to recognize that he could readily kick start creative capitalism all by himself—by rethinking the investment strategy of the $40 billion corpus of his own Foundation and connecting it strategically with the grant-giving side.

The Yale Endowment

It is always somewhat risky to criticize an icon, and I do so here with considerable trepidation. The Yale University Endowment (with over $22 billion in assets) and its highly acclaimed Chief Investment Officer David Swenson have achieved almost mythological status among institutional investors around the world. Indeed, these may be the very first critical words ever published regarding the Yale Endowment! By conventional criteria, this reverential status is well deserved: the Endowment has consistently achieved top-quartile investment performance, far outstripping the average of its peers. In addition to its exceptional returns, the Yale Endowment has also been a thought leader in asset allocation and portfolio strategy—it was one of the first major institutions to make significant "bets" on such "alternative" investments as hedge funds, private equity, commodities, and other nontraditional asset classes. In a typical year, the Endowment's 17 percent plus returns generate over 30 percent of Yale's entire operating budget. In 2007, the investment team generated exceptional returns of 28%, and added a staggering $5 *billion* to the overall Endowment's value. Fuelled by its outstanding returns, the Endowment has increased in size *10-fold* in the past decade.

So what's the problem? What's not to like here? How can we dare to criticize such a self-evidently successful approach? Well, in fact, it is precisely the disjunction between the Endowment's reputation for innovation and success and its studied avoidance of sustainability investing that makes its example so compelling.

Like most American campuses, Yale has its share of student activists pressing the University to invest its assets in a more "socially responsible" manner. Swenson and his staff have, however, unequivocally rejected such suggestions, usually trotting out the same myths we examined in Chapter 2 as the investment logic for their refusal to even consider such a thing.

There is little debate that Yale is indeed one of the world's great universities. In fact, President Richard Levin refers explicitly to Yale's role as a truly global university, advancing the frontiers of knowledge and educating future leaders, not only for the United States but for the entire world. Against such a backdrop, the Endowment's dogmatic refusal to even *consider* addressing major global megatrends, such as sustainability in its investment strategies, seems all the more puzzling. Once again, like the Gates Foundation, were the Yale Endowment to even publicly *consider* integrating sustainability considerations into its investment process, the positive impact on its peers worldwide would be immense.

The Endowment publishes no "responsible investment" principles or guidelines regarding ES factors; indeed, it publishes no investment principles of *any* kind. In a world in which the World Economic Forum in Davos has declared climate change to be "the business issue of the millennium," and the net exposure of major U.S. companies to climate risk can vary by over *30 times* even within the same industry sector, the failure to investigate these exposures systematically would seem to be a nontrivial lapse in due diligence and fiduciary responsibility.

In addition to the purely financial risks that the Endowment is courting because of its de facto boycott of sustainable investing, it is also incurring unnecessary reputational risk, both for itself and for the entire University. In 2002, for example, Yale shifted over $10 billion from publicly traded equities to private equity. This substantial allocation invested in a series of limited partnerships, one of which planned to purchase the Baca Ranch in the San Luis Valley in Colorado and pump large volumes of water from an underground aquifer across the mountains to the City of Denver. Predictably, the local community objected strenuously, characterizing Yale as engaging in "the rape of the community,"[16] since it owned 50 percent of the limited partnership and had an invitingly high public profile. After the controversy, the land was sold to the Nature Conservancy for subsequent conversion into a national park, although Yale received virtually none of the credit and most of the blame for what had gone before.

A more recent example of ES-driven reputational risk emerged in 2007, when the Endowment (along with those from Harvard, Princeton, Columbia, and others) was sued for usury—yes, charging an unconscionable amount of interest! One of the Endowment's investment vehicles, Realty Financial Partners, was alleged to be making loans with an interest rate of 42 percent—twice the legal limit.[17] An attractive yield to be sure—had it been legal—but hardly a tonic for the reputations of the sophisticated endowment investors—*or* their donors. To be fair to the institution, however, neither its Ivy League peers nor Stanford is currently pursuing sustainable investment with any more vigor or enthusiasm than is Yale.

Environmental NGOs:
The Emperors Have Few Clothes

Nongovernmental organizations (NGOs) with an environmental mission have, over the past decade, achieved unprecedented levels of sophistication, financial and technical resources, credibility, and impact. They have clearly become major players in the Sustainability Revolution and have catalyzed an enormous amount of progress, particularly among corporations. What is *less* well known, however, is that they could achieve even *greater* credibility, legitimacy, and real-world impact if they more consistently put their money where their mouths have already been for quite some time now.

The Nature Conservancy

The Nature Conservancy is a U.S.-based endowment with global program activities and a mission that can be accurately inferred from its name. (Actually, come to think of it, in the United States not-for-profit sector, in which completely and deliberately disingenuous organizational names abound, this alone can be considered something of an achievement!) The Conservancy's purpose is to preserve plants, animals, and natural ecosystems throughout the United States, Canada, Latin America, the Caribbean, Africa, and Asia Pacific. Its primary revenue sources are government grants, private donations (including gifts of land), and investment income from its $2 billion endowment. (In 2007, the investment income exceeded $225 million.) It uses these funds to acquire, protect, and rehabilitate a variety of different ecosystems around the world. In addition to its own resources, the Conservancy also leverages complementary resources from elsewhere; it helped secure a $400 million allocation from the World Bank's Global Environment Facility to strengthen national park systems in developing countries and an additional $10 million to help 35 countries conduct scientific audits of their biodiversity resources.

This is all great stuff. But, once again, we must ask the inconvenient question: what about the *investment* side of the house? The allocation and investment of $2 billion could unquestionably have a considerable impact—for good *or* for ill—on environmental quality. So, what percentage of the $2 billion is currently invested in any one of the top-performing sustainability funds, such as the Winslow Green Growth Fund, Generation Investment Management's global sustainability fund, or Jupiter's Global Green Fund? You guessed it: zero.

What is even more disturbing is that *not one dime* of the endowment's $2 billion investment capital is subjected to even a cursory assessment of the environmental performance or impact of its investee companies. It is entirely possible that the Conservancy is invested in the worst polluters imaginable, directly undercutting its own program objectives. We simply don't know. And, more importantly, neither do they.

Unfortunately, the Nature Conservancy is far from the only prominent—and otherwise highly competent—environmental NGO in this position. Environmental Defense, one of the most high-profile and effective of those in the United States, is similarly bereft of environmentally sensitive strategies or even research when it comes to the investment of its $100 million endowment, as are many other leading organizations such as the World Resources Institute. Surely these are lost opportunities.

Organized Labor

Few would dispute that organized labor has played—and continues to play—a critical role in economic, political, and social development in countries all over the world. However, and as is the case with multilateral financial institutions, public pension funds, endowments and foundations, and NGOs, organized labor has fallen well short of the potential impact it *could* have were it to use its capital resources more strategically.

Do Like We Say, Not Like We Do: The AFL-CIO

Organized labor *should* be at the very least sympathetic to the social and environmental concerns of sustainability, if not in the forefront of their advocacy. The American Federation of Labor and Congress of Industrial Organizations (AFL-CIO) is a voluntary federation of 55 national and international labor unions. The AFL-CIO union movement currently represents some 10.5 million members, including teachers, taxi drivers, musicians, miners, firefighters, farm workers, bakers, bottlers, engineers, editors, pilots, public employees, doctors, nurses, painters, truck drivers, and plumbers. The self-described mission of the AFL-CIO is

> . . . to improve the lives of working families—to bring economic justice to the workplace and social justice to our nation. To accomplish this mission we will build and change the American labor movement.

At a major institutional investor summit on climate risk in New York City in February 2008 hosted by the United Nations, AFL-CIO President John Sweeney boasted that organized labor "controlled" $5 *trillion* of investable assets in the United States alone. By any measure, that is a serious quantum of economic power—if only it could be utilized strategically and effectively. The AFL-CIO's Office of Investments is—at least rhetorically—a major advocate of the concept of "Workers' Capital"—using the capital markets as a catalyst to move toward a more socially equitable, "stakeholder-centric" system as opposed to a "shareholder-centric" one. The Office leads the AFL-CIO's "capital stewardship" efforts to protect workers' capital for their future retirements. These efforts include educational and advocacy programs on corporate governance, executive pay, and retirement security. The Office has also developed a comprehensive set of *proxy voting guidelines* that lay out the AFL-CIO's positions on corporate governance as well as social and environmental issues.

The guidelines have been developed to provide pension fund trustees with a consistent framework for voting their funds' shareholder proxies at companies' annual general meetings in an effort to affect their policies and behavior. The concept of "active share ownership" is, quite properly, important to the AFL-CIO as investors. Voting shareholder proxies to try to influence company behavior is an absolutely basic—if limited—weapon in the active shareowner's arsenal. Doing so using a consistent, coherent set of guidelines should help maximize whatever effectiveness this practice can have.[18] The guidelines are applied to both of the AFL-CIO's principal investment vehicles, the AFL-CIO Staff Retirement Fund and the AFL-CIO Reserve Fund. The Retirement Fund is the pension plan for staff employees and is a separate legal identity from the AFL-CIO, with its own separate board. Strangely enough for an organization that often crusades for openness and transparency from *companies,* there is no publicly available information about even the *size* of the Retirement Fund, never mind any of its investment policies. The AFL-CIO Reserve Fund is part of the AFL-CIO itself and had investments worth $31 million at the end of 2004, the most recent date for which publicly available information exists.

In addition to dealing with corporate governance and executive pay issues, the AFL-CIO's proxy voting guidelines also have a section on "Corporate Social Responsibility" that recommends support for shareholder proposals encouraging the adoption of policies on corporate conduct, labor principles and human rights, the CERES environmental principles, equal employment opportunity, and fair lending. Not surprisingly, in the wake of the subprime mortgage market meltdown in 2007–2008, demands for improved risk disclosure topped the current labor proxy voting agenda. The creation of succession plans for company CEOs was another, somewhat surprising major concern. ES issues, however, received short shrift in the latest labor proxy voting season.

In any event, proxy voting is all well and good, but in our view it represents only the first and most basic and timid step on the evolutionary ladder toward truly active share ownership and the use of economic power. Occasionally, it has admittedly been effective in modifying corporate behavior. It should *not,* however, be confused with the thorough integration of ES factors in the process of deciding which securities to purchase in the first place. In our view, as long as shareholder resolutions can be and are routinely ignored by the management and boards of companies, it will be much more effective for large institutions to actually *invest* according to clearly articulated environmental and social objectives. Talk is truly cheap.

The AFL-CIO publishes the proxy voting records of its two funds twice a year. Sadly, however, that seems to be the alpha and omega of ES integration in the investment of the unions' pension funds, at least as far as any evidence from public documents is concerned. There is absolutely no disclosure on how either of the two major funds is actually invested. The latest financial report available on the internet is, inexplicably, for the year 2004. The investment strategies, asset mix, and other details are not clearly disclosed. It is not even possible to obtain information on the overall *size* of the fund!

With that level of opacity concerning even the most elementary *traditional* financial information, it is hardly surprising to discover that the AFL-CIO funds have absolutely no investment principles or guidelines concerning ES issues. What *is* somewhat surprising, however, is the yawning gulf between the principles the organization proposes that *others* follow and those it is prepared to observe itself. On the proxy voting side, that is, when it comes to how *other* organizations ought to behave, the AFL-CIO is quite vocal about poor corporate governance, excessive executive pay, accountability, and social and environmental issues. These are, after all, the same folks who publish documents with titles such as *Failed Fiduciaries* and *Enablers of Excess.*[19] When it comes to its *own* investment criteria, however, the group is absolutely mute.

Take the high-profile issue of climate change, for example. American labor leaders have been quite outspoken in their support of the idea of addressing climate risk in investment strategies. As noted above, AFL-CIO

President John Sweeney was one of several prominent labor leader con-
veners of the Institutional Investor Summit on Climate Risk at the United
Nations headquarters in New York City in February 2008. He was also
one of the featured speakers, along with UN Secretary General Ban Ki-
Moon and Al Gore. (Another prominent speaker was Connecticut State
Treasurer Denise Nappier, whom we discussed earlier in this chapter.)
We could be forgiven for assuming, therefore, that the AFL-CIO might
actually be taking concrete steps to ensure that its investments were routinely scrutinized to assess their level of risk exposure to climate change.
After all, as we have seen, risk levels can vary by a factor of *30* among
companies in the very same industry sector and country, and climate risk
can have a demonstrable impact on the share price performance of companies.[20] Indeed, that was one of the basic premises underpinning the
Investor Summit in the first place.

Unfortunately, however, nothing of the sort is true. There is no
indication of any organized labor investment whatsoever in any specific
vehicles designed either to mitigate climate risk or to exploit climate-
driven opportunities on the upside, such as clean technology (solar power,
wind power, biofuels, and so forth). Far worse in our view, there is similarly no evidence that *any* of the AFL-CIO's external fund managers
have been instructed to address climate change, or indeed any other ES
risks or issues, in *any* of the organization's investment portfolios. Once
again, the evidence that we shall discuss in Chapter 4 suggests that this
failure may well be leaving financial returns on the table. What is beyond
dispute is that it is also leaving potentially positive social and environmental impact on the table, not to mention creating a glaring gap between the AFL-CIO's rhetoric and the investment reality on the ground.

To be fair, it must be acknowledged that the AFL-CIO *is* using at
least some of its investment capital to pursue explicit economic and social objectives. The externally managed AFL-CIO Building Investment
Trust has, over 20 years, invested over $6 billion in commercial real estate
designed to create both economic growth and union jobs. On the housing and urban revitalization side, the AFL-CIO has created a mutual
fund vehicle, the Housing Investment Trust, focused on investing in
community housing in cities such as New York and Chicago, via high-
grade debt securities. Over the past decade, the Trust has helped build or
rehabilitate over 80,000 housing units, improving the supply of affordable housing and, again, creating employment for union members.

Once again, all of this is commendable stuff, but does not even
scratch the surface of what could be accomplished by strategically mobi-
lizing the *full* power of organized labor's investment capital across all of

the asset classes and geographies in which it invests. And it is certainly a far cry from the labor movement's high-minded rhetoric!

Company Pension Funds: The Sounds of Silence

No account of lost investment opportunities for asset owners would be complete without remarking on the virtually complete absence of *corporate* pension funds from the sustainable investment landscape. With only a handful of exceptions, several of which we shall highlight in Chapter 9, company pension funds have so far stayed away from the Sustainability Revolution in droves. This is true even of companies that have given sustainability a high priority in their actual business operations, and indeed have succeeded admirably there. As we have seen with multilateral financial institutions, public sector pension funds, endowments and foundations, "green" NGOs, and organized labor, however, there appears to be a complete conceptual disconnect between the operating side of the organization and the investment of its workers' pension assets. I suspect that unlike their public sector counterparts, corporate pension funds have not explicitly rejected the sustainable investment hypothesis; they have simply never even *considered* it in the first place. Perhaps they will do so soon; if not, the opportunity cost in terms of both financial returns and positive sustainability impact will inevitably be high.

The foregoing examples throughout this chapter make for somewhat depressing (if not infuriating) reading. If nothing else, however, they provide ample evidence of the power of the ideological headwind that the sustainable investment thesis has been facing for over 15 years now. At the same time, however, the optimist (Pollyanna?) in us tends to view the situation as a glass half *full*—an enormous opportunity just waiting to be seized. Just imagine the impact if even 10 percent of the assets controlled by multilateral financial institutions, pension funds, endowments and foundations, NGOs, and organized labor could be harnessed and shifted onto a more sustainable trajectory!

Before that can happen on any scale, however, we need a conceptual framework for investment into which such an approach could fit. It is to the task of constructing one that we shall turn in Chapter 5. First, however, let us consider the actual financial performance track record of sustainability investment. Skeptics and opponents of the sustainable investment thesis often refer to this body of "evidence" to buttress their case. Sadly, it seems that relatively few have actually bothered to examine it, and fewer still have interpreted it correctly. But let's see for ourselves.

Chapter 4

But What Does the Evidence *Really* Say?

A constant barrier to the widespread acceptance of sustainable investment has been the misconception that it automatically translates into underperformance.

—MERCER INVESTMENT CONSULTING AND UNEP-FI

As we have seen, those mainstream investment analysts and portfolio managers who have considered sustainability factors at all seem fervently convinced that there is, "out there" somewhere, a solid body of empirical financial performance evidence that convincingly repudiates the sustainable investment hypothesis. I myself came face to face with this belief system in 1997.

At that time, I had the opportunity to "pitch" the sustainable investment thesis directly to the chairman of one of Wall Street's leading investment banks, a highly knowledgeable and well-respected individual. I began, "In the twenty-first century, environmental and social issues are becoming more and more important to companies' competitive success. They are also relatively new, unfamiliar, and often devilishly complex.

Companies capable of dealing with them more effectively than their competitors are, therefore, likely to be simply better-managed, more strategic companies overall. And as such, they are quite likely to be better *financial* performers as well." As I continued, he stopped me in mid-sentence and said, "Your investment thesis is *total* nonsense! *All* of the *performance* evidence runs in the other direction."

Needless to say, I found this response somewhat disconcerting. The implications for me personally were stark indeed: I'd clearly wasted the past 30 years of my life and now appeared poised to waste the next 20 years as well! As I pondered this gloomy scenario for several seconds, the proverbial "lightbulb" suddenly went off in my head: I realized in a flash of blinding insight that he was bluffing. He was simply repeating the conventional wisdom he'd heard from his peers and that surrounded him everywhere he went, both professionally and socially.

Taking a chance, I told him that I had actually brought with me a number of reasonably sophisticated academic studies that did in fact support my case[1] and respectfully requested that he ask one of his junior colleagues to review them and *then* tell me what he thought "all the evidence" actually said. (After all, each of the studies I had cited had been published in the *investment* literature, not by Greenpeace or Mother Jones!) To his eternal credit, he actually did so, and our conversations ultimately led to an 18-month live simulation conducted over 1998–1999 of a "sustainability-tilted" portfolio of U.S. large capitalization stocks. The experiment was conducted by his own highly skilled quantitative team using external research on the environmental performance of the companies. To isolate and highlight any impact of the environmental and social factors, great care was taken to filter out the effects of traditional investment factors, such as company size, industry sector, and price momentum. In other words, the only thing that distinguished the test portfolio from the underlying Standard and Poor's 500 benchmark index was a relative overweighting of companies that were above average sustainability performers and a corresponding underweighting of sustainability laggards. The results after 18 months were a 190 basis point (1.9 percent) "sustainability out-performance premium" and a much more receptive investment bank chairman.

I recount this story not to demonstrate that the chairman was wrong (although he was), but to illustrate the fact that even exceptionally bright, knowledgeable, and experienced investment professionals can carry sufficient intellectual baggage that their instinctive reflex is one of negativity toward the sustainable investment thesis.

Regrettably, the chairman is far from alone in this regard; his views continue to represent the majority view among investors even today. Indeed, quite recently I heard one of Wall Street's most respected analysts state in a major public speech: "there is not one shred of respectable academic evidence to support the sustainable investment thesis." At the time, I happened to be thumbing through the then-current issue of the *Financial Analysts Journal,* the peer-reviewed, literary Olympiad for financial analysts. And right there, large as life, on page 51, was an article by the head of research for one of the three largest pension funds in the world (and part-time investment finance professor), providing what seemed to my untrained eye to be precisely the sort of credible academic evidence that we were solemnly being told by a respected expert did not exist.[2] No wonder the path toward the Sustainable Investment Revolution has been such a difficult and tortured one!

So what does the evidence *really* say? We shall try to summarize it in this chapter. One major caveat needs to be made at the outset, however. The majority of the bourgeoning academic literature exploring the relationship between ES performance and financial returns is simply *not* directly relevant here. The reason is this: most of it analyzes the performance of *traditional* SRI funds, which are typically based on a variety of negative, values-based company exclusions—not only "sin stock" companies in the tobacco, pornography, armaments, and (sometimes) alcohol industries, but also entire high-impact sectors, such as oil and gas, mining, forestry, and chemicals. Our thesis in this book is that the latter group of industries is both indispensable in a practical sense *and* representative of a huge swath of the global economy. To try to build a viable investment portfolio without including them is to court enormous risk by concentrating our "bets" on much too narrow a range of companies. The trick for sustainability investors, therefore, is to research and find the *best-in-class* companies in each sector.

Having said this, we will briefly review the literature on the performance of traditional SRI funds, if only because that too has been largely misunderstood and misrepresented by the mainstream. Figure 4.1 summarizes the results of a study commissioned by the U.K. Environment Agency.[3] This "meta-study" reviewed nearly 100 separate, third-party studies conducted over the past decade to examine the impact of environmental, social, and/or governance factors on financial performance. The literature review found strong evidence for the existence of a positive relationship between environmental management quality and financial performance: 79 positive correlations, 11 neutral relationships, and only 9 negative correlations.

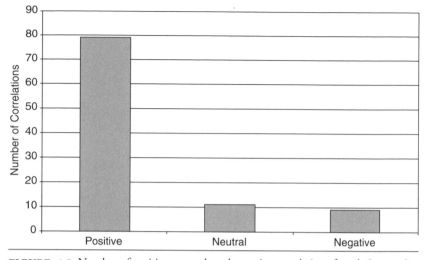

FIGURE 4.1 Number of positive, neutral, and negative correlations found. Source: Innovest Strategic Value Advisors

As gratifying as these results will be to traditional SRI advocates, inasmuch as they completely contradict the conventional "wisdom" of the sustainable investment skeptics, they are not particularly germane or helpful for our precise purposes here. As seen in Chapter 2, the exclusions-based, "neoclassical socially responsible investment" approach that permeated most of these studies is simply *not* the style of investing we are either examining or advocating here. Just to refresh the reader's memory, "sustainable investment," as we use the term in this book, is *a style of investing that explicitly and systematically examines performance and positioning of companies on environmental and social issues as part of the basic investment evaluation discipline. Importantly, it does so by using that performance as a proxy for management quality and future financial outperformance, not as a basis for ethical value judgments about the companies and their executives.* Any conclusions drawn from this traditional literature would, therefore, while broadly encouraging, not be particularly relevant to sustainable investing as we have defined it for our purposes.

The Sustainable Investment Literature

For that reason, therefore, we have confined ourselves here to the much more limited, but more directly relevant, research that has been conducted on *returns-seeking* approaches that seek to generate superior financial performance by adding ES analysis. In this chapter, we shall examine three separate bodies of such "evidence":

- Practitioner and academic research
- Research by "sell-side" investment banks
- Actual performance results from real-world "sustainability" funds

In examining this literature, one further caveat will be required. As with any study of *any* investment style or philosophy, definitions are crucial, and direct apples-to-apples comparisons are extraordinarily difficult to come by. For those reasons, sweeping or generalized conclusions are dangerous and should be avoided. Each study referred to will be at least somewhat unique in the following:

- Its precise definition of "sustainability"
- Which ES factors receive particular emphasis—e.g., climate change versus human rights—and how much;
- The risk/return objectives of the particular fund;
- The degree of emphasis accorded to each of the myriad of traditional investment factors; and
- The specific time period, geography, and market conditions in which the fund performance being studied was operating.

For all of these reasons, very few authoritative and generalizable conclusions can or should be drawn from "the evidence." Having said that, however, given the overwhelmingly negative *perception* of what the evidence actually says, it will be highly instructive to examine the facts.

Contrary to what is still a surprisingly widespread popular belief in traditional investment circles, there *is* in fact a large and growing body of both academic and empirical evidence to support the sustainable investment thesis.

Practitioners and Academics

The first example, a quantitative study undertaken by investment practitioners, comes from Boston and the Advanced Research Center of State Street Global Advisors (SSgA). One of the three largest money management firms in the world, SSgA currently has over 2 trillion dollars under management.[4]

In that study, Kim Gluck and Ying Becker examined whether the environmental performance and strategic positioning of the company provided an independent, noncorrelated source of outperformance for SSgA's actively managed portfolios.[5] SSgA used Innovest environmental ratings as proxies for the quality of its environmental management and performance. Using SSgA's own proprietary quantitative models, the study ranked each company in the investment universe (the largest publicly traded U.S. companies—the S&P 500) on traditional investment factors such as earnings estimates, analyst sentiment, price momentum patterns, and earnings quality. The effects of the environmental factors were carefully parsed out and isolated. The results showed that the "environmentally enhanced" portfolio outperformed both the passive S&P 500 benchmark *and* SSgA's actively managed stock-picking fund. These results included transaction costs and other constraints (such as portfolio turnover limits) that we would normally encounter in a real-life portfolio management process.

The results strongly suggest that combining "sustainability" overlays with an underlying fundamental investment process can indeed generate incremental performance gains. The "sustainability premium" observed in this study was 119 basis points (1.19 percent) per year, a nontrivial margin in the world of professional investors. Moreover, the portfolio's "information ratio" (the ratio between the level of outperformance and the volatility of those returns) also improved substantially, from 0.86 to 1.22. In Figure 4.2 the lowest of the three lines represents the benchmark itself, the middle line the SSgA outperformance portfolio, and the top line the SSgA portfolio, "turbo-charged" by sustainability factors.

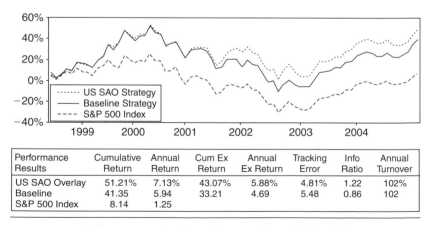

Performance Results	Cumulative Return	Annual Return	Cum Ex Return	Annual Ex Return	Tracking Error	Info Ratio	Annual Turnover
US SAO Overlay	51.21%	7.13%	43.07%	5.88%	4.81%	1.22	102%
Baseline	41.35	5.94	33.21	4.69	5.48	0.86	102
S&P 500 Index	8.14	1.25					

FIGURE 4.2 Performance results. Source: Innovest Strategic Value Advisors

A second, broadly similar study was undertaken in 2005 by a team of Dutch finance academics led by Dr. Rob Bauer, who at the time also had a "day job" as head of research for APG, the Dutch public pension fund that is the largest in Europe. (We shall learn more about APG in Chapter 9.) Bauer, Jeroen Derwall, and others analyzed the difference between the financial performance of "best in class" ecoefficient companies and those of the "worst in class" group.[6] Once again, the authors used Innovest data as a proxy for the "eco-efficiency" of the companies. A multifactor analysis was used, controlling for traditional investment factors such as fund manager style, company size, industry sector, and momentum effects. The authors' analysis was based on the performance of companies relative to same-sector peers facing similar environmental challenges, as opposed to simply excluding the companies in high-impact sectors such as mining, energy, and chemicals, as is typical of many traditional "SRI" funds.

The authors constructed portfolios by ranking each company according to its "eco-efficiency" score in each of the industries. Then they created two portfolios—one of highly rated companies and one of poorly rated companies. The two portfolios were equal in size and mutually exclusive (i.e., no company appeared in both the portfolios). The results showed that the "best-in-class" portfolio outperformed the "worst in-class" portfolio by fully 350 basis points (3.5 percent). The portfolio Sharpe ratios (another commonly used measure of the ratio of risk to return) indicate that the performance difference persisted even after adjusting for the two portfolios' volatility. When transaction costs were included, the outperformance margin increased to over 3.8 percent, since the worst in class portfolio had greater turnover than the best in class one. Overall, the authors concluded that "the benefits of considering environmental criteria in the investment process can be substantial."[7]

An even more recent academic study was conducted in 2008 by Alex Edmans, a finance professor at the highly regarded Wharton School of Business at the University of Pennsylvania.[8] Edman's study is of particular interest here in that it focused on a sustainability factor traditionally neglected in the academic literature—human capital. Using *Fortune* magazine's "Best Companies to Work for in America" lists as proxies for companies with strong human resource management, Edmans created equally weighted portfolios of the 100 top performers, rebalanced annually when the new year's list was announced. The study reviewed the portfolio's performance over the period 1998–2005, making appropriate adjustments for industry sectors, company size, and other factors. The results showed that companies with superior human capital management achieved over *double* the average market return! On an annualized, risk-adjusted basis, the model portfolio outperformed the market benchmark by fully 7.7 percent.

While unquestionably sophisticated, all three studies might be looked at askance by critics, inasmuch as they were backward-looking exercises, focused on the *preceding* 6- to 8-year period. Indeed, the possibility of "look-back" bias and "contaminated" results cannot be dismissed entirely. The same criticism cannot, however, be leveled at our next piece of "evidence."

This case was a *live,* 3-year, real-time simulation involving four actual portfolios held by a smallish California county pension fund, with roughly $1.3 billion in assets. However, here the sustainability "bets" were made in advance, and the *subsequent* performance of the companies was then tracked. Rather than analyzing hypothetical portfolios, these simulations used as benchmarks and starting points the *actual* portfolios that the pension fund and its external asset managers already had in place. During the simulation, the actual portfolio stock holdings remained exactly the same for all the simulated portfolios; the only thing that changed was the relative *weights* each stock received. New weightings were established, based on each company's relative ES rating from Innovest Strategic Value Advisors. Leaders were overweighted slightly; laggards were underweighted.

The entire point of the simulation was to answer the "what if?" question: what—if any—financial performance impact would sustainability factors have had if they had been added to the analysis of the fund's four external managers, who collectively managed virtually all of the pension fund's assets. The simulation ran for 3 full years, from 2002 to 2005.

Importantly, to avoid any unintended "bets" on particular industry sectors, company size, p/e ratios, and other traditional financial factors, the simulation portfolios contained *exactly the same* companies as the underlying, real portfolios. Not a single company was deleted or added; the existing portfolio was simply "tilted" according to the sustainability ratings of its constituent companies. Top-rated companies were overweighted in the simulation portfolios; poorly rated companies were underweighted. Each portfolio was given three different levels of "tilt": by 50, 100, and 200 basis points overall (0.5, 1, and 2 percent). Each simulation portfolio was rebalanced quarterly, in parallel with the underlying actual portfolios. The pension fund's external consultant supervised the simulation directly in order to ensure its integrity and objectivity.

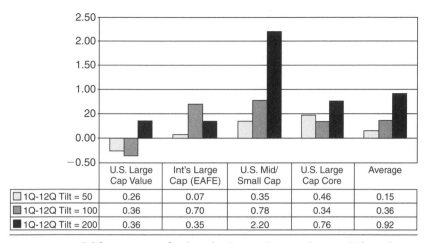

	U.S. Large Cap Value	Int's Large Cap (EAFE)	U.S. Mid/ Small Cap	U.S. Large Cap Core	Average
☐ 1Q-12Q Tilt = 50	0.26	0.07	0.35	0.46	0.15
▨ 1Q-12Q Tilt = 100	0.36	0.70	0.78	0.34	0.36
■ 1Q-12Q Tilt = 200	0.36	0.35	2.20	0.76	0.92

FIGURE 4.3 California pension fund results. Source: Innovest Strategic Value Advisors

Despite considerable differences among asset managers, investment styles, and geographic focus, the results demonstrated that all four portfolios would have generated additional returns had their managers systematically integrated sustainability ratings into their investment processes at the maximum—but still relatively modest—level (Figure 4.3).

On average, this particular pension fund would have boosted its returns by over 90 basis points (0.9 percent) had it used the sustainability overlay across its entire portfolio. In the context of a $1.3 billion fund, this represents nearly $12 million in pensioners' retirement savings that was left "on the table" by failing to integrate sustainability research. Interestingly, the individual asset manager whose portfolio would have benefited the most (the U.S. small and mid-capitalization manager) happened to be the very same manager who was the most vociferously hostile to the concept of adding sustainability research before the study began.

A second live simulation is still in progress today. It is based on the "Global 100," a hypothetical portfolio created over 3 years ago by Innovest for the World Economic Forum in Davos, Switzerland. The companies are described as "the 100 most sustainable companies in the world" —perhaps a somewhat extravagant description, given the variety of industry sectors involved, and the almost infinite variety of working definitions of "sustainable" companies. Having made that disclaimer, however, the list is by no means completely arbitrary, nor does it contain "apples-to-oranges" comparisons between, for example, software companies and mining companies. Each company on the list has been selected

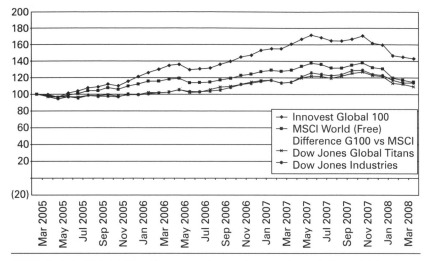

FIGURE 4.4 Global 100 performances. Source: Innovest Strategic Value Advisors

as among the best-in-class, based on evaluations against same-sector peers. The list includes companies such as France's Lafarge (a cement company), the Anglo-Dutch oil company Royal Dutch/Shell, and Japan's Mitsubishi Heavy Industries. (It is worth noting that few of them would have found their way into a traditional SRI portfolio.) The most recent Global 100 list is reproduced in Appendix 3.

Since its inception in February 2005, the Global 100 list has outperformed its MSCI World Benchmark by more than 600 basis points per year, a substantial margin (Figure 4.4).

The skeptics may still protest that even if the simulations were live and not retrospective, the fact that there was no real money behind them renders them somehow invalid and/or unpersuasive. For their benefit, we turn now to a brief summary of some research undertaken by mainstream asset managers and investment banks.

Sell-Side Research

A recent study by the United Nations Program Finance Initiative's Asset Management Working Group (which includes notable asset managers such as HSBC, BNP Paribas, Henderson, Morley, Hermes, ClearBridge, and RCM) as well as Mercer Investment Consulting examined both academic and broker research on links between ES factors and financial performance.

The broker research (including reports from leading firms such as Bernstein, Citigroup, Goldman Sachs, and Lehman Brothers) reviewed the materiality of ES factors on investment performance. Overall, out of the 30 studies and broker reports reviewed, 13 identified positive relationships with financial/investment performance, 10 were neutral, 3 were negative, and 4 identified either a neutral-positive or neutral-negative relationship.[9]

Real-World Evidence

Once again, however, a hard-core skeptic might believe that all of these studies are "only" studies and clamor for some "real-world" evidence. For them, one concrete example is provided by a global portfolio that has been in operation for over 3 years and currently has roughly $100 million invested in it. The portfolio is being managed by Credit Agricole Asset Management, a leading European asset manager, and is a conservative, "enhanced index" approach, designed to outperform its benchmark by a modest 1–2 percent per year. In this fund, sustainability factors are the single largest differentiator from the benchmark, and the annualized "sustainability premium" in this case has been over 130 basis points, or 1.3 percent (Figure 4.5).

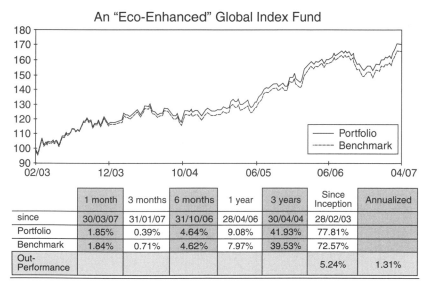

	1 month	3 months	6 months	1 year	3 years	Since Inception	Annualized
since	30/03/07	31/01/07	31/10/06	28/04/06	30/04/04	28/02/03	
Portfolio	1.85%	0.39%	4.64%	9.08%	41.93%	77.81%	
Benchmark	1.84%	0.71%	4.62%	7.97%	39.53%	72.57%	
Out-Performance						5.24%	1.31%

FIGURE 4.5 Global portfolio results. Source: Innovest Strategic Value Advisors

It must be conceded that a single example hardly makes for a compelling, scientific proof statement. Indeed, perhaps even this entire collection of academic and broker research, live simulations, and a real-world example will not be sufficient to persuade some die-hard sustainability skeptics. Given both the rigor of the methodologies and the pedigree of the organizations involved, however, they should be more than sufficient to at least give some pause to those who deny even the *possibility* of such sustainability-driven outperformance. And they certainly disprove the oft-repeated refrain that "there is not a shred of academically respectable evidence to support the sustainable investing hypothesis."[10]

In this chapter we have reviewed a reasonably large body of evidence about the link between the performance of companies on key sustainability factors and the financial returns they have generated for investors. That evidence has come from a variety of very different sources. In our view at least, the weight of evidence argues heavily *in favor* of the sustainable investment thesis, not against it. At the very least, it should convincingly call into question the blithe dismissal of the thesis by its many critics, as well as their breezy assurances about the existence of a robust body of "evidence" that supports their case. This mythical body of research quite simply does not exist.

There is one further, and critically important point. Even if this considerable body of evidence had *not* been so compelling, this would hardly repudiate the case for sustainable investment. *All* of this evidence, by definition, is *historical* or, at best, contemporary. What really matters to investors is the *future*. And if the reader concurs with even part of our assessment of major global megatrends in Chapter 1, the case for sustainable investment *going forward* becomes virtually irrefutable.

Before looking more closely at how it's actually done, however (and who's already doing it), we now attempt to provide a logical and robust conceptual framework so that investors can place the sustainable investment thesis in its proper historical and theoretical context.

Chapter 5

Toward a New *Post*modern, Sustainable Portfolio Theory

Certain perils that lurk in investment strategies cannot be spotted by the use of the models commonly employed today by financial institutions.

—WARREN BUFFET, LETTER TO BERKSHIRE HATHAWAY
SHAREHOLDERS, FEBRUARY 2007

While it must be confessed that sustainability and ES-driven "perils" were—and are—undoubtedly the furthest thing from Mr. Buffet's mind, the general point made by the legendary investor and billionaire remains a perfectly valid one. (And, in any event, I was taught as a small child *never* to argue with a multibillionaire about how to make money!) The risks to which he was referring, of course, relate to the sort of financial land mines that feature prominently in current business and financial headlines. Those dizzyingly complex (and opaque) financial instruments include collateralized debt obligations (CDOs), the prime culprits in the subprime meltdown of 2007–2008), collateralized mortgage-backed securities (CMBSs), as well as credit derivatives.[1] The hidden risks with which *we* are concerned here are much less publicized, but no less real or dangerous. They are the *sustainability*-driven financial risks, that is, those created by environmental or social factors, which only rarely show up on Wall Street's radar screens.

To manage those risks, *and* seize the sustainability-driven *opportunities* that go with them, twenty-first century investors will need to address them systematically. To do that, it would be profoundly helpful to have a theoretical and conceptual framework with which to do so.

In this chapter we shall attempt to provide some of those theoretical underpinnings. In doing so, we borrow liberally from four very different schools of financial and investment thought:

• Modern Portfolio Theory and the Efficient Markets Hypothesis
• Behavioral Finance
• The "Adaptive Markets" Hypothesis
• "Intangibles" Investing

Each will be discussed briefly in turn.

First, however, it is worthwhile to pause and reflect briefly on why all of this is necessary. In a nutshell, it is because the traditional methods of investment analysis have proven woefully inadequate. If they were ever satisfactory, they are certainly not up to the task today of guiding investors through the treacherous shoals of the Sustainable Investment Revolution. In the next section, we explore some of the most serious weaknesses of the accounting-based numbers that have historically provided the "raw feedstock" for investment analysis as it is conventionally practiced today. Squeamish—or excessively credulous—readers may want to skip this next section; it will be far from reassuring.

A Crisis of Legitimacy for Accounting-Driven Analysis[2]

The spate of high-profile corporate governance scandals several years ago has clearly been a major, if indirect, factor in helping propel ES issues into a more prominent and credible place on the agenda for international investors. They did so by dramatically weakening public and investor confidence in traditional financial institutions and methods and creating a new openness to innovative alternative approaches, including sustainability investing.

The sudden and spectacular implosions of companies, such as Enron, WorldCom, Tyco, Parmalat, Global Crossing, and Ahold, have seriously—

TOWARD A NEW *POST*MODERN, SUSTAINABLE PORTFOLIO THEORY **75**

and quite possibly irrevocably—shaken investor confidence in the financial numbers generated by companies and their accountants in the first place, to say nothing of what analysts do with those numbers *after* they get them. Subsequent revelations about seriously conflicted (if not outright fraudulent) Wall Street research have only exacerbated those concerns by calling into question both the quality and the objectivity of the analysts. Compounding all of this, then New York State Attorney General Eliot Spitzer launched a high-profile attack on many of the structural, systematic defects and conflicts inherent in the traditional Wall Street research model. The issues were sufficiently egregious that a group of 10 leading investment banks paid a total of $1.4 billion in fines and undertook some significant organizational reforms designed to reduce the likelihood of recurrences. That "rogues' gallery" included such Wall Street stalwarts as Salomon Smith Barney, Merrill Lynch, and Credit Suisse First Boston. Throw in the mutual fund late trading scandals of 2004/2005, where a number of investment management firms played fast and loose with stock trading rules for the benefit of favored clients, and we have an environment positively ripe for reform. In the late trading cases, mutual fund household names including Prudential, Janus, MFS, and Bank of America were forced to disgorge over a billion dollars in fines and restitution to investors. Needless to say, none of this did a whole lot to reassure investors from "Main Street" that Wall Street had their best interests at heart.

In my own view, this widespread disenchantment is by no means an entirely bad thing; if nothing else, it has provided a powerful impetus for examining new, alternative approaches and analytics. As a result, the door to including "nontraditional" factors, such as environmental and social risk, into investment research became open more widely than had ever been the case before. Traditional Wall Street analysis had been shown to be—to put it mildly—limited and deeply flawed. It is at least arguable that up to now, the last truly major conceptual breakthrough in financial analysis occurred in the fifteenth century, with the introduction of double-entry bookkeeping by the Italian monks. A bit of a rethink 500 years later would hardly, I think, be premature!

Let's face it, accounting-based performance numbers are the raw material for virtually all contemporary investment analysis. The limitations of this traditional approach, while little noticed until relatively recently, are both legion and extremely serious. Collectively, they make a mockery of the usual dismissal of ES analysis as woolly minded, subjective, and imprecise. (Remember, precision is all relative right?) And if the *inputs* to the investment analysis process are fundamentally defective, what can we safely assume about its later *outputs?*

Intellectual Foundations Made of Sand

One obvious and egregious flaw in the accounting numbers is that they provide, at best, a static, retrospective, "rear-view mirror" view of the finances and competitive positioning of companies. A second serious failing is their extreme sensitivity to what might be politely termed some rather malleable accounting assumptions. Allow me to illustrate this with a few examples from recent history. With a single changed accounting assumption, the combined earnings of high-profile U.S. companies Intel, Cisco, and Dell would have changed in an instant from a $4.4 billion profit to a *loss* of $1.4 billion for the first three quarters of 2002. The assumption in question, which underpined the positive number, is that stock options for executives should not be treated as a company expense in the current year, but rather should be amortized on the books over a number of years. However, most accounting academics and even accounting standards boards now recommend that this practice be reversed. If we make that single change, the $1.4 billion *loss* figure becomes the one that more fully reflects the company's real financial situation to investors.

And these are not exactly obscure companies with little analyst coverage that we're talking about here; their financial statements have been scoured by some of the most sophisticated financial and industry analysts around. If even *they* could not reliably tell their clients whether these high-profile companies actually *made* money or lost it (and we're not looking for six sigma accuracy here, just a simple "thumbs-up" or a "thumbs-down" signal—a nice "happy face" sticker or else a "skull and crossbones" toxic symbol) we really must question not only the omniscience but even the *utility* of traditional financial analysis altogether.[3]

Another common accounting device is the increasingly widespread use of so-called "pro forma" accounting techniques. They are *supposed* to give investors a clearer picture of financial positions of companies by removing certain "nonrecurring," "one time," or "extraordinary" items, such as the "restructuring" expenses that are often incurred when companies merge or acquire one another. Since pro forma earnings are not subject to the same reporting rules and level of regulatory oversight as traditional generally accepted accounting principles (GAAP)-based figures, the latitude for companies to interpret their own results is considerable. And since each company can make its *own* assumptions, comparisons among them become virtually useless. Pro forma accounting emerged during the dot-com boom, when companies whose expenses vastly exceeded their revenues were casting about for ways to provide some encouraging news for analysts. This allowed the 100 largest technology companies on the U.S. NASDAQ stock exchange, for example, to show their investors a combined profit of $10 billion in one year. Had the more conservative U.S. GAAP been used instead, they would have shown a combined *loss* of $71 billion![4] Depending on the set of numbers on which we wish to rely, Cisco's third quarter results at the time were either a profit of $230 million or a *loss* of $2.7 billion.

If, after five *centuries* of refinement, *this* level of precision is the best that the accountants and financial analysts can manage, their critiques of the "sloppiness" and imprecision of ES analysis would seem to ring rather hollow. People in glass houses . . . .

Even the U.S. Securities and Exchange Commission has warned investors and companies of the perils of pro forma accounting:

> Pro forma financials should be viewed with appropriate and
> healthy skepticism. Because pro forma financial information, by
> its very nature, departs from traditional accounting conventions,
> its use can make it difficult for investors to compare an issuer's
> financial information with other reporting periods and with other
> companies[5]

The U.S. standard-setters and regulators have, to their credit, actually taken steps to at least attempt to protect both ordinary and "sophisticated" investors from misleading pro forma information. The much-celebrated Sarbanes-Oxley Act of 2002 was an important part of that effort. Sarbanes-Oxley was a direct response to the Enron and other corporate accounting scandals and was an aggressive and comprehensive attempt to improve information transparency for investors.[6] Its measures did in fact have a salutary impact, but they have proven to be limited. Despite the new laws and regulations, many companies continue to push the envelope to the breaking point, through devices such as locating their pro forma results in the most prominent places possible in their earnings press releases. In some cases, this has included actually putting them in the headlines! This virtually guarantees at the very least a substantial degree of confusion among investors as to which set of numbers, pro forma or GAAP, should be relied upon most heavily.

The point being made here is simply this: despite literally centuries of evolution and refinement, traditional accounting numbers can provide only a partial, static, retrospective, and potentially grossly misleading picture of a company's true investment risk profile and competitive positioning. Assumptions must be made about the treatment of the following:

- The true value of "goodwill" from mergers and acquisitions, including the value of company brands
- Stock option costs—how and when to calculate them
- Company pension fund liabilities and expected returns
- Research and development costs
- The value of unsold inventory
- Depreciation rates for capital expenditures
- "Restructuring" charges

Both the number and financial magnitude of these accounting assumptions make the resulting outputs questionable at best.[7] And let us remember, those outputs are also the most essential *inputs* for traditional investment analysis. And we have omitted—for now—what is arguably accounting's single greatest shortcoming of all for our purposes—its inability to deal with "intangibles," including such central sustainability concerns as human capital, environmental risks, and human rights. We shall return to this fundamental shortcoming later in this chapter.

A substantial portion of the case for sustainability investing thus rests on the contribution it can make to overcoming at least some of the limitations of traditional accounting-driven analysis and to providing investors with a much more comprehensive, dynamic, and forward-looking picture of the companies in which they are may invest. Let us now turn, then, to constructing at least the beginnings of a "theory" of sustainability investment, beginning with some of its key intellectual antecedents from the world of mainstream finance.

The Building Blocks: Modern Portfolio Theory

"Modern" portfolio theory (MPT) was arguably born in 1952, with the publication of Harry Markowitz's seminal article "Portfolio Selection" in the *Journal of Finance*.[8] Markowitz and other key contributors to MPT, such as William Sharpe, were recognized with Nobel prizes, albeit roughly 40 years after the groundbreaking work itself was done. The central tenets of modern portfolio theory are as follows:

- It is important to shift the focus of investment beyond the individual security to address the statistical relationships among the much larger number of securities in an overall investment *portfolio.* In other words, the risks and expected returns of a given stock should *not* be viewed in isolation, but rather in terms of how they interact with the *other* securities in the portfolio. It is the risk and return characteristics of the *entire* portfolio that ought to be of greatest concern to investors.

- There are significant benefits in constructing a *diversified* portfolio of securities (or even of entire portfolios) to mitigate the risk inherent in each individual security. Statistically, Markowitz demonstrated that diversification allows the risk level of the total portfolio to be *less* than the sum of the risk of its individual components.

- Investors are rational and self-interested, and markets are inherently efficient. Therefore, investors will always seek to maximize their expected return for a given level of risk or minimize the risk at a desired level of return. They will take additional risk *only* if they have good reason to believe that they have a reasonable likelihood of receiving a higher return if in fact the "bet" pays off. (Any horse racing aficionado will be familiar with this basic precept, although things can get considerably more complicated with investment portfolios.)

- It is possible to calculate an "efficient frontier"—an imaginary line on a graph at which financial returns could be maximized for any given level of risk or, alternatively, the risk minimized at any given level of return. Rational investors of the MPT would want all of their investment choices to fall along this efficient frontier.

Modern portfolio theory has had—and continues to have—an enormous impact on actual investor thinking and behavior today. From the standpoint of sustainability investment, however, it is MPT's assumption of efficient markets that is most problematic.

One of the most enduring—if sterile—debates in academic finance circles concerns this "Efficient Markets Hypothesis" (EMH). Proponents of the EMH, such as the University of Chicago's Eugene Fama,[9] argue that markets are indeed highly efficient and that therefore stock prices fully and rapidly reflect all the available and material information about companies. There are several important assumptions and corollaries attached to the EMH:

- Information is roughly equally available to all market participants;
- Investors are rational and act in their own objective self-interest; and
- Because all relevant information is fully, accurately, and promptly incorporated into market prices, it is extraordinarily difficult, if not impossible, to outperform the market.

It must be said that there is much more empirical evidence to support at least the conclusion of the third point than the first two. The first hypothesis was convincingly repudiated nearly 30 years ago by Columbia University economics professor, Nobel Prize winner, and former chief economist of the World Bank Joseph Stiglitz. His work on the *asymmetrical* nature of information flows and financial markets effectively demolished that particular pillar of the EMH.[10] In a nutshell, Stiglitz demonstrated in elegant academic fashion what ought to have been intuitively obvious in the first place: everyone does *not* have equal access to information, nor are all equally capable of *interpreting* it. This point is of central importance to the sustainable investment hypothesis. We would argue strongly that **in the case of ES information and analysis, markets are woefully inefficient; information is by no means universally available, and it is certainly not widely considered credible or even potentially useful. Therefore, it cannot possibly be fully reflected in current stock prices.** The *good* news for investors, however, is that it is precisely this same market information inefficiency regarding sustainability issues (such as climate change or supply chain disruptions due to human rights violations) that provides investors with the opportunity to achieve exceptional financial returns. Investors who take the time and trouble to dig more deeply for sustainability information and analysis *can* indeed develop a significant information advantage.

For example, if an investor is one of the relatively small group of people who knows *which one* of the 26 largest publicly traded electric utilities in the United States may be *30* times more exposed to the financial consequences of potentially forthcoming climate change regulations, *that* information can be acted upon. And until the (far-off) day dawns when ES information is both universally available *and* taken seriously, there will always be a significant arbitrage opportunity for investors to exploit that information inefficiency. In our example here, investors might want to underweight or even "short" those utilities with the largest net risk exposures,[11] using information that is not yet in the broader market. This is a classic example of the information advantage sustainability investors will enjoy, at least until the day—if it ever occurs—when sustainability analysis is both available and used nearly universally. What's more, this information advantage is likely to be even more pronounced in the emerging markets of the developing world, where ES information is even more difficult to access than it is in the so-called advanced economies. And if our diagnosis of global megatrends in Chapter 1 is even remotely accurate, that information advantage will become even larger in the future than it is today.

When all is said and done, we have rejected more than we have accepted from MPT. Nonetheless, by simply raising a number of important questions and stimulating vigorous debate, MPT has been an important building block in our construction of a theory of sustainable investment. We turn now to a second intellectual precursor—the rapidly growing field of behavioral finance.

Behavioral Finance

The emergence and growth of the field of behavioral finance have been a direct response to and repudiation of the assumption of investor rationality that formed an integral part of the EMH. Behavioral finance devotees believe that investors' emotions, fears, and cognitive biases play a significant role in their ultimate investment choices and behavior. This applies both to individual investors and to the well-known "herd mentality" and mass psychology of large *groups* of investors—sometimes also known as "the market." All of this clearly stands in sharp contradistinction to the EMH's portrayal of investors as bloodless, wholly rational, automatons.

The seminal figures in behavioral finance were Amos Tversky and Daniel Kahneman, who began publishing in the mid-1970s.[12] Briefly, advocates of the increasingly influential behavioral finance approach argue that in the real world, a host of cognitive and psychological biases effectively *preclude* investors from exhibiting the purely rational behavior that is the cornerstone of the EMH. Among the most important of these cognitive frailties are the following:

- *Anchoring*—the tendency to filter, frame, and interpret new information to conform to preexisting beliefs. For our purposes here, the most important anchoring that occurs is the persistent belief that ES factors are either irrelevant or even harmful to financial returns. With this mindset, apparent evidence of sustainability-driven superior returns is almost reflexively dismissed as being due to other factors.
- *Conservatism*—a close relative of anchoring: the reluctance to alter our beliefs, even in the face of emerging new evidence that would appear to contradict them.
- *Availability bias*—the tendency to base investment decisions on information that is readily available, whether or not it is actually germane or valuable. The slavish use of p/e ratios on which we commented in Chapter 2 is a perfect case in point: p/e numbers may be next to

useless, but they have three great virtues: they're simple, everyone else uses them, and they are readily *available*. No real intellectual elbow grease is required. The connection here with the sustainable investment hypothesis is an obvious one: ES information is generally not only unavailable, but as we have seen, even when it is both available and robust, it is rarely used. We shall see some concrete examples later in this chapter of cases in which sustainability analysis could have been *extremely* useful to investors. The subprime mortgage debacle in general, and Bear Stearns' demise in particular, provide object lessons in this regard.

- *Recency bias*—the tendency to extrapolate excessively from recent events and to imbue them with disproportionate weight in investment decisions, while underweighting the full, long-term historical record. Otherwise put, this is betting on what *has* worked, especially recently. This behavioral bias, almost by definition, creates a *backward*-looking cast of mind that looks askance at any new, "unproven" approaches such as sustainable investment.
- *Overconfidence.* Enough said.

Readers recalling our discussion in Chapter 2 of the cognitive biases specific to the integration of sustainability factors will recognize each one of these five tendencies of behavioral finance as directly relevant.

Behavioral finance has had a sufficiently profound impact that Kahneman was awarded the Nobel Prize in economics in 1992. (His colleague Tversky unfortunately died or he too would undoubtedly have been similarly honored.) Investment guru and writer Peter Bernstein summarizes the case for behavioral finance this way:

> On a consistent basis, excess return has to come in some shape or form from the behavioral side. Otherwise alpha wouldn't exist. If people didn't let their emotions dominate, mis-pricings wouldn't exist or would be ephemeral.[13]

In other words, if all investors had the same information, at the same time, and interpreted it with the same analytical quality and degree of optimism or pessimism, it *would* become literally impossible to outperform the market. Luckily for sustainability investors, *none* of those preconditions generally prevails.

Behavioral finance has thus contributed important insights that have helped us construct a theory of sustainable investment. The next intellectual ingredient emerged even more recently.

The Adaptive Markets Hypothesis

First propounded by MIT finance professor Andrew Lo in 2004, the Adaptive Markets Hypothesis (AMH) is an attempt to reconcile and synthesize the key but apparently mutually contradictory tenets of both the EMH and behavioral finance.[14] Lo's central thesis is that *both* previous schools of thought are correct—at least to a point. Using insights and analogies from both evolutionary biology and cognitive neuroscience, Lo argues persuasively that while markets are indeed largely efficient, more importantly, they are also *adaptable*.

In Lo's ecology of finance, concepts such as competition among species, mutation, diversity, and natural selection are of critical importance. He views investors as far from the rigid, predictable robots of the EMH; rather they respond and adapt to the changing environment in which they work, creating multiple feedback loops and impacts that change investors' thinking and behavior. Factors such as the magnitude of available profit opportunities, the number and nature of the competitors vying for them, and the responses of those actors to changing information and market conditions can all elicit adaptive behavior in response. Investors' objectives, risk appetites, resources, and investment time horizons can and do change markedly over time, all of which can change their investment behavior. Nor, most importantly, will all investors be alike in these regards in the first place. Thus, the market is influenced not by some homogeneous, predictable force, but rather by the interaction among a dynamic multiplicity of disparate, differentially motivated players who themselves change, adapt, and evolve over time.

Lo's AMH is compelling, and adds nuance and practicality to both the EMH and behavioral finance approaches that preceded it. It represents another building block as we move toward constructing a theory of sustainable investment. It is, however, incomplete in one important respect for our purposes. Like its predecessor models, Lo's AMH does not fundamentally question the reliability, completeness, or utility of the accounting-based numbers on which all traditional investment analysis ultimately depends. In short, it fails to recognize the bourgeoning importance of "*intangibles,*" including sustainability factors. It is to that last ingredient that we now turn, for sustainable investment is a direct and more specific outgrowth of the thinking around intangible value more generally.

Capturing Intangible Value

The most basic, powerful, and direct conceptual roots of the sustainable investment hypothesis can be found in the body of academic thinking and writing around "intellectual capital" and "intangible value." The core proposition is this: while the business world itself has changed beyond recognition since the 1400s, the accounting system through which it keeps score has not. Italian monk and mathematician Luca Pacioli invented double-entry bookkeeping in Venice in the fifteenth century; this was arguably the last truly fundamental conceptual advance in accounting.

Pacioli's world was a world of tangible assets—land, grain, livestock, ships, machinery, and so on. In the twenty-first century, however, economic value is now being created primarily by *in*tangible assets such as ideas, brands, innovation capacity, the quality of strategic alliances, unique work processes, and databases. Such attributes are notoriously difficult to capture and value systematically, but as we have seen, they typically comprise 80–85 percent of a company's true market value.[15] Put differently, *fully 80–85 percent of both the risks and value potential in companies' "iceberg balance sheets" lies below the surface, beyond the easy reach of traditional profit and loss statements, balance sheets, and accounting numbers.* Former investment banker and U.S. Securities and Exchange Commission chairman Bill Donaldson puts the case nicely:

> To state an obvious, but often over-looked fact—quarterly earnings do not reflect companies' long term viability. Identifying the factors that will drive long-term growth—such as personnel, strategy, financial strength and flexibility, internal corporate governance, innovation and customer service—may be more difficult to quantify, but they offer a more accurate and more complete portrait of a company's future.[16]

Sustainability factors are simply a subset—albeit a critically important subset—of that dominant, subsurface portion of the "iceberg balance sheet" that we encountered in Chapter 1.

Proponents of the sustainable investment hypothesis are far from the first to observe and attempt to wrestle with the growing disconnect between the market value of companies and the value that can be gleaned from traditional finance analysis. Some of the most important intellectual pioneers in this area have been Leif Edvinsoon, Karl-Eric Sveiby, Goran Roos, and Tom Stewart, the current editor of the prestigious *Harvard*

Business Review.[17] None of these writers adopted the perspective of the *investor,* however; each approached the subject from the perspective of company managers and executives, and how they could best identify, quantify, mobilize, and manage these hidden and elusive assets on behalf of the companies themselves. What they *did* contribute to the foundations of the sustainable investing hypothesis, however, was a sharp and exclusive focus on the *non*traditional factors that in fact drive most of contemporary companies' investment risk *and* their future potential to create competitive advantage and exceptional returns in the future.

To bring the *investor* perspective to the intellectual capital debate, it fell to New York-based accounting and finance professor Baruch Lev, arguably the most prolific and influential figure in the "intangible value" debate. Working at the Stern business school at New York University, Lev has, since 1996, published two books and over 30 articles on intangibles, valuation, and the limitations of conventional accounting. In Professor Lev's words:

> We are all making investment decisions based on accounting information that is, at best, limited and, at worst, badly distorted. All of us need better information so that we can make better investment decisions.[18]

Although the connection is rarely if ever explicitly recognized in the literature, we believe that all of this work has helped to create the intellectual preconditions for sustainability investing, with its focus on one particular constellation of "nontraditional" risk and value drivers.[19] Sustainable investing simply makes these linkages more transparent, viewing ES factors as generators of many of the key components in companies' "competitive DNA," including incremental reputational capital and brand value; differentiation; superior capacity to attract, retain, and motivate top-flight human capital; product and process innovations; increased market share; relationships with regulators, customers, employees, suppliers, and communities; and attracting superior alliance partners.

In the preceding sections, we have reviewed four important strands of investment thinking:

- Modern Portfolio Theory;
- Behavioral Finance;
- The "Adaptive Markets" Hypothesis; and
- "Intangible" Investing.

In the next section, we shall attempt to combine and build upon them to create a kind of *post*modern portfolio theory—a theory of sustainable investing.

Toward a Theory of Sustainable Investing

In addition to building on the work of several different branches of finance theory, our approach to sustainable investing also rests on a number of key assumptions, hypotheses, and investment beliefs. Let us first briefly review the ones that we proposed in the first chapter.

The Investment Logic

We believe the following:

- Traditional financial analysis cannot possibly provide a complete picture of the true competitive risks, value potential, and future performance of companies. Typically, at least 80 percent of a company's value is now driven by "intangibles," which cannot be adequately captured in financial statements.[20]
- "Management quality" is arguably the most important of these intangibles—the factor most critical to companies' competitiveness, profitability, and—ultimately—their share price performance.
- ES issues are, and will remain, among the toughest, most complex management challenges of the next 20 years and are therefore a potent, forward-looking litmus test and proxy for a company's overall management quality.
- Companies with superior positioning and performance on ES factors tend to be
  - More forward-looking and strategic
  - More agile and adaptable
  - Better managed companies in general; and therefore
  - Likely to be *financial* outperformers as well.
- ES factors will become even *more* important to companies'—and investors'—competitive and financial success over the next 3 to 5 years.
- Despite this, however, they are grossly underrecognized and underresearched by mainstream investors. This creates a significant and

growing market inefficiency. Those prepared to do the research and analysis will be rewarded with a substantial information advantage.

To these, we would now add the following more general propositions about investing:

- Investment success is actually less dependent on understanding the "fundamentals" of companies than it is on identifying any disparities between the prices warranted by those fundamentals and the markets' *expectations* of the companies.[21]
- Changes in investor expectations are the primary trigger of stock price changes.
- The most critical challenge for investors is to *anticipate* any revisions to those expectations.
- Those changed expectations are in turn triggered by "catalysts for change."[22]
- Today, change catalysts are increasingly found among "nontraditional" or "intangible" factors, including ES ones.
- ES factors can and should be integrated with more traditional investment analysis to generate more accurate forecasts of critical investment factors such as the likely duration of a company's period of competitive advantage; the rate at which that advantage may erode; and the magnitude, sources, and timing of future cash flows.

Adding Investment Insight

At the end of the day, the case for sustainable investment involves one simple proposition: ***integrating sustainability considerations into investment analysis provides a fuller, more comprehensive, and more forward-looking understanding of both the risk profiles of companies and their future ability to create competitive advantage and investor returns.***[23] Indeed, it is extremely difficult, at least for us, to conjure up any compelling arguments *against* acquiring additional information and understanding.

Let's take a look at the specific sustainability issue of climate change, for example. Figure 5.1 nicely illustrates, across seven different industry sectors, the enormous range of the levels of financial exposure of companies to this increasingly important investment risk factor. Each of the bars in the graph represents the potential percentage of the various companies'

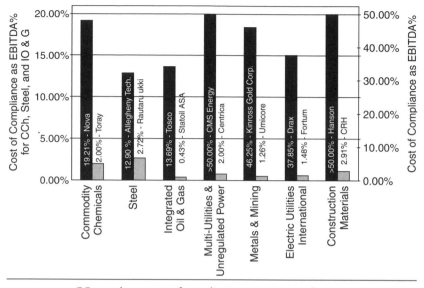

FIGURE 5.1 CO_2 regulatory cost of compliance across seven industry sectors.
*EBITDA is earnings before taxes and depreciation allowances.
Source: Innovest Strategic Value Advisors

earnings that could be at risk if a future regulatory regime imposed some sort of tax or cost on carbon dioxide emissions.[24] This has in fact *already* occurred in Europe, and most knowledgeable observers believe that similar regulations are inevitable in the United States, regardless of who wins the 2008 Presidential election. The only question is when.

The dark bars in Figure 5.1 represent the most risk-exposed company in each industry sector; the lighter bars represent the companies with the least risk exposure. Note that to scale the graph properly, some bars had to be artificially truncated when they hit over *50* percent of company earnings!

In the Multi-Utilities and Unregulated Power sector, for example, the two bars near the center of the chart reveal that CMS Energy has over *25 times* the net risk exposure of Centrica.

Now, let us be clear here: the sustainable investment hypothesis does *not* automatically compel asset managers and fiduciaries to avoid CMS Energy like the plague or to automatically load up on Centrica stock for sustainability and climate change reasons alone. There are, quite properly, a myriad of other considerations that should weigh on any final investment decision, not least of which is the current share price of companies. Earnings history and momentum, historic capital efficiency, analyst sentiment, and a variety of other, more traditional factors are also important. The most "sustainable" company does not necessarily make the best investment candidate, particularly if it is grossly overpriced at a given point in time. But, having said that, *climate change (and other sustainability factors) need to be at least **part** of the analytical and decision-making mix.* Simple financial prudence and fiduciary responsibility demand it. The relative weights accorded to sustainability factors—and indeed all of the others—are quite properly the province of asset managers; indeed, that's what they are getting *paid* for. But it is the truly exceptional chief investment officer, portfolio manager, or fiduciary today who could even *begin* to tell which companies lie where on the climate risk spectrum. And what is perhaps even more troubling, there is not exactly a stampede afoot at present from those demanding to find out!

Climate change is, of course, only one of many sustainability issues, albeit arguably the most important today in several industry sectors. Had mainstream analysts been playing close and systematic attention to ES factors, they might well have been much quicker to spot other looming financial icebergs:

- The Tyco, Parmalat, and HealthSouth governance and accounting scandals and subsequent financial implosions.
- Monsanto's disastrous commercial foray into Europe with a genetically modified food product.
- The Aventis Starlink corn recall incident, which cost the company $200 million, plus a share price hit.
- DuPont's 15 percent share price drop over a 3-month period in 2005, after its problems with the Teflon chemical PFOA became public.
- Growing public and legislative resistance to permitting new coal-fired power plants, particularly in the United States.
- Community opposition successfully derailing Royal Dutch/Shell's drilling program off the North Shore of Alaska in 2007.
- The forced cancellation of a planned on-shore liquefied natural gas (LNG) facility in Long Beach, California in 2007 because of community environmental concerns. The project was a joint venture between Mitsubishi and Conoco.
- The forced closure of Canadian gold miner Eldorado's new Kisladag mine in Turkey in 2007 because of alleged water contamination by cyanide used in the leaching process. This effectively extinguished 50 percent of the company's total global production capacity.

- Community and NGO pressure disrupting Petrobras' exploration program in the Amazon in 2007 and 2008.
- The mortal strategic risk to automakers, particularly in Detroit, from their excessive exposure to gas-guzzling sports utility vehicles (SUVs).
- Corporate culture incompatibilities, particularly in the ES area, between the Royal Bank of Scotland (RBS) and its Netherlands-based acquisition ABN-AMRO in 2008. RBS may still live to regret its underestimation of both the quality and importance of ABN-AMRO's superior ES risk management architecture—*and* its ability to capture commercial opportunities on the upside.

And the list goes on. Certainly the top sustainability analysts spotted problems in each of these companies, and typically did so much earlier than traditional Wall Street analysts.

Subprime: The Poster Child for Sustainability Analysis

At present, global securities markets continue to be roiled by what is termed for shorthand convenience "the subprime mess"—or "meltdown," or "fiasco," take your pick. Whatever one calls it, it has already eliminated more than $300 billion from the balance sheets of major financial institutions. It has also cost the jobs of the then CEOs or Presidents of Merrill Lynch, Citigroup, Morgan Stanley, and others, and the end is nowhere in sight.

Here's how the subprime mortgage debacle began. Investment banks such as Merrill Lynch, Citibank, Lehman Brothers, UBS, and Bear Stearns created "arm's-length" vehicles to which they then transferred large volumes of mortgage loans. This device was intended to allow them to keep the new loans off their balance sheets, making it easier to meet new international requirements for banks' capital adequacy.

The new vehicles then repackaged and "sliced and diced" those receivables into complex securities such as CDOs and CMBSs and then sold them to outside investors, largely major institutions, such as pension funds and insurance companies. The vehicles then pocketed the "spread" —the difference between what the institutions ultimately paid and the (supposedly lower) rates at which the new vehicles themselves had bought the mortgages from the banks in the first place.

It was supposed to be a "win-win" situation: the banks charged the vehicles (essentially, *themselves*) a hefty investment banking fee for creating and maintaining the new financial structures, and the vehicles themselves also made a tidy little profit on the spreads. And here's the best part: because of an accounting convention (quirk?), the banking fee was the only revenue that had to be reported on the banks' profit-and-loss statements. Under the accounting rules, however, the banks *were* required to estimate any potential losses from the vehicles, record them as an expense on their balance sheets, and disclose them in the Management Discussion and Analysis section of their securities filings.[25] Sure enough, each of the aforementioned banks estimated those potential losses to be "immaterial" in their filings, right up to the subprime meltdown in August 2007.

Now, I suppose each of us has our own definition of "material" (and so indeed do the accounting rules!), but so far this accounting-driven "distortion" has produced over $300 *billion* in bank writedowns and repeated, seemingly endless, earnings restatements. In the case of Citigroup alone, these "off balance sheet" vehicles were responsible for more than $40 billion in writedowns—i.e., *losses.* So much for keeping risks away from their balance sheet! And there is no real end in sight to the financial carnage.

It is reasonably clear now, with the gift of hindsight, that either Wall Street did not see the subprime locomotive coming or, alternatively, it did, but internal conflicts of interest prevented the banks from advising their clients about the dangers, since some of them were actually "shorting" the very same securities for their own accounts that they were simultaneously selling to their clients![26] Whatever the cause, the first inkling that the average investor had of the problem was through published research reports in mid-2007. Meanwhile, at least one sustainability analysis house had begun alerting its clients as early as October 2006.[27]

Why? I would like to believe that it was because of my Innovest colleagues' superior brainpower—certainly not my own. Alas, I believe instead that it was more likely a function of looking at that particular subsector of the financial services industry from a very different perspective, and through a different lens—an ES lens.

Here's how it happened: the head of Innovest's financial services analyst team, Greg Larkin, routinely examines the social impact of banks' lending activities in poorer, more vulnerable communities. At issue is whether the banks are acting responsibly or exploitatively. (Historically, such concerns seem to have rarely troubled mainstream bank analysts unduly.) In September 2006, however, Innovest's U.S. financials team became concerned and decided to dig deeper. What they found was quite disquieting; they had essentially stumbled across the tip of what turned out to be an exceptionally large, subprime iceberg.

The first thing that the team found was that the volume of housing loans given to people with impaired or no credit histories and/or without legal immigration status had *quintupled* between 2001 and 2005 to reach $625 billion. This surge had been fueled by a then booming real estate market, cheap credit, ample liquidity, and a tremendous proliferation of mortgage securitization, using fancy new instruments such as CDSs (credit default swaps) and CDOs. CDSs, which have notional values in the trillions, are essentially instruments that provide investors with "insurance" against companies defaulting on their loans. CDOs, as we have seen, are securities created by packaging together hundreds of individual loans (mortgages, car loans, etc.) and then "slicing and dicing" them into different tranches with differing levels of risk. Those securities are then sold by the lenders and investment banks, typically to large institutional investors. The securities are notoriously complex and opaque and create a considerable—and dangerous—distance between actual borrowers and the entity to which they ultimately became indebted. The true level of risk can easily be obscured, as indeed occurred in the subprime mortgage market crisis. The percentage of these exotic new securities linked to the subprime market had increased *8-fold* between 2003 and 2005.

The second major concern unearthed through the ES "lens" was that there was in fact no data to suggest that all of these new borrowers could actually *afford* their new housing loans. On the contrary, U.S. payrolls were stagnant, and household savings rates had turned negative for the first time since the Great Depression. The team then discovered another worrisome, 10-year trend: downturns in household savings rates have, historically, generally been accompanied in lock-step by commensurate increases in loan defaults. Under such circumstances, how could all of these new homeowners suddenly afford their new mortgages? The simple answer was that they couldn't. And they didn't.

Mortgages were typically offered at very attractive initial rates, but contained "reset" clauses whereby the rates were automatically bumped up later. This reset "feature" appears not to have been clearly communicated to or at least well understood by the buyer. The typical subprime home buyer was essentially (if unwittingly) betting that their incomes would increase by some 20 to 30 percent over the next few years. To be able to afford the newly increased mortgage rates, they absolutely *had* to. This proved to be an extremely aggressive and optimistic bet, and it was implicitly also being made by the large institutions that packaged up and sold (or bought) the mortgage-backed securities that had aggregated thousands of individual loans together.

Then the inevitable happened: individual household incomes did *not* grow sufficiently to cover the mortgage rate resets, defaults skyrocketed to unprecedented levels, housing values collapsed, and the value of the subprime securities plummeted like a stone. *Voilà:* one subprime crisis.

The point of this ($300 billion, and counting) example is simply this: when analyzing individual companies and even entire market segments, adding an ES perspective can alert investors to both risks and opportunities that traditional investment analysis and perspectives tend to overlook.

Bear Stearns: Giving New Meaning to the Term "Bear Market"

As noted previously, the most notable individual corporate casualty of the subprime fiasco was the once-impregnable Wall Street investment bank Bear Stearns. Here again, an ES analytical perspective proved extremely valuable in identifying risks that had passed completely under "the Street's" radar.

In June 2007, Bear Stearns had just made a $3.2 billion secured loan to one of its own hedge funds, which had incurred severe losses on its subprime positions. Nonetheless, Credit Suisse, CIBC, and Merrill Lynch all reiterated their "Outperform" ratings on Bear Stearns. UBS and Sanford Bernstein maintained a neutral rating, but set a target price of $170 a share. At that point, Bear's stock was trading at $150 a share.

At least one sustainability research house swam against the tide, however, and gave Bear Stearns a below-investment grade rating of BB, almost entirely because of the researcher's ES focus and perspective. Relative to its Wall Street rivals, Bear seemed to view ES risk management as a costly distraction with little or no discernible ROI potential. Despite the fact that Bear was up to its eyeballs in the subprime market, it seemed to regard responsible lending as though it were a distraction from its core mission of making profits for itself and delivering value to its shareholders.

Ultimately, however, it was this very risk—the insolvency of the borrowers that essentially acted as collateral for so much of the bank's assets—that caused Bear's investors and clients to lose confidence and withdraw their capital so quickly and dramatically.

In its July 2007 report, the sustainability research house had written:

> There is no evidence that Bear Stearns has a centralized system for identifying and managing key ES threats at the executive level or in the risk management division. **The bank's ES risk radar is reactive rather than anticipatory,** which sets it behind sector leaders and exposes the company's earnings to unanticipated environmental and social shocks **(especially in the sub-prime sector).**[28]

Prophetic words indeed, and where there was smoke, there did indeed turn out to be fire. Bear Stearns' risk management architecture—or lack thereof—in the ES space turned out to be a proxy and leading indicator for its *overall* risk management capabilities. And for a firm whose core business *was* risk, this proved to be an absolutely fatal shortcoming.

Bear Stearns' collapse illustrates with chilling clarity that key environmental and/or social drivers (in this case, the financial and reputational risks to the banks from flogging totally inappropriate products to low-income communities) are reconfiguring the entire investment risk landscape. Investors who have not yet evaluated how ES risk might affect future earnings, credit quality, and cashflows would be well advised to take Bear Stearns' implosion as a *serious* wake-up call. Whether or not they actually *will*, of course, remains to be seen.

Some Forward-Looking Questions for Investors

The foregoing, however, are all *historical* examples of investment "mistakes" that might well have been avoided or at least mitigated with high-quality ES analysis. Hindsight, of course, is generally 20/20. (In fairness, though, several of the examples cited here *were* predictions made *ex ante*.) As investors, of course, we are much more concerned about the *future*. Going forward, astute investors will want to consider—or have their advisors consider—the following sustainability-driven questions:

About Climate Change
• To what extent will climate-driven water shortages in northern Chile affect the *mining companies* that consume roughly 70 percent of the

region's water? Which mining companies are best positioned—BHP Billiton, Xstrata, Grupo Mexico, or Antofagasta?

- Which *electric power producers* will be most successful at diversifying their generation assets into wind, solar, and other renewable energy sources? Iberdrola? Florida Light and Power?

- Which *coal-based U.S. electric utilities* are most likely to weather the inevitable transition to a carbon-constrained regulatory and economic environment? AEP (American Electric Power)? FirstEnergy? Pinnacle West? Dynegy?

- Who will win the global race to commercialize CCS (carbon capture and storage)—a potentially game-changing technology in the fight against climate change? Norway's diversified oil and gas company Statoil Hydro? Italy's major electric utility Enel? BP or Royal Dutch Shell?

- Which *insurers* are most likely to create successful new products driven by the growing global concerns about climate change? Swiss Re? Munich Re? Zurich Financial? AIG?

About Social Issues
- Which major *pharmaceutical companies* are best positioned to navigate successfully through the sociopolitical and competitive challenges of "solving" the thorny problem of access to medicines in emerging markets—Merck, GlaxoSmithKline, Novartis, Sanofi-Aventis, Pfizer, or others?

- Which *companies active in Latin America and Asia* are most likely to succeed in figuring out how to create and access new customers at the "base of the pyramid"—those subsisting on incomes of less than 2 dollars a day? Companies such as CEMEX and Unilever have shown considerable early promise, but it's still very early in the base of the pyramid sweepstakes.

- How rapidly and successfully will *global food companies* manage the necessary strategic transition to becoming "health, science, and wellness" companies? Which will be the winners and which will be the losers—Nestle, Cargill, Archer-Daniels, Midland, Danone?

- Which major *mining companies* active in Africa will be most successful in wrestling with the devastating impact of the HIV/AIDS pandemic on the skill base and productivity of their work forces? Anglo American? De Beers? Golden Fields? Xstrata? And what about "black empowerment," an increasingly critical economic and sociopolitical issue in Africa?

About Technology
- Which major *automaker* will best solve the challenges of low-pollution, next-generation power trains? Toyota or Honda? Ford or GM? Or will it be India's innovative Tata Motors, or an upstart company from China?
- Which of the *oil and gas majors* will most successfully use nanotechnology to improve data collection about the physical characteristics of new reservoirs, to improve their rates of recovery and efficiency? Royal Dutch/Shell? Occidental Petroleum?

About Natural Resources
- Which *forest products company* will wrestle most successfully with the demands of a global marketplace that is increasingly sensitized to the imperatives of sustainable forestry? Based on recent track records, it is more likely to be a Scandinavian company such as Stora Enso or Holmen AB than a North American rival such as Temple Inland or Great Southern.
- Which *beverage companies* will best adapt to an emerging competitive environment where, by 2025, water scarcity will leave an estimated one-third of the world's population without access to adequate drinking water? Coca Cola? Pepsico? Diageo?

Overall, which global banks are best positioned to both manage the downside risks and capture the upside investment opportunities presented by the sustainability revolution? HSBC? JP Morgan? Standard Chartered? Citigroup?

These are the types of questions that investors and their advisors and money managers should be asking—and they should be asking them now! Each set of companies mentioned, in each of the varied and diverse industry sectors cited above, contains *wide* discrepancies between the best and worst company performers. Can *your* investment managers tell you which is which? And these are emphatically not trivial issues or questions; they are virtually certain to have a profound impact on global investment returns for at least the next 20 years. Those investors who cannot or will not ask these questions—*and* get good answers—should expect to be left behind, or worse.

Chapter 6

Why Does It All *Matter* Anyway?

The State of the World

Sustainability is here to stay or we may not be.

—NIALL FITZGERALD
K CEO, UNILEVER

Before moving on to what I expect will be much more uplifting and optimistic material in Chapters 7 through 12, it will be helpful to pause and remind ourselves why sustainability investing is such a critical imperative.

At the risk of sounding excessively melodramatic, current environmental and social conditions—*and* forward-looking trends—should be enough to give *all* investors pause. Unfortunately, most don't spend much time thinking about them (with, of course, the conspicuous exception of the enlightened readership of this book), but they absolutely *should*. Unless these trends can be halted and reversed, there will be relatively little *point* in investing; we will simply not have the sort of world in which anyone would *want* to work, raise children, or spend their retirement. So this chapter is intended to be a brief "refresher course" on the State of the World, with particular focus on what it means for investors.

There is absolutely no shortage of comprehensive—and utterly depressing—accounts of the extent and gravity of environmental and social problems in the world today. Among the most recent (and least despondent, inasmuch as it actually offers some promising recipes for change, hope, and concrete *action*) is Jeffrey Sachs' recent *Common Wealth: Economics for a Crowded Planet.*[1] When read together with two major intergovernmental publications, the *Millennium Ecosystem Assessment* (2005)[2] and the UN Environment Program's *Global Environmental Outlook 4* (2007),[3] the reader receives an excellent, in-depth picture. All are recommended reading.

Here, we will attempt to do no more than summarize some of their key findings, along with those of a few other researchers. Our objective here is not to replicate or compete with that excellent body of existing work, but rather simply to highlight what it all means for private sector companies and, in particular, for their *investors*. Buried beneath the avalanche of facts and figures are both risks and opportunities for corporate leaders and investors. Company executives who can understand the powerful and changing underlying global dynamics will be well on their way to avoiding many of the risks and capitalizing on at least some of the opportunities. Those who either ignore or fail to come to grips with the issues are almost certainly doomed to mediocrity at best and commercial extinction at worst. And precisely the same fate will await their investors.

Our "State of the World" review will, of course, be seen through a *sustainability* lens. If the reader accepts anything like the "Four Pillar" definition of sustainability that we proposed in Chapter 1—Environment, Human Capital, Stakeholder Capital, and Strategic Governance— it is easy to see that virtually *no* company on earth will be unaffected by at least one of the sustainability issues and megatrends discussed here. So, even in the unlikely event that readers are sublimely disinterested in the fate of the planet being left to their children and grandchildren, financial self-interest alone should make sustainability a top-of-mind issue. But what *types* of companies need to be concerned about sustainability issues? Well, the list is an extremely long one:

- Companies highly dependent on their brand strength and, therefore, particularly vulnerable to having it tarnished (e.g., McDonalds, Nike, Gap, and Coca Cola).
- Companies with a major direct environmental impact (e.g., Royal Dutch/Shell, Rio Tinto Alcan, and DuPont).

- Companies dependent on natural resources for their core products (e.g., clean water for Coca Cola or Pepsi, healthy forests for companies such as International Paper, and productive soil for agriculturally based companies such as Nestlé, Cargill, and Archer Daniels Midland).
- Companies dependent on natural resources as an important input in their supply chains (e.g., pure water supply for semiconductor chip makers, such as Intel and AMD).
- Companies with major social and community impact (e.g., Occidental Petroleum drilling for oil in the Ecuadorean jungle near aboriginal populations; sporting goods companies and clothing manufacturers with major manufacturing facilities in Asia).
- Companies facing the imminent prospect of increasing regulations (e.g., electric utilities in the United States, such as AEP).
- Companies whose workforces are in danger of being decimated by major diseases, such as HIV/AIDS. Mining companies with significant operations in Africa (Anglo American, for example) spring readily to mind here.
- Companies facing competitive markets for top talent (e.g., just about everyone!).

As can immediately be seen from even this brief list, *just about every company on earth* stands to be impacted by the Sustainable Investment Revolution. Sustainability, therefore, is neither a mere "nice to have" or a niche concern; it will be increasingly important to both corporate executives everywhere *and* to the investors evaluating their companies.

We will now briefly summarize some of the most striking and worrisome factors and trends with respect to a number of the key sustainability issues.

Eleven Major Sustainability Challenges

While not exhaustive, the list of 11 major sustainability challenges that follows should be daunting enough.

Population Growth and Urbanization

Global population growth, most of it in the developing world, is combining with increasing incomes and urbanization to place intolerable strains on both the natural carrying capacity of the earth and our ability as societies to manage these issues. They are arguably the number one sustainability challenge and are fundamental drivers of most of the others as well.

Poverty and Social Inequality

Obviously problems in their own right, poverty and social inequality are also prime causes of many of the other environmental issues, as well as severe and widespread human health problems.

Climate Change and Energy

Accelerating fossil-based energy use is creating massive air and water pollution and is, of course, the prime culprit in the climate change challenge. Climate change itself is already affecting a number of different industry sectors and, as we have seen, is rewriting the international rules of competitive advantage.

Human Rights

The sometimes violent repression of freedom of speech and association, as well as labor and children's rights, is, again, both intolerable in principle in its own right *and* imposes enormous productivity and opportunity costs, both for business and for the broader society.

Water Scarcity and Quality

Water quality and availability issues are becoming increasingly serious all over the world, causing and spreading disease and death, exacerbating violent conflicts, and constraining business growth and, even, survival.

Air Pollution

Particulates, smog, and volatile organic compounds are creating increasingly serious health problems in both the developed and developing worlds at a cost of hundreds of billions of dollars each year. They are also impairing the quality of life and hurting worker productivity.

Human Health

Disease and premature death are not only unacceptable from a purely humanitarian perspective, but they also impose enormous financial costs on both business and society as a whole.

Waste and Waste Management

Solid waste management is a growing issue for communities in both the developed and developing worlds. In addition, chemicals, heavy metals, and toxic waste create a greater risk of cancer and reproductive harm for humans, plants, and animals.

Soil Degradation and Loss

The progressive deterioration in both the quality and quantity of soil undermines agricultural productivity, increasing famine and poverty and placing additional stress on forests, which are then cut down to provide new agricultural land.

Deforestation and Deterioration of Forests

Unsustainable harvesting of timber in countries such as Brazil and Indonesia exacerbates climate change, accelerates soil erosion and biodiversity loss, and increases flood risk.

Biodiversity Loss

Natural ecosystems are essential for human life. Habitat destruction threatens a variety of interrelated ecosystems, often in unexpected ways.

While we shall summarize and discuss these issues separately in this chapter, it should be clear that this division is an entirely artificial one. In point of fact, most of these problems are tightly interrelated and exacerbate one another. Climate change, for example, far from being a "stand-alone" issue, has a direct bearing on the quantity and quality of agricultural soil, water quality and availability, human health, forests, and biodiversity, just for starters. Population growth and urbanization affect all of those, *plus* air quality. And so on. Indeed, it is precisely the tightness of the interrelationships that makes the problems so profound and seemingly intractable. The *good* news, of course, is that any significant *improvement* in any one of these sustainability challenges tends to have immediate and positive spillover effects on the others.

For these reasons, therefore, the reader should be cognizant that while the sustainability issues are presented here separately for convenience, they are very much interwoven with one another.

The implications for those investing are stark. Just as it is ultimately impossible to have successful, enduring companies within societies and physical environments that are degraded and failing, so too it is impossible to have successful investors. The winners of the twenty-first century will be those who understand these sustainability megatrends and imperatives, allocate their financial resources to those companies that also "get it," and can navigate those trends better than their competitors. By "navigate," we mean both the ability to minimize and manage the downside risks *and* to identify and capture opportunities by providing solutions on the *upside.*

Just to clarify the reader's expectations, however, what follows is *not* intended to be an exhaustive catalog of all the sustainability challenges worthy of attention, nor is it designed to provide a comprehensive, in-depth discussion of the ones that we do emphasize. Equally importantly, it does not attempt to provide anything close to a complete enumeration of all of the specific investment risks and opportunities associated with each sustainability issue or theme. What it *is* intended to provide, however, is just a bit of a flavor of both the breadth and the depth of those possibilities, both positive and negative. In Chapter 7 we shall provide 10 specific minicase studies of companies that we consider to be capitalizing on one major sustainability trend or another. For now, however, we shall content ourselves with simply setting the stage.

With all of those caveats out of the way, let us now review some of the specific business—and therefore *investment*—risks and opportunities driven by sustainability factors.

The Key Sustainability Issues

Issue: Population Growth and Urbanization

Snapshot State of Play

- The world's population is currently growing approximately 75 million a year.
- The UN Population Division's *median* growth forecast predicts an increase from 6.7 billion in 2008 to 9.2 billion in 2050—an increase of 2.5 billion people.
- The majority of this projected population growth will occur in the already-impoverished developing world.
- The scale of human economic activity ("gross world product") has increased by *eight times* since 1950.[4] The UN projects a further 6-fold increase by 2050.

Impacts

- The World Wide Fund for Nature (WWF) estimates that the *current* population already exceeds the earth's carrying capacity by at least 20 percent.
- The combination of population growth, greater per capita income and economic activity, and urbanization is beginning to place intolerable stress on both the earth's own natural resource carrying capacity and our own manufactured physical and social infrastructure.
- In China alone, over 300 *million* people are expected to migrate from rural areas to the cities over the next 15 years. Among the many environmental impacts of this migration, each of these people will likely require and consume *three times* as much energy in their new urban settings as they do today. Given that China's energy consumption per unit of gross domestic product (GDP) is *already* nine times greater than that of Japan, the potential implications and impact are almost beyond imagination.
- Also in China, increases in the size and income of the population are, among many other impacts, resulting in a dramatic increase in the amount of meat eaten. This, in turn, creates increased demand for animal feed, which, in turn, has fueled a sharp increase in the volume of soybeans China imports from Brazil. That then has accelerated the deforestation of Amazonia in order to grow more soybeans. This then exacerbates climate change, which may in turn hurt agricultural yields. And so the cycle continues. In the world of sustainability, *everything* is connected to everything else!
- Another example of the compounding sustainability impact of the potent combination of population growth and increased income in China is that automobile production has already increased by 350 percent since the year 2000. This is in response to demand from a growing and increasingly affluent and urbanizing population. Even at that, however, only 18 of every 1000 people in China currently own a car. Just imagine the environmental impact and resource consumption that will be unleashed when that ratio is quadrupled—or if it ever even remotely approaches that of the United States, which is currently *40 times* larger than that of China!

Risks

The global economic center of gravity and dynamism is shifting profoundly and irrevocably from developed markets to emerging ones, particularly the "BRIC" countries (Brazil, Russia, India, and China). Organisation for Economic Co-operation and Development (OECD)-based companies without compelling emerging markets strategies are likely to face mature, saturated, and stagnant markets in their traditional countries of focus.

Opportunities

- The BRIC countries generally, as well as the so-called "N-11" countries ("next" 11: Bangladesh, Egypt, Indonesia, Iran, Mexico, Nigeria, Pakistan, Philippines, South Korea, Turkey, and Vietnam), will become increasingly dynamic and attractive markets.
- In countries with "aging" demographics, increased opportunities in health care and "healthy living" products and services will abound.
- Urban infrastructure—roads, public transit, wastewater treatment, education, health care—will require massive investment. Much of it will likely be accomplished through public–private partnerships, which will require new management and investment appraisal skills.
- The "Base of the Pyramid," the 4 billion people in emerging markets with annual incomes of less than $1500, represents both an enormous pool of talent and entrepreneurship, as well as a largely untapped customer and consumer base.

Issue: Poverty and Social Inequality

Snapshot State of Play

- Fully 15 percent of the people in the world today live in extreme poverty.[5] The wealthiest 10 percent of the world's population earns fully 48 percent of its total income; the poorest 10 percent earns only 1.6 percent.
- Twenty percent of the population consumes 86 percent of the world's goods and services today; the other 80 percent consumes only 14 percent.
- The 200 wealthiest *individuals* in the world today have more assets than the least wealthy 4.5 *billion* people combined.[6]
- World poverty was further exacerbated in 2008 by dramatic increases in the cost of basic staples. In the short period between January and April, the price of rice—a staple for fully 50 percent of the world's population—increased by *400 percent!*

Impacts

- Serious adverse effects on human health and life expectancy.
- Extensive human suffering and misery.
- Enormous loss of human productive capacity.
- Economic desperation often drives environmentally destructive behavior (e.g., deforestation for fuel in emerging markets).
- Loss of potential talent pool and consumer markets for business.

Risks for Investors

- There is a generic risk that if poverty and social inequality persist or, worse still, become exacerbated, even existing market opportunities are likely to be jeopardized by social unrest and dislocation. The worldwide food riots of 2008, triggered by skyrocketing food costs, provide a sobering leading indicator.
- In terms of *opportunity* costs, persistent poverty obviously precludes literally billions of people from becoming either customers or productive employees.

Opportunities

Again, at the "Base of the Pyramid," there are 4 billion people living on less than $1000 per year. As we shall see in Chapter 7, contrary to intuitive expectations, this population actually represents an enormous and potentially viable consumer market. Investment opportunities at the Base of the Pyramid include the following:

- Financial services, such as microcredit and microinsurance.
- Telecommunications services—the provision of cellular telephone and wireless data exchange, even in rural villages.
- Housing construction.
- Consumer goods and services.

These opportunities are not likely to be available to investors directly. The best way to participate will likely be to invest in one of the growing number of microfinance funds, several of which are offered by major, mainstream money management houses.

Issue: Climate Change and Energy

Snapshot State of Play

- Scientists have observed a growing increase in average global temperatures of 0.7°C over the past century. This average overall figure, however, masks more extreme changes in particular regions.
- We *currently* add roughly 17 billion tons of CO_2 to the atmosphere every year, which stays in the atmosphere for 70–100 *years.*
- Of the 12 warmest years on record since 1850, 11 have occurred over the past 12 years.
- Business as usual will create atmospheric concentrations of CO_2 and other greenhouse gases that exceed tolerable limits for minimizing climate change. Even significant reductions may not be sufficient. The current consensus is that a rise in average temperatures of 2°C or more would cause unacceptable risks. Preindustrial concentrations were roughly 280 parts per million (ppm) of CO_2 equivalents. Just since 1960, it has already increased from 315 to 380 ppm.
- Until very recently, most scientists had agreed that a stabilization target of 450 ppm would be adequate. (A "business-as-usual" scenario would leave us at a totally unacceptable 560 ppm by 2050.) In the past few months, NASA scientist James Hansen, one of the world's leading climate scientists, has urgently argued that even 450 ppm will likely be inadequate and that even a 1°C temperature rise above 2000 levels could be highly disruptive. He has, therefore, proposed the much more stringent target of 400 ppm.
- Considering that China alone adds the equivalent of the total U.K. power generation capability *every week* via coal-fired plants, the magnitude of the climate challenge becomes both clear and stark.
- Perhaps most worrying is that most scientists agree that climate impact is likely to be both unpredictable and discontinuous, with geometric increases beyond the tipping point that is unknown.
- Each new piece of peer-reviewed scientific research emphasizes that climate change is occurring both more widely and more rapidly than was predicted even 12 months previously.

Impacts

- There has been a significant increase in violent storms and extreme weather events (floods, droughts, heat waves, hurricanes, windstorms). Heat waves in Europe in the summer of 2005 alone caused 30,000 deaths. Floods in Myanmar in 2008 caused a loss of life several times larger still.

- Shrinking mountain glaciers. In Africa, Mount Kilimanjaro has lost 80 percent of its ice and thawing permafrost in the Arctic. The U.S. Rockies has reduced the snowpack by over 16 percent.
- Earlier breakup of river and lake ice.
- Altered growing seasons and agricultural productivity.
- Shifts of plant, animal, and insect geographic ranges.
- Increased disease transmission (e.g., malaria in Africa at elevations that were previously too cool for transmission of the disease).
- Changing precipitation patterns and ocean currents and chemistry.
- Rises in sea level.
- Forest destruction (e.g., pine beetle infestation in British Columbia, Canada, because of changed weather patterns).
- Potential major impact on energy, agriculture, forestry, infrastructure, and tourism industries.

Risks for Investors

- Companies in sectors such as agriculture, forestry, and tourism that depend on the specific location of their facilities could face serious risks to either their core business itself or to an important part of their supply chains. Tourism activities directly dependent on pristine beaches and coral reefs or reliable snow cover for ski resorts could find their very *raison d'être* threatened.
- Companies in sectors such as energy utilities, oil and gas, mining, and chemicals with poorer "carbon efficiency" than their competitors will face greater regulatory costs and stakeholder risks as we move into a "carbon-constrained" future.
- Companies with vulnerable inputs and supply chains, such as food processing and pulp and paper companies, are likely to be less directly but no less injuriously affected.
- Insurers—and reinsurers, such as Swiss Re and Munich Re—are facing economic losses from extreme weather events that are *10 times* larger than they were in the 1950s.

Opportunities

- "Pure-play" renewable energy providers in the solar, wind, geothermal, and biofuels subsectors will be attractive. Major companies as diverse as Walmart, AMD, Starbucks, and Johnson and Johnson have all made firm commitments to obtaining a significant portion of their energy requirements from renewable sources. In several cases, the target level is actually 100 percent!

- Major companies in a variety of sectors with superior "carbon efficiency" and better strategic exposure to "next-generation" energy sources, energy efficiency, and conservation will enjoy significant competitive advantages and are likely to be better investment candidates than their same-sector peers.

- Companies providing the "plumbing" for the coming low-carbon economy—such as "smart" meters and energy management software, power converters, and superconducting materials to connect solar and wind power to grids, and much more. These "plumbing" companies (such as American Superconductor) have the great virtue for investors of removing the necessity of picking tomorrow's specific winning clean energy technologies and companies. Good "plumbing" will be needed by *all* of them.

- Harnessing the economic opportunities in the forestry sector by "monetizing" the ability of companies to capture and sequester carbon dioxide.

- The same insurers and reinsurers that are exposed to climate risk on the downside are also the potential beneficiaries of opportunities for new products and services on the upside.

Issue: Human Rights

Snapshot State of Play

- Over the past decade, armed conflict has killed 2 million children, disabled 4 to 5 million, and left 12 million homeless and more than 1 million orphaned or separated from their parents.[7]

- There are approximately 250 million child laborers worldwide: Asia accounts for 153 million and Africa for 80 million.[8]

- Of the children engaged in child labor, 150 million are working in agriculture.[9] Child agriculture workers frequently work long hours in scorching heat, haul heavy loads, are exposed to toxic pesticides, and suffer high rates of injury, exposing them to lasting physical and psychological harm.

- Seventy-five percent of the refugees internally displaced in the world are women and children under the age of 16 years who have lost their families and their homes.[10]

- In the last decade, there were approximately 300,000 child soldiers.[11]
- Between 2000 and 2005, Amnesty International issued more than 400 Urgent Actions on behalf of individuals whose human rights were believed to be at immediate risk of violation.

Risks for Investors

- Poor stakeholder relations. The security of the "social license to operate" of companies can easily be threatened, along with business relationships with governments, business partners, trade unions, subcontractors, and suppliers.
- Risk of consumer protests and damage to corporate reputation and brand image from human rights abuses anywhere in the global supply chains of companies.

Issue: Water Scarcity and Quality

Snapshot State of Play

- Only 1 to 1.5 percent of the world's water supply is currently available for human use; the majority is salt water.
- Major drivers of water stress include population growth, increased incomes and consumption patterns, increasingly intensive agricultural and industrial processes requiring more water, and climate change.
- World water demand increased 6-fold between 1900 and 1995, although the population growth was "only" three times its base level.[12]
- Contamination affects and compromises the water supplies of as many as 3.3 billion people today; at least 1 billion lack access to clean drinking water.
- Serious water stress is already evident in the North China Plain, the Sahel, the Horn of Africa, Northern India, the Murray-Darling Basin in Australia, the southwestern United States, and elsewhere.
- In industry, it currently takes 3000 gallons of water to produce a single semiconductor, 62,000 gallons to produce a single ton of steel, and 39,000 gallons to produce a single car.[13]
- By 2025, some 1.8 billion people will be experiencing "absolute scarcity"—insufficient water for drinking, sanitation, irrigation, and industry.
- In the developing world, as much as 95 percent of all sewage and 70 percent of industrial waste currently goes, untreated, directly into rivers, lakes, and oceans.

Impacts

- Lost agricultural productivity from droughts in China, Australia, and sub-Saharan Africa.
- Violent social and political conflicts over an increasingly scarce resource, e.g., in Darfur, Sudan, and Somalia.
- In China, grain production has dropped by the equivalent of the entire production of Canada over the past 6 years.
- Lost educational and economic opportunities result because gathering water consumes huge amounts of time (usually for women) in emerging markets.
- Famine, disease, and mass migration occur.
- Over 75 percent of the world's fisheries are already overexploited and past the point of sustainable renewal.

Risks for Investors

- Companies in the agriculture, manufacturing, semiconductor, and beverage sectors, among others, will come under growing competitive and economic pressure and disruption in water-stressed parts of the world. In Kerala, India, for example, Coca Cola's plant was shut down for 2 years over concerns about the company's excessive water consumption. The importance that Coca Cola places on water today is nicely captured by the job title of its top sustainability executive— VP of Environment and Water. In the forest products sector, Celulosa Arauco's $1.4 billion pulp and paper mill at Valvidia, Chile, was closed for 3 months after a water pollution incident, at a cost to the company of over $10 million.

Opportunities

- Large companies with diversified holdings along different parts of the "water-value chain" will be of special interest to sustainability investors. Companies with a global scale, such as Suez, Veolia, and ITT, are involved in the provision, purification, and management of water supplies.
- Large companies in sectors highly dependent on water that are capable of using the resource more efficiently will have a growing competitive advantage. This is already apparent in the mining and agricultural sectors in Australia, for example.

- Smaller "pure-play" companies are engaged in water purification, desalination, management, and efficiency.

Issue: Air Pollution

Snapshot State of Play

- A World Bank survey of more than 100 cities in industrial and developing countries that had data on emissions of sulfur dioxide or nitrogen dioxide found that the air in many urban areas remains unhealthy.[14]
- Twenty-nine percent of the world's cities recorded sulfur dioxide emissions (often associated with power plants) above maximum levels allowable under World Health Organization (WHO) guidelines, and 71 percent had nitrogen dioxide emissions (often associated with automobile use) that exceeded WHO maximums.[15]
- Developing countries are less likely to meet WHO standards. Cities in China are particularly hard hit. More than 80 percent of them in the World Bank list had sulfur dioxide or nitrogen dioxide emissions above the WHO threshold.[16] Nearly half of all cities in China have excessive sulfur emissions registered levels at more than double the WHO standard.[17]
- Over the past 2 decades, a sharp increase in fossil fuel burning that has accompanied economic expansion has caused smog to form at levels that cut the amount of sunlight reaching the earth's surface by 10 to 15 percent.[18]

Impacts

- A 2000 World Bank study projected that on average 1.8 million people would die prematurely each year between 2001 and 2020 because of air pollution.[19]
- 137.2 million Americans—including as many as 29.8 million children under the age of 14 and close to 2 million children suffering from asthma attacks—are potentially exposed to unhealthful levels of ozone (smog).[20]
- In the United States alone, estimates of the annual human health costs of outdoor air pollution range from $14 billion to $55 billion annually.[21]
- Globally, an estimated 200,000 to 570,000 people die each year from ambient air pollution.[22]

- Each year, pollution claims 70,000 lives in the United States.[23]
- Globally, an estimated 2.8 million people die each year from exposure to particulate matter pollution indoors, primarily due to the heavy use of fossil fuels (wood, coal) for home heating and cooking in many parts of the world.[24]
- Air pollution also adversely affects agriculture. The measurable, regional-scale impact on crop yields caused by tropospheric ozone has been estimated to cause economic losses for 23 arable crops in Europe in the range $5.72 to 12 billion/year.[25] There is evidence of significant adverse effects on staple crops in some. With the growing demand and subsequent rising price of food, such costs are likely to be unsustainable.
- More than half a dozen comprehensive studies in the United States and Europe since the 1980s have shown that yield reductions from ozone are economically significant.[26] A 2002 study of European farming, for example, determined that ozone was costing farmers more than EUR 6 billion annually.[27]
- For American adults, asthma is the fourth leading cause of work absenteeism, resulting in nearly 15 million missed or lost workdays each year. This causes an estimated total cost of nearly $3 billion in lost productivity.[28] Asthma causes and exacerbations are directly linked to poor air quality.

Risks for Investors

- Higher health-care costs result, leading to lower profits and higher taxes for companies. Company health costs will be an increasingly important strategic issues for investors. In the United States, for example, health-care insurance costs have surged by 250 percent since 2000. Since there are wide differentials in the ability of companies to manage "wellness" with their employees, sustainability investors will look carefully at company-specific health-care management and costs.
- Lower worker productivity is also a major issue for companies and a risk factor for their investors.
- Not only is human capital directly impacted, but so too is the cultivation of our natural resources, as particulates and smog reduce the intensity of sunlight reaching the earth's surface, thereby harming agricultural productivity.
- The increased concern for air quality will also lead to more stringent regulations on burning fossil fuels.

- The United States, where corporate average fuel economy (CAFE) regulations have been nearly unchanged since introduced in 1975, is extremely likely to make dramatic increases in fuel economy standards because of growing concern over the impact of fossil fuel burning on air quality and climate change. Companies with greater "ecoefficiency" stand to benefit.

Opportunities

- Globally, the market for "cleantech" products and services in 2007 was over $280 billion, more than triple its size 2 years earlier. Over the next decade, it is expected to grow to $1.3 *trillion.*[29] A sizable percentage of that cleantech market will be devoted to goods and services aimed at air pollution.
- In 2004, world air pollution control industry *profits* were estimated at $3.2 billion. Profits are forecast to grow to $21 billion in 2015, with $3 billion generated from the supply of systems, $11 billion from the supply of products, and $7 billion from the supply of services.[30]
- Significant new multipollutant air regulations are also on the horizon. U.S. President Bush's proposed Clear Skies Act, the most visible of these new air pollution initiatives, is expected to require over $40 billion in new pollution control investments by 2020.
- There is significant growth potential in this area in emerging markets as well. The air pollution control, monitoring, and testing market was close to $200 million in 2003. Moreover, it is expected to grow 15 percent annually over the next decade as air pollution becomes a growing concern. In China, for example, the world's leading emitter of sulfur dioxide and other air pollutants, demand for air pollution control equipment is expected to grow by 18 percent annually through 2010.[31]

Issue: Human Health

Snapshot State of Play

- Serious nutritional deficiencies in parts of the developing world.
- High child mortality rates in parts of the developing world.
- Major water-borne diseases—cholera, childhood diarrhea.
- The number of people living with HIV worldwide in 2007 was estimated at 33.2 million; in 2008 deaths worldwide from HIV/AIDS were 2.2 million.

- Since 1970, approximately 35 *million* people worldwide have died from HIV/AIDS.[32]
- In 2007, 2.1 million children under 15 years of age were living with HIV, 290,000 children died of AIDS, and 420,000 children were newly infected with HIV.
- By 2007, over 15 million children under 18 years of age have lost one or both parents to AIDS.[33]
- New disease vectors from climate change—e.g., malaria, where there were none before.
- Lack of access to affordable medicines in emerging markets.
- Reemergence of diseases, such as tuberculosis, which had previously been brought under control.
- Emergence of extremely dangerous, drug-resistant disease adaptations.

Impacts

- Quite apart from their profound and devastating humanitarian implications, disease and premature deaths can obviously be a major inhibiting factor on economic productivity and competitiveness.
- Malaria alone kills up to 3 million people per year, most of them children in Africa.

Risks for Investors

- Investors should be alert to company-specific capabilities for minimizing and managing diseases. In the mining sector in Africa, for example, the HIV/AIDS pandemic has had a major deleterious impact on worker productivity and health-care costs.

Opportunities

In general, in the emerging markets, health-driven risks to investors significantly outweigh any opportunities. In this one case, it is largely a question of downside risk.

- Having said that, companies headquartered in the OECD markets can, nonetheless, create enormous value for their global franchises by contributing meaningfully to mitigating health problems in emerging markets, even if those contributions themselves (deeply discounted or even free medicines, for example) are not commercially profitable.

- In developed markets, by contrast, "diseases of affluence," such as obesity, poor nutrition, and, in some cases, diabetes, offer investors significant opportunities in companies capitalizing on a variety of "healthy lifestyle" and "wellness" products and services. The runaway commercial success of Whole Foods Supermarkets is only one example of a beneficiary of the spectacular growth of the "LOHAS" market—"lifestyles of health and sustainability."

Issue: Waste and Waste Management

Snapshot State of Play

- In the United States, each person on average creates nearly a ton of solid waste per year (1600 pounds). This is, not altogether surprisingly, more than any other nation on earth.
- Close to 30 percent of the waste generated in the United States is packaging material; 55 percent of this waste ends up in the form of residential garbage. The remaining 45 percent comes from manufacturing, retailing, and commercial trade in the U.S. economy.[34]
- Only about one-tenth of all solid garbage in the United States currently gets recycled.
- As of 1992, 14 billion pounds of trash were dumped into oceans annually around the world.
- The European Union (EU) produces 1.3 billion tons of waste each year, an average of nearly 1200 pounds per person. Roughly 40 to 45 million tons of this are classed as hazardous, or particularly dangerous.[35]

Impacts

- Existing landfill capacity in some urban centers is becoming scarce, but proposals for new sites often generate community opposition and compete with more productive uses for increasingly valuable land.
- The breakdown of biodegradable waste in landfills forms methane. This gas can create odor problems, kill surface vegetation, and is an extremely potent greenhouse gas.
- Methane from landfills currently constitutes roughly 4 percent of the EU's greenhouse gas emissions. It has a much greater climate-warming potential than CO_2 per molecule, but fortunately the absolute volumes involved are not as large.[36]

- Leaching from landfills can also cause the contamination of groundwater.
- Emerging market cities, such as Beijing, are facing particularly explosive growth rates in the size of their waste management problems.

Risks for Investors

- The increasing cost of waste. Governments, especially in Europe, are stepping in to regulate the end-of-life disposal of computers, cell phones, and other electronic equipment. All of this makes waste much more costly. This requires new "cradle-to-grave" approaches to product design whereby, for example, cars are "designed for disassembly" right from the outset.
- Sustainability investors will want to pay attention to the level of waste generated by companies per unit of profit or revenue. Companies that are not sufficiently "ecoefficient" will find themselves at a growing competitive disadvantage going forward.

Opportunities

- The energy content of waste products can be harnessed directly by using them as a direct combustion fuel or indirectly by processing them as another type. The waste-to-energy market in Europe is growing and is expected to do so for at least 10 years. Europe's waste-to-energy capacity is expected to increase by approximately 13 million tons. Almost 100 new plants will come on line by 2012.[37] To offset the high initial investment costs of biomass power plants compared to conventional fossil fuel-fired technologies, governments and agencies have introduced various incentives and subsidies, in some cases up to 50 percent of the investment costs.
- Growing landfills, coupled with the higher cost of oil, could lead to a greater demand for landfill gas extraction systems to extract the landfill gas as an alternative energy source.
- The recycling business has an annual turnover of $160 billion and employs 1.5 million people worldwide.[38]
- Recycling an aluminum soda can saves 96 percent of the energy used to manufacture it and produces 95 percent less air pollution and 97 percent less water pollution.
- One ton of paper from recycled pulp saves 17 trees, 3 cubic yards of landfill space, 7000 gallons of water, 4200 kilowatt hours (enough

to heat your home for half a year), and 390 gallons of oil. It also prevents 60 pounds of air pollutants.

- Producing recycled white paper creates 74 percent less air pollution, 35 percent less water pollution, and 75 percent less process energy than producing paper from virgin fibers.
- Sixty percent of the world's lead supply currently comes from recycled batteries.
- As emerging markets become more industrialized, they will generate more waste and will need an infrastructure to handle the large amount of postconsumer recycling and waste management.

Issue: Soil Degradation and Loss

Snapshot State of Play

- Degradation of soil quality affects 25 percent of all potentially arable land, and the overall pace of degradation has accelerated in the past 50 years.[39]
- Productivity has declined substantially on approximately 16 percent of the agricultural land in developing countries, especially in croplands in Africa and Central America, pasture in Africa, and forests in Central America. Almost 75 percent of Central America's agricultural land has been seriously degraded, as has 20 percent of Africa's and 11 percent of Asia's.[40]
- Estimates of land as a result of degradation vary widely, from 5 to 12 million hectares every year. Assuming that land loss continues at current rates, an additional 150 to 360 million hectares would go out of production by 2020.[41]
- Changes in temperature, rainfall, and climatic extremes will only add to the stress on agricultural resources in regions where land availability and degradation, food price shocks, and population growth are already major concerns. Climate change, salination, and increases in ground-level ozone from fossil fuel combustion threaten further deterioration.

Impacts

- Agricultural yields in the developing world are generally lower. Crop yield losses in Africa from 1970 to 1990 as a result of water erosion alone are estimated to have been 8 percent.[42] Some researchers project a 1 to 2 percent decline in *overall* global agricultural yields.[43]

- In South and Southeast Asia, estimates for total annual economic loss from soil degradation range from under 1 to 7 percent of agricultural gross domestic product (AGDP). Estimates for eight African countries show annual economic losses ranging from under 1 percent of AGDP in Madagascar to 9 percent in Zimbabwe.[44]
- During the 1980s and 1990s in Zimbabwe, soil erosion resulted in an annual loss totaling $1.5 billion. During the same time period in South Asia, the annual economic loss was estimated at $600 million for nutrient loss by erosion and $1.2 billion because of soil fertility depletion.[45]
- Besides affecting aggregate food supply, soil degradation also diminishes agricultural income and economic growth.
- Land degradation and desertification may account for as much as about 30 percent of the world's greenhouse gas releases. These changes to the land also alter the water, temperature, and energy balance of the planet.[46]

Risks for Investors

- Less productive land equates to higher input prices and further food price inflation, which is already a major global humanitarian, economic, and security issue. These issues will have obvious, direct impact on companies in the agricultural and food and beverage sectors.

Opportunities

- Greater political and popular acceptance of genetically modified foods and seeds, as well as other methods and technologies that enhance productivity in agriculture, will occur (e.g., Monsanto and Bio-Agriculture).
- Greater demand for high-quality agricultural land (because of constrained supply) will lead to more robust land prices for companies that have positioned themselves strategically.

Issue: Deforestation and Deterioration of Forests

Snapshot State of Play

- Thirty-seven million acres of forest are being cut down each year. At the current rates of loss, between now and 2020, the world will lose almost 6 percent more of its total forest cover.[47]

- Since 1990, the world has lost forest cover equal to the combined land areas of Texas, California, and New York, or Spain and France.
- In the OECD countries, original old-growth forests are being cut down and replaced by secondary growth and "monoculture" tree farms, which require chemical fertilizers and pesticides to survive. So, while the total area of forested lands has not declined markedly over the past decade, the forests' *quality* has.
- Acid rain has had a substantial deleterious impact of forests in both Northern Europe and North America. While the problem has since ameliorated in those regions, dramatically increased levels of air pollution in Asia foreshadow very serious problems there.
- A climate change-driven pine bark beetle infestation in British Columbia and Alaska and reduced maple tree production in Vermont have occurred.

Risks for Investors

- Losses in both the quantity and quality of forest feedstocks pose an obvious and direct threat to both lumber and pulp and paper companies.
- Forest production companies are subject to boycotts from key customers for unsustainable forestry practices, both from nongovernmental organizations (NGOs) such as Forest Ethics and from major customers such as Walmart, Kinkos, and Limited Brands (Victoria's Secret and catalogs). Companies such as International Paper and Boise Cascade have already suffered from such boycotts.

Opportunities

- The other side of the forest degradation coin has been an increase in the value of the high-quality forests that do remain. This has accelerated the emergence of timber as a new asset class for investors. Timberland investing has become particularly popular with large, sophisticated institutional investors, who value the fact that its financial returns tend not to be correlated with those of the equity and bond markets. This adds diversification benefits to their overall portfolio and dampens down the volatility of their returns to some extent. Major asset managers, such as the Hancock Timber Response Group, Brookfield Asset Management, Citigroup, and UBS Timber Investments, are very active in this market.

- Forests also play an important role in the global effort to combat climate change by capturing—sequestering—carbon dioxide from the atmosphere. While the current rules and mechanisms of the Kyoto Protocol make it difficult at present, it is likely that ways will emerge for investors to monetize forests' environmental contribution by way of creating, buying, and selling emission reduction credits. This already occurs in the voluntary markets, but not yet in the regulated one.
- Forest products companies, especially those from Scandinavia and Brazil, are leveraging the branding value of certified sustainable forest management practices to capture both market share and premium pricing in increasingly sensitive customer markets.

Issue: Biodiversity Loss

Snapshot State of Play

- According to the World Conservation Union, 103 plant and animal species have become extinct since 1800, indicating an extinction rate 50 times greater than the natural rate.[48]
- According to the World Wide Fund for Nature, global biodiversity has declined by almost one-third over the past 35 years. Land-based species were reduced by 25 percent, ocean-based species by 28 percent, and freshwater species by 29 percent.[49]
- Fully two-thirds of the major marine fisheries are categorized as either already depleted, overexploited, or fully exploited.[50]
- It is estimated that global warming of 2°C or more would threaten 20 to 30 percent of plant and animal species with extinction.[51] Ocean warming and acidification, for example, would create an environment in which some species could no longer survive.

Risks for Investors

The contributions of biodiversity-dependent ecosystem services to national economies are substantial. And as the following figures illustrate, biodiversity is highly valuable.[52]

- Annual world fish catch—$58 billion.
- Global herbal medicine market—roughly $43 billion in 2001.
- Anticancer agents from marine organisms—up to $1 billion/year.

- Honeybees as pollinators for agriculture crops—$2–8 billion/year.
- Coral reefs for fisheries and tourism—$30 billion/year.

A growing need to protect biodiversity may create significant barriers to business growth and subsequent financial value.

- In April 2004, for instance, the share price of Associated British Ports plummeted 10 percent after the U.K. government rejected plans for a new container terminal in Dibden Bay near Southampton. One of the major factors behind the government's refusal was the potential impact of the terminal on local wildlife.
- Customers are switching to suppliers that offer ecocertified products (e.g., the Body Shop's "animal-friendly" products are taking market share in the cosmetics market).

Opportunities

- New investment models are now emerging that make the environment a profit center and will dramatically alter the commercial basis of land management and biodiversity/ecosystem preservation.
- This move toward the monetization of "ecosystem services" leads to opportunities for business to sell services provided by ecosystems, e.g., ecotourism.[53]
- Over the past decade, ecotourism has grown at a year-on-year rate of between 4 and 10 percent. In 2007, ecotourism constituted close to 7 percent of the total international tourism market.
- Other market-based mechanisms are creating new rights and value for the use of natural resources. These rights can then be traded, in the same way that greenhouse gas emission permits are already traded in Europe today.
- The growing market for wetlands banking[54] in the United States is one innovative example. At the end of 2006, the market for wetland banking was estimated to be $1 billion.[55]
- Banks and investors could tap into growing markets for sustainable biofuels, along with markets for certified commodities, such as fish, timber, and organic food. Estimates suggest a potential market size of about $60 billion annually by 2010.
- In November 2007, an Australian-based forestry investment firm, New Forests Pty Ltd., created an innovative partnership with the Sabah state government in Malaysia. Under the deal, biodiversity

credits are created that will allow palm oil producers to participate in forest conservation. New Forests Pty Ltd. and the state in East Malaysia will help protect about 34,000 hectares in the Malua Forest Reserve, which is home to orangutans, Sumatran rhinos, and clouded leopards. In return for an estimated $10 million investment to create a conservation bank, New Forests receives "biodiversity credits" from the government, with the Malaysian government retaining actual ownership of the forest. The credits can then be sold in a secondary market. Malaysia has been expanding rapidly into the palm oil market, contributing substantially to global deforestation, so this innovation has the potential for considerable positive impact.

Well, there you have it. A rather rushed, breathless tour of 11 of the most powerful sustainability trends confronting international investors today. Each of them is likely to be persistent, and each creates both risks and opportunities. None of them is likely to disappear any time soon, so forward-looking investors had better get used to them. To the extent that they do so, we believe that serious inroads *can* in fact be made in combating and reversing their harmful effects. And here's the best part: investors can actually generate superior returns while they're doing so! In the next chapter, we profile a number of major companies that have understood and capitalized on at least one of those 11 major sustainability issues. We would argue that they are precisely the sorts of companies that twenty-first century investors need to seek out.

Chapter 7

Sustainability and Competitive Advantage

The New Corporate Imperative— and Some Success Stories

The key is to go where the puck will be going, not where it is now.

—ICE HOCKEY LEGEND WAYNE GRETZKY

We have argued throughout this book that the performance of companies on sustainability issues is becoming an increasingly powerful determinant of their competitiveness and financial performance. In my experience, however, this changing dynamic has generally been much more widely appreciated by corporate executives than by investors. Indeed, on the *corporate* side, sustainability is rapidly becoming the new competitive orthodoxy, and the case for it, from the company perspective, has already been made well elsewhere.[1] In this chapter, however, we shall attempt to show why *investors* should care just as much, or even more, than company executives.

From the investor's standpoint, what is driving this growing nexus between the performance of companies on environmental and social (ES) issues and their investment returns is the fact that those issues can directly and profoundly affect *both* the risk and return sides of the investment equation.

The Downside Risk Side of the Coin

On the downside, ES factors can create a wide variety of potential financial risk exposures for companies and their investors:

- *Operating risk:* Managing emissions and waste product discharges, coping with product liability risk, dealing with issues regarding permits and "ecotaxes," as well as handling delayed or canceled projects, acquisitions, or divestitures can divert substantial financial and managerial resources away from more productive business activities. Typically, resource extraction companies in sectors such as mining, oil and gas, and forestry can easily rack up environmental expenditures totaling 10 to 30 percent of their total annual operating costs. Those types of numbers, of course, become even *more* significant in today's environment of turbo-charged competition, falling stock prices, and razor-thin profit margins.
- *Balance sheet risks:* Historical and contingent liabilities can have a major negative impact on a company's market value. The decommissioning of mines and the cleanup of derelict industrial sites, for example, can become a serious financial burden if appropriate preparatory measures have not been taken. The threat of litigation on a large scale because of past business practices can also damage a firm's stock price severely. To illustrate, at various times Haliburton, Dow, and ABB have each lost as much as 40 percent of their total market capitalization over investor fears of retroactive asbestos litigation in the United States.
- *Capital cost risk:* Pollution control expenditures, product redesign costs, and other capital outlays as a result of changing or anticipated environmental standards and regulations and customer expectations can become significant budgetary items. During the 1990s, for example, the oil refining industry spent approximately $30 billion to comply with governmental environmental regulations, a trend that looks as if it will continue because of ever-tightening fuel and air quality standards. In the electric utility sector, installing "scrubbers" to reduce SO_2, NO_2, and particulate emissions can easily cost more than $300

million for a single 850-megawatt (MW) plant. And even that level of expenditure won't make a serious dent in the plant's greenhouse gas emissions, which are nearly certain to be regulated and constrained over the next few years in the United States. Another recent example of environmentally driven capital expenditure comes from Canada's oil sands. In this case, the financial exposure belongs to Exxon Mobil, courtesy of its 70% ownership stake in Suncor, a major player in the oil sands. In early 2006, the Canadian federal government tightened its standards, lowering the permissible level of sulfur in petroleum products. The price tag for Suncor's retrofit was $500 *million*.

- In some cases, investor concerns about the company's sustainability performance can actually increase its cost of both debt and equity capital, or even make the capital unavailable altogether.

- *Business sustainability risk:* Companies in many industries face risks arising from the intrinsic lack of sustainability of their products and services. To give just one example, government plans to address climate change concerns could disrupt coal markets and significantly curtail demand. The Japanese government's public musings about imposing a carbon tax on imported high-sulfur coal in order to reduce climate change provide a sobering example. Those musings alarmed coal company investors who worried (justifiably) that the taxes could reduce demand, shrink company profits, or both. Those anxieties proved sufficient to lop nearly 10 percent off the total market value of one European coal company, Xstrata. That reduction, in turn, was sufficient to drop Xstrata out of the elite FTSE 100 company index in Britain, thereby depriving the company of hundreds of millions in investment capital from large institutions that "automatically" buy the entire index as a block. Interestingly, despite the evident growing public and governmental concern about climate change, the subject had received precisely *one line* of discussion in the multi-hundred page securities filing submitted 18 months earlier when the company had gone public. The top-tier Wall Street investment bank handling the transaction had apparently not deemed the issue worthy of serious attention.

- *Brand and reputational risk:* This may be the most important sustainability risk factor. Major corporations remain heavily dependent on their "social license to do business," which can be revoked summarily over perceived environmental or social transgressions Opposition from local communities, governments, and major nongovernmental organizations (NGOs) can delay or even totally derail major, billion-dollar projects and can besmirch company brands and reputations for years. Exxon Mobil is still suffering today from the reputational damage inflicted by the notorious Exxon Valdez oil spill nearly 20 years ago. More recently, in 1995, Royal Dutch Shell was trounced in a major public relations battle by the NGO Greenpeace. At issue was the most environmentally appropriate way to dispose of a decommissioned North Sea oil platform, the Brent Spar. Royal Dutch Shell's proposed solution was actually technically and scientifically superior, as Greenpeace later conceded. But in the modern era of stakeholder capitalism, technical merit alone, along with 5 dollars, would buy Royal Dutch Shell executives a large latté, but not much more. Greenpeace won the public relations battle hands down. The result was the loss of fully 30 percent of the company's market share in Germany within a month; it took more than 18 months to regain it. More recently, Royal Dutch Shell has suffered similar commercial damage from critics charging that the company has been complicit in human rights abuses in the Niger river delta in Nigeria. In a similar vein, Exxon Mobil has become a chronic target for shareholder activists and consumers because of its high-profile resistance to aggressive action on climate change. Another example of sustainability driven reputational risk is the backlash against several major pharmaceutical companies, such as Pfizer, Wyeth, and Schering Plough, for resisting the provision of HIV/AIDS medicines at or below cost in Africa.

In addition to having a direct impact on companies' customers, damage to corporate brands from ES-driven incidents can also be a major impediment to recruiting the very best talent. Indeed, brand or reputational value can be so large—measured in billions of dollars for some firms— that the Financial Accounting Standards Board (FASB) in the United States is currently considering a proposal that would recognize this vital "intangible asset" on corporate balance sheets.

But Opportunities on the Upside Abound

On the *other* side of the coin, however, companies can also create a real competitive advantage, reinforce "brand equity," and boost profits and shareholder value by superior sustainability performance. That performance can create new value by doing the following:

- Attracting, retaining, and motivating top talent.
- Anticipating changes in the regulatory and business environments ahead of competitors.
- Generating revenue growth through new products, services, and technologies.
- Increasing customer and investor loyalty.
- Improving relations with regulators, local suppliers, local communities, and other key stakeholders.
- Securing, retaining, and enhancing a "social license to do business," particularly in emerging markets countries.
- Reducing operating expenses through measures such as improved energy efficiency and waste minimization.
- Reducing the risk of legal liabilities and fines.
- Accessing and affording greater investment capital.
- Improving innovation and adaptation in the corporate culture.

As we shall see later in this chapter, many companies are already generating top-line revenue growth with new products and services predicated on sustainability outperformance. Executives at companies as diverse as Honda (automobiles), Iberdrola (electric utilities), and HSBC (banking) are absolutely convinced that their superior sustainability performance and reputations have generated both competitive advantage and concrete shareholder value. They have done this through improved relations with customers, suppliers, employees, regulators, and other key stakeholders.

We shall devote the balance of this chapter to a number of brief case studies of companies that are successfully capitalizing on the *opportunity* side of the sustainability coin. Despite their wide variety of both industry sector and geographic origin, all of the companies profiled have at least one thing in common: they have all recognized the *risk* dimension of the sustainability challenge, and they have also identified and seized competitive opportunities on the *upside*. They have understood that just like any previous global industrial restructuring, the Sustainability Revolution is far more than simply the sum of its downside risks. It also creates a plethora of commercial opportunities on the upside. Winning companies will have the ability to both recognize and capture them.

Precisely the same logic also applies to *investors*. In the twenty-first century, the winners will be those with a superior ability to recognize the companies with the best strategic management, greatest agility, and most fully developed abilities to see over the horizon consistently. *Investors need to recognize that today—and for at least the next 20 years—those competitive attributes will be in demand as never before. And the top sustainability companies have them in spades. That's why they should be of extreme interest to investors.*

Broadly speaking, there are at least three different ways for investors to capitalize on the upside opportunities created by the Sustainability Revolution:

1. Invest in "pure-play" clean technology companies in fields such as solar energy, wind, biomass, and geothermal energy. These are typically smaller companies with a strict focus on a particular environmentally beneficial technology. This market has already grown to an estimated $200 billion per year and continues to enjoy explosive growth.[2] Those companies can be accessed by investors most easily through a myriad of cleantech funds and indices, including the U.S.-focused Clean Edge and Wilder Hill indexes, the FTSE/Impax ET 50 index in the U.K., and the global Cleantech Index.

2. Invest in the new and bourgeoning "carbon markets." Increasingly, the right of industry to emit greenhouse gases, such as carbon dioxide and methane, is being restricted by law. This is already the case in Europe, and state and provincial regulations for the same purpose have also been enacted in parts of the United States, Canada, and Australia. Increased "carbon regulation" is now a worldwide certainty; the only real questions remaining are the pace and severity of the restrictions. This effectively "monetizes" what had previously been a free good—the unrestricted ability to emit greenhouse gases (GHGs) into the atmosphere. In essence, the right to emit GHGs will henceforth come with a price tag. In Europe, the current cost of the right to emit 1 ton of carbon dioxide (or its equivalent) is approximately $35. Under a so-called "cap-and-trade" system, such as the current European Trading System, overall quotas and limits for GHG emissions are first established—amid furious lobbying from all sides—by the regulator. Companies that can reduce their emissions below their targets through greater energy efficiency or other means can earn "credits," which can then be sold to companies that cannot otherwise meet their targets as economically.[3]

Traders and investors now buy and sell those emission credits and create specialist funds with which to do so. (We shall discuss one such fund in Chapter 10.) The carbon markets, nonexistent only a few years ago, are worth approximately $60 billion per year today, an increase of fully 80 percent over the previous year. A further 50 percent increase to over $90 billion is projected for 2008. By 2020, estimates are for a staggering $3 trillion market, if, as expected, the United States becomes an active participant in what should by then be a global carbon market.[4]

One warning for both individual and institutional investors alike, though: the carbon markets are no place for amateurs. They are markets that are both created and heavily driven by government policy and regulation, and they require extraordinarily specialized knowledge to navigate successfully. The process for certifying emission reduction projects is Byzantine at best, and even experienced experts have been badly burned.[5] Do *not* try this stuff at home! The *only* sensible way to "play" the carbon markets is through investing in a company or fund that does this for a living (we shall discuss one of them, Climate Change Capital, in Chapter 10); even then it's a risky business that is not for the faint-hearted investor.

3. Invest in large, diversified companies that although not "pure plays" on sustainability trends, have nonetheless identified and are successfully exploiting sustainability driven trends to the benefit of their overall businesses. These will be the real winners in the Sustainability Revolution; they have correctly diagnosed the major megatrends and have begun to position themselves accordingly.

All three sets of opportunities are worthy of serious and ongoing attention from sustainability investors, but it is this third set of opportunities that will be the focus of this chapter for two reasons. First, this third category will absolutely dwarf the other two in terms of its sheer overall size and importance in most investors' portfolios, whether they be individuals or institutions. The first two categories combined—private equity and commodities[6]—will rarely account for more than 10 percent of an investor's total portfolio and, frequently, significantly less. Large-cap public equities, by contrast, will likely have *at least* five times as many assets allocated to them by institutional and individual investors alike.

The second reason is that the first two categories have already received an enormous amount of attention in both the investment and popular press, and their prices have already been bid up accordingly. Opportunities in the third category, however (large and mid-cap companies), have *not* yet been broadly recognized, and so a significant "sustainability premium" remains for investors in that asset category.

In this chapter, we shall examine a group of large international companies that by dint of superior management and strategic positioning stand to benefit from the sustainability megatrends we discussed in Chapter 1 more than their competitors. *These* are the types of twenty-first century, "future-proof" companies that should be of great interest to far-sighted investors. They are turning major sustainability issues, such as climate change, the energy efficiency imperative, access to affordable medicines in emerging markets, and even structural poverty in the developing world, into business opportunities and competitive advantages. They are *also* making a substantial, concrete contribution to improving the sustainability of the planet. Here, as a representative sample, are 10 of their stories.

Clean Coal Is *Not* an Oxymoron: Mitsubishi Heavy Industries

"Heavy" and "industry" are not necessarily the first two words that spring to mind when we think about the sustainability of the planet. Indeed, to many, they would seem to be its very *antithesis.* Certainly you will not find Mitsubishi Heavy Industries (MHI) on the "buy lists" of too many traditional "socially responsible" investment funds; the company simply operates in the "wrong" sectors for their purposes. And yet investors looking to combine sustainable development and superior financial returns—and who wish to do something *positive* about sustainability rather than simply *avoiding* companies—and even entire industry sectors —would do well to take a closer look at MHI.

Japan's MHI is the quintessential example of a company with potentially massive environmental impact understanding the *zeitgeist* of the global sustainability imperative —and positioning itself accordingly to take commercial advantage. The particular sustainability driver that animates MHI the most is the worldwide search for cleaner, lower-carbon energy. This in turn is being propelled and accelerated primarily by mounting concerns over climate change. And Mitsubishi has spread its bets both widely and wisely; it is a major player in developing both incremental improvements to conventional fossil fuel energy production *and* the emerging alternative energy and renewables market space.

In the conventional energy area, MHI manufactures high-efficiency gas turbines, integrated gasification combined-cycle (IGCC) coal plants, and gas turbine combined-cycle (GTCC) systems. IGCC plants represent a roughly 20 percent reduction in CO_2 emissions relative to conventional coal power; they also offer potentially cheaper carbon capture and storage (CCS) for the carbon dioxide that *is* emitted than traditional technologies. GTCC technologies, through a combination of gas and steam turbines, can boost energy efficiency while reducing the environmental footprint of plants. Mitsubishi expects to capture as much as 50 percent of the U.S. market for coal-fired power plants by selling its "clean"—i.e., gasified—coal technologies. MHI is also a manufacturer of "clean diesel" power plants.

But Mitsubishi can also read the writing on the wall. Even in the United States, often viewed as the last major refuge of the "climate deniers," obtaining approval for conventional coal and other fossil fuel-powered plants is becoming more and more difficult. TXU, for example, the largest electric utility in Texas, was forced by public and political pressure to cancel *10* coal-fired plants in late 2007. Similar proposals in Kansas, Nevada, and all other states ran into increasingly virulent—and effective—opposition in 2008. So MHI is pursuing renewable and "alternative" energy solutions with at least as much gusto as its clean coal initiatives. MHI, it should be noted, has been in the wind turbine business for nearly 30 years and is the largest manufacturer in Japan. In addition, MHI has recently received its largest order yet—for over 440 turbines for deployment in the United States.

The company also produces solar batteries, fuel cells, and photovoltaics, as well as biomass systems. MHI even has a significant presence in the geothermal energy market, where heat occurring deep underground is used to make steam for power turbines. It has already constructed geothermal plants in 13 countries around the world, including Kenya, Iceland, Costa Rica, and the United States. Geothermal power generates no CO_2 emissions and thus represents another weapon in the battle to minimize climate change. Indeed, while it attracts less publicity than some of the other renewable energy sources, geothermal energy may well prove to be the "dark horse" of the clean energy race. In total, MHI has already installed some 3000 MW of geothermal power—enough for nearly 2.5 million households.

More controversially, Mitsubishi is also one of the world's leading manufacturers of nuclear power plants. Nuclear power seems to be enjoying something of a political renaissance in at least parts of the "green" community; as a generator of absolutely no greenhouse gases, it is becoming increasingly acceptable as a part of the emerging energy mix in the post-Kyoto, carbon-constrained world.

Thus, MHI is extraordinarily well positioned for the Sustainability Revolution. It has not only made significant and diversified investments in "transition" technologies, such as clean coal and nuclear power, but it has a very strong strategic position with respect to "next generation" renewables. It is a good bet indeed for sustainable investors.

Climate Change and Energy Efficiency: Rio Tinto Alcan

Rio Tinto Alcan, the product of Rio Tinto's corporate acquisition of Alcan in 2007, is currently the largest producer of aluminum in the world. It provides another textbook illustration of an organization well positioned to leverage global sustainability trends for increased competitive advantage and profitability. In 2008, the aluminum industry is expected to grow by nearly 10%, from a base of nearly $100 billion. Aluminum prices have already nearly doubled between 2004 and 2008. Rio Tinto Alcan can expect to capture *more* than its fair share of that growing market, in significant part because of its skillful exploitation of sustainability drivers and trends.

Let's start with the growing global imperative for energy efficiency. A potent combination of rapidly rising oil prices, concerns about the security of energy supply, and growing public and regulatory responses to climate change is placing an unprecedented financial and competitive premium on energy efficiency. On the input side, aluminum production is notoriously energy intensive; industry experts anticipate that energy costs will represent nearly 30 percent of the total cost of aluminum by 2010. With the acquisition of Alcan, however, Rio Tinto acquired access to a low cost, zero-carbon-emission fuel source—hydroelectric power. Unlike many of its competitors, Alcan generates fully 40% of all of its energy requirements from that renewable source. Moreover, Alcan is improving its energy efficiency by nearly 20 percent per year, despite increasing production. So the new company is already ahead of the game in a world in which fossil fuel energy costs are growing rapidly and unpredictably, and companies are increasingly subject to carbon constraints, taxes, or both.

But that's just the beginning. These same concerns over energy costs, fuel efficiency, and climate change create benefits for Rio Tinto Alcan on the *output* side of its business as well. They are driving a major push for "lightweight" materials in the auto, aircraft, and other transportation industries. This plays directly to aluminum's strengths and therefore to Rio Tinto Alcan's. In the auto sector, Toyota, BMW, Audi, and Jaguar have all recently introduced aluminum vehicles. Aircraft manufacturers are also shifting to aluminum-titanium alloys to decrease weight while improving durability and resistance to corrosion. Alcan has already been a supplier to both of these lightweighting industry sectors and fully intends to capture an even larger market share going forward.

Alcan has also been highly effective in *marketing* the superior sustainability characteristics of its aluminum products. By partnering with its customers, Alcan has essentially become a value-added design partner, leveraging its expertise into a much stronger—and better-compensated—competitive position. With Jaguar, for example, Alcan provided both key materials and technology for the new, aluminum-intensive XJ Sedan. The company is also working on a broader level with other auto manufacturers and governments to promote more fuel-efficient vehicle design more generally. (This objective just happens to be heavily dependent on aluminum for its realization.) In a similar vein, Alcan has also collaborated with other suppliers and customers to design more energy-efficient commuter trains through lightweighting.

The company is also aggressively expanding its production of titanium dioxide—the principal feedstock for titanium. Major capital projects in both Canada and Madagascar will add significant capacity in that area. With a strong competitive footprint with respect to two of the most important lightweighting metals currently known (aluminum and titanium), Rio Tinto Alcan is now extremely well positioned strategically to dominate its competitors in tomorrow's world, where the race is likely to go to the most energy efficient and least carbon intensive—in other words, to the *lightest,* if not the swiftest.

The Energy Efficiency Opportunity: United Technologies Corporation

United Technologies Corporation (UTC), like many of the companies profiled in this chapter, would rarely, if ever, find itself in the portfolio of a traditional "socially responsible" investor. For one thing, many of UTC's products have a significant environmental impact. For another, at least one of its business lines—aerospace—is uncomfortably closely linked with military activities. (Although the same helicopter the company produces also happens to be the most popular in the world for medical emergency rescue missions.)

But this chapter—and indeed this entire book—is *not* about identifying the most pristine companies, nor is it about splitting hairs about whether the helicopter's humanitarian contribution does or does not offset its military application. For that matter, we do not wish to wade into the even larger ethical quagmire of debating whether military force is itself justified, and when. Instead, what both this chapter and the entire book *are* about is simply this: identifying companies that demonstrate a superior understanding of sustainability trends and dynamics and an ability to *translate* that understanding into competitive advantages and new sources of profit. As they do so, that process generally, and not incidentally, translates into a significant, positive environmental and/or social impact as well. UTC is one such company. And its financial results are substantial: over the past decade it has achieved cumulative shareholder returns of 388 percent—roughly five times better than its benchmark, the Standard and Poor's 500 index.

UTC's core business is providing high technology products and services to the aerospace and building systems industries worldwide. The UTC Group operates through six separately branded companies, which run the gamut from manufacturing passenger and freight elevators to providing engines, spare parts, and aftermarket and fleet management services for the aerospace industry. Many of UTC's products and services, such as elevators and aircraft engines, are highly energy intensive and, as such, are potentially significant contributors to greenhouse gas emissions. The increasing demand among industries for greater fuel energy efficiency, combined with growing cost and regulatory constraints, provides both major strategic and operational challenges *and* a set of promising new business opportunities for UTC.

What follows are just a few examples of how UTC and its group companies have capitalized on the growing imperative for energy efficiency:

- Otis Elevator's innovative new Gen2 elevator system eliminates the need for lubrication and is 50 percent more energy efficient than conventional systems. Gen2's environmental and energy efficiency benefits will be a particularly important competitive weapon for UTC's market penetration in China. Not only is China currently the fastest growing segment of the world elevator market, but its political leadership has become increasingly concerned about energy and environmental issues. This plays perfectly to UTC's advantage.
- Years ago, UTC's Carrier division pioneered the development of air conditioning systems using CFC alternatives to avoid the depletion

of the atmosphere's ozone layer. This was an early indication of the company's long-term view of the market, as well as its ability to gain competitive advantage and innovate ahead of regulations. Today, new U.S. regulations demand that residential air conditioning systems shipped in the United States after 2007 must achieve 30 percent better energy efficiency than previous designs. Not only are the new standards better for the environment, they are clearly better for UTC as well.

- Pratt & Whitney's Green Engine Program is focused on aircraft fuel efficiency, extended ranges and payloads, and reduced emissions and noise. The company's new PW6000 engine is more fuel efficient than those offered by competitors, while also ensuring a longer period of use, thus reducing the environmental impact from disposal. Pratt & Whitney has also introduced a new type of engine, the geared turbofan (GTF), which is expected to offer up to 12 percent better fuel efficiency in longer-range regional airliners, the fastest growing segment of the industry. The GTF's advantages are also propelling it to the top spot in the competition to power the next generation of Airbus and Boeing regional narrow body airliners.

In anticipation of future market-driven demand for even higher efficiencies, UTC is also searching for opportunities in next generation technologies, such as fuel cells. In 2004 UTC released the PureCell™ 200. The system generates 200 kW of clean, reliable electricity and 900,000 BTUs of usable heat suitable for cogeneration applications. The PureCell™ 200 technology has now been installed in 19 countries on five continents, ranging from a New York City police station to a science center in Japan.

UTC's ability to anticipate and adjust consistently in a new environment of increasingly stringent regulations and customer demands for greater energy efficiency is already paying off. UTC is a prime example of a company attuned to the changing market imperatives of the twenty-first century. As the Sustainable Investment Revolution continues to gather momentum, UTC is precisely the sort of company in which far-sighted investors should be interested.

The Next Generation Carmakers: Honda

To most casual observers of the global automobile manufacturing sector, Toyota is the company whose name has become virtually synonymous with environmental excellence. Without in any way minimizing that company's considerable achievements in this regard, though, I believe that the Honda story is no less remarkable, considerably less well known, and therefore well worth telling here.

The 100+ percent increase in retail gasoline prices over the past 5 years is almost certainly indicative of a long-term, secular trend. The fundamental supply and demand realities driving current gas prices are primarily a function of four converging factors: a dramatic growth in global demand, fueled by explosive industrial and economic growth in "emerging" markets such as China and India, as well as increasing levels of car ownership in newly affluent sectors of society; the relative inaccessibility and high costs of next-generation resource discovery and recovery; refining capacity bottlenecks; and, of course, geopolitical instability in many of the highest-potential areas.

At least two things appear certain: we have reached the end of the era of cheap gasoline, and carbon-based fuel prices will continue to be highly volatile. These two apparently permanent new realities present a game-changing challenge for the auto industry, one that promises to realign profit and risk opportunities completely for investors.

Fuel economy regulations are tightening in all major auto markets, driven primarily by concerns over local air quality and climate change. The European Union has entered into voluntary agreements with automobile manufacturers' associations to achieve fuel economy averages of roughly 40 miles per gallon (mpg) by 2009 and 43 mpg by 2012. Regulations (and "voluntary" agreements enforced by threat of regulation) have already been introduced in various European countries, including the United Kingdom and Spain, that would impose fines on automakers exceeding 43 mpg after 2012. Today's focus on fuel economy may well lead to the eventual extinction of the traditional, internal combustion gasoline engine. This threat has galvanized a worldwide search for "next generation" power trains, a search in which Honda has excelled.

Even in the United States, where corporate average fuel economy (CAFE) regulations have remained virtually unchanged since they were first introduced in 1975, dramatic increases in fuel economy standards seem inevitable—and likely to arrive soon. A revised CAFE bill introduced in the U.S. Senate in June 2007 looks set to pass, possibly with some minor loosening, in the House of Representatives. The State of California has already preempted new federal CAFE standards through fuel economy regulations of its own, which are currently being challenged by automakers in the U.S. courts. The California law has been copied by a number of other states, including Connecticut, Massachusetts, Vermont, Rhode Island, Maine, New Jersey, and New York. The end result of this political and economic dynamic is clear: fuel-efficient cars will grow in their dominance of the market. Hence, if car makers wish to remain competitive, fleet fuel efficiency must become a top strategic priority.

Honda has been a leader in the production of fuel-efficient vehicles for nearly three decades now. It is currently running neck and neck with Toyota in the race to become the best CAFE performer; its U.S. model year 2005 passenger cars achieved an average of 33.5 mpg, with its light trucks managing 24.5 mpg. These numbers give Honda the highest overall fuel economy in the United States. Given the upward trajectory of the trend for Honda's fuel efficiency over the past four years, there is every indication that this leadership position will be retained and even strengthened.

Above all, however, it is Honda's track record at commercializing leading-edge power train R&D that may make it an even *more* promising sustainability leader than Toyota. Unbeknownst to most people, it was actually Honda—not Toyota—that launched the first hybrid vehicle in the U.S. market—the 70 mpg Insight. Its latest hybrid, the CR-Z (which stands for Company Renaissance Zero), uses new high-tech materials to push the lightweight/fuel efficiency envelope even further. Honda is also investing more in fuel efficiency R&D than any other car maker, including Toyota. One of the fruits of that R&D effort is the next-generation FCX Clarity. The Clarity is a zero-emission, hydrogen-powered fuel cell car. It is expected to make its on-road debut in late 2008, and will initially be available by lease in (where else?) southern California.

However the battle for the future of the auto industry ultimately ends up, for the present at least Honda and its Japanese competitor Toyota are setting the pace globally. Detroit's Big 3 have been reduced to gasping in their wake—*and* licensing their technology.

The Future Is Renewables: Iberdrola

Iberdrola S.A. is a Spanish-based electric utility whose principal activities are the generation, transmission, distribution, and marketing of electricity for industrial, commercial, and domestic use. The company currently serves 25 million customers in Europe and the Americas and owns hydroelectric, fossil-fuelled, nuclear, and renewable power generation facilities with a total capacity of more than 42,500 megawatts (MW).

Iberdrola's overall energy mix is one of the most "sustainable" of any major electric utility in the world: it is made up of 30.8 percent combined cycle, 22.8 percent hydroelectric, 18.1 percent renewable energy, 11.1 percent thermal, 7.9 percent nuclear, 6.8 percent fuel oil, and 2.5 percent cogeneration. As of today, Iberdrola is the number one provider of wind power in the world, with 7.7 gigawatts (GW) of installed capacity, with another 42 GW in its project pipeline.

Over the past seven years, Iberdrola has nearly quintupled in size and has increased its stock market value to nearly $80.5 billion. It has recently expanded in Latin America and acquired electric generation and distribution companies in Brazil, Bolivia, Chile, Guatemala, and Mexico. It became a major global player with the 2007 acquisition of Scottish Power for $22.5 billion. The company is now the fourth largest electricity company in the world, with a stock market capitalization of almost EUR 52 billion as of December 2007. Renewable energy has become a major strategic priority for Iberdrola; its 2008–2010 strategic plan targets a renewable energy capacity of 13,600 MW, nearly double the current level of 7700 MW, which itself represents a 75 percent increase over its capacity at the beginning of 2007.

Iberdrola's shift into clean energy began in 2001. After a rapid period of consolidation and expansion, its renewable energy division has become the largest wind energy company in the world in terms of total installed capacity. It is now present in 19 countries, and in 9 of the 10 markets in the world showing the greatest potential for growth and development of the industry.[7] In 2006 the Renewable Energy division accounted for 14 percent of the group's total profits, which is projected to reach 22 percent by 2010.[8] In 2006 Iberdrola signed a $4.09 billion deal with a major Spanish wind-turbine maker, Gamesa SA, to build a number of additional wind farms in the United States. Iberdrola has also made strategic bets all along the wind energy value chain; it also holds a 24 percent equity stake in Gamesa.

In late 2006, Iberdrola's entire portfolio of renewables assets was consolidated and spun out as a separate division, Iberdrola Renovables. On December 13, 2007 Iberdrola floated 20 percent of its new renewables subsidiary, which immediately became one of the top 10 Spanish companies in terms of market capitalization: almost EUR 24,000 billion at the end of fiscal year 2007. The financing put over 4 billion euros into Iberdrola's coffers and was the largest-ever initial public offering (IPO) in the sector.

While Iberdrola's renewables portfolio is overwhelmingly focused on wind, the company is also placing modest strategic bets on at least three other renewable energy sources: solar thermal, biomass, and wave energy. In 2007 it began construction of its first thermosolar plant in Puertollano, an industrial city in Spain on the high-speed train line from Madrid to Seville. This pioneering facility will have an installed capacity of 50 MW and will require the investment of more than 200 million euros. At the same time, the company has also begun construction of a prototype wave-energy plant at Cantabria in Spain.

In May 2008 Iberdrola announced that it planned to invest $8 billion in renewable energy in the United States between 2008 and 2010. The company has targeted a 15 percent share of the wind power market in the United States by 2010. We would not bet against them.

Banking on Sustainability: HSBC

There is absolutely no shortage of stirring "green" rhetoric flowing from major international banks these days. On the contrary, there is probably a *surplus,* considering the yawning disconnect between much of that rhetoric and the reality of the banks' actual performance. HSBC Holdings PLC is a conspicuous exception. It is, we think, fair to say that sustainability considerations are more thoroughly interwoven throughout the "corporate DNA" of HSBC today than they are within any other major global bank.

HSBC (formerly the Hong Kong and Shanghai Banking Corporation) is currently the world's third-largest bank by market capitalization and also one of its most truly international. It has operations in over 80 countries and, uniquely, strong roots in both Europe and Asia that stretch back over a century. An appreciation of sustainability-driven risks and opportunities can be seen across at least four dimensions of HSBC's activities: its commercial lending, its asset management, its research and awareness-building work, and its internal operations.

In its lending activities, HSBC makes a concerted and systematic effort to assess the environmental and social risks confronting its borrowers (and therefore itself); it has developed detailed, sector-specific lending guidelines to help govern the tough, case-by-case decisions that inevitably confront bankers. This is not to suggest that HSBC makes no loans in high-impact sectors, such as oil and gas, mining, forestry, or chemicals; far from it. Indeed, given the realities of the current business environment, it would be economic suicide for any bank rash enough to do so. What its sustainability guidelines and research *have* accomplished, however, is to allow HSBC to make loans with its eyes wide open, to price the risks that they are willing to take more appropriately, and to refuse unacceptable risks altogether.

But many global banks today have similar lending policies and practices. Where HSBC *really* stands out is in its asset management activities. It has a dedicated six-person, in-house environmental, social, and governance (ESG) research team, headed by Xavier Desmadryl and based in Paris and London. The group conducts its own original research and is also responsible for synthesizing a large volume of both company-specific and thematic sustainability research from external providers, including Vigeo and Innovest. This research platform provides the intellectual capital base for a variety of sustainability funds and products available to both HSBC's individual and institutional clients. At the moment, HSBC manages over $1.5 billion in a variety of different sustainability funds, and this figure is likely to increase substantially going forward.

Climate change is a recurring and important theme in both HSBC's investment product lineup and its ongoing research programs. In late 2007, HSBC launched a Global Climate Change Index, explicitly designed to identify companies particularly well positioned to weather the coming global megashift toward a lower-carbon economy. The Index contains 300 companies with significant exposure to one or more of three climate-related themes: lower-carbon energy production, energy efficiency and management, and waste, water, and pollution management and control. The Index, which is designed to provide investors with comprehensive exposure to the broad range of opportunities driven by climate change, appears to have real outperformance potential, based on historical back-tests. The Index is investable, as are subindexes devoted to each of its three overarching themes. The low-carbon energy production subindex contains solar, wind, biomass, and geothermal companies. The energy efficiency group includes companies contributing to improved fuel efficiency in the automobile sector, fuel cells, and energy management technologies, while the third subindex is focused on waste and water recycling technologies and pollution control. HSBC also offers a more concentrated, actively managed portfolio composed of 50 or 60 stocks selected from the 300-name index as well as a smaller, 100-company climate index.

The last major dimension of HSBC's sustainability thrust is in research and awareness building. One of the centerpieces of this effort was the creation in late 2007 of a Climate Change Centre of Excellence in London. The Centre's first head is Nick Robins, one of the most highly respected leaders in the sustainable finance field and the former head of the sustainability unit at Henderson's Global Investors. The new Centre's mission is evident in its name; its mandate is to catalyze a broader and deeper understanding of the scientific, regulatory, and economic dimensions of climate change, both for the bank itself and for a broader group of its clients and other stakeholders. The new Centre initiates and coordinates input from a wide variety of both internal and external sources. It clearly and unapologetically has a commercial dimension to its mandate as well: to help HSBC's various business groups identify both risks and business opportunities. One important resource for both the Centre itself and HSBC more broadly is Sir Nicholas Stern, who became a senior advisor to the bank in mid-2007. Stern, the former chief economist of the World Bank and lead author of a hugely influential and eponymous report for the British cabinet on the economic implications of climate change, is one of the most recognized figures in the world in the climate field.

Importantly, HSBC's knowledge-building and awareness-raising efforts are not confined to the boundaries of the bank itself. In May 2007, it launched the ambitious and unprecedented $100 million, 5-year HSBC Climate Partnership. Under the Partnership, HSBC is providing substantial, multiyear funding to four world-class NGOs: the World Wide Fund for Nature, the Climate Group, Earthwatch, and the Smithsonian Tropical Research Institute. The Partnership's major activities have already included a high-profile global awareness campaign among CEOs, local mayors, and other "influencers"; research on carbon capture, sequestration, and storage; and a major effort to assist the Asian cities of Mumbai, Delhi, and Beijing to become low-carbon cities of the future.

The last major manifestation of HSBC's sustainability commitment can be seen in its internal operations. Bank executives, such as chairman Stephen Green and global sustainability chief Jon Williams, reasoned that before launching a bevy of climate-themed investment products for others to buy they really ought to get their *own* house in order first. And they did. They announced the bold corporate objective of becoming "carbon neutral," i.e., having an overall net carbon emissions impact of zero. The bank seconded Francis Sullivan from the World Wildlife Fund to quarterback the effort, which has included massive energy efficiency and conservation campaigns, as well as the purchase of "offsets" (e.g., emission reduction "credits" generated by tree planting and clean technology projects) to neutralize the impact of those emissions it could not eliminate outright. In late 2005 HSBC became the first major global bank to achieve carbon neutrality.

Taken together, HSBC's efforts in the sustainability space in general and on climate change in particular are truly impressive and have been launched over a remarkably short space of time. Other global banks have now begun to *talk* a very good game on these topics; HSBC is actually *playing* one.

Capitalizing on the New Climate for Insurers: Swiss Re

The bane of the financial sector has always been the existence of so-called "fat-tail" risk. These are events whose likelihood of occurrence is statistically extremely remote, but whose *consequences,* should they occur, are potentially severe.[9] Climate change, of course, is a classic example of precisely this type of risk, and Swiss Re was aware of it much earlier than most of its competitors. One concrete indication of the seriousness with which Swiss Re is taking the climate challenge can be seen in the fact that the file is managed directly by the CEO and the Chief Risk Officer—the two most senior executive positions in the entire company.

Zurich-headquartered Swiss Re is the world's second largest global reinsurer, with more than 70 offices in 30 countries. As well as reinsurance, the company provides a range of other financial and insurance products for major companies through its three principal business divisions: property-casualty, life and health, and financial services. The impact of climate change has significant direct implications for all three. For example, more frequent flooding and violent storms significantly alter the risk profile of property insurance. Climate change's effects on the incidence and transmission patterns of disease have implications for its life insurance underwriting business. And, as we shall see, climate change can also pose both reputational and financial risks for the companies that Swiss Re insures.

A critical component of Swiss Re's overall strategic response to climate change has been an unusually strong focus on research, dialogue, communication, and awareness building. The company published its first major piece of climate risk research nearly 15 years ago. Since that time, Swiss Re has published at least a dozen major studies and concept papers on climate change, attempting to educate both its own clients and the wider public. Swiss Re is also active in sponsoring a number of innovative climate research partnerships with organizations including Switzerland's National Centre of Competence in Research on Climate, the Swiss Federal Institute of Technology, and the City University of Hong Kong.

In 2000, after a 6-month, group-wide feasibility study, Swiss Re created its Greenhouse Gas Risk Solutions (GHGRS) unit. Its mandate was to facilitate climate-driven business opportunities, develop new insurance product solutions, and work closely with each of the three major business divisions to help them identify both commercial risks and opportunities. One specific product that Swiss Re has identified as a possible climate-driven opportunity is company directors and officers liability insurance. Reasoning that climate change has now become a truly strategic business risk in many industry sectors, Swiss Re asks specific questions on climate change in its discussions with prospects and clients about both new and renewed insurance policies for company directors and executives. The answers have become a significant factor in determining both the levels of insurance coverage and its costs. In extreme cases, Swiss Re may even decline to provide coverage altogether.

Swiss Re has also developed insurance products that directly facilitate emissions trading. As we have seen, there remains considerable uncertainty attached to the complex process of securing carbon emission reduction credits under the Kyoto Protocol. Typically, project financing must be committed before it is entirely clear whether the United Nations' staff will actually approve the carbon credits as legitimate. This creates a clear role and opportunity for insurers. In 2006 Swiss Re cocreated the world's first insurance product specifically designed to manage Kyoto Protocol-related risks. The new instrument covered the risks attached to monetizing the carbon credits from two landfill gas emission reduction projects in Argentina.[10]

Another area of innovation and business opportunity for Swiss Re is in providing insurance for renewable energy projects. The company recently underwrote the construction of a wind farm off the Welsh coast. As more wind farms are built offshore, becoming larger and more costly, the demand for insurance products can be expected to increase because of the large amounts of money at risk.

A third climate-related insurance product area is "weather derivatives" —financial instruments that, in essence, provide protection against the financial consequences of droughts, hailstorms, and other extreme weather events. Swiss Re currently has a 30 percent market share in that sector, as well as a 40 percent share of the global "cat" (catastrophic) bond market.

In addition to its purely commercial trading and sales of weather derivatives, Swiss Re has also been working with Columbia University's Earth Institute to create the Climate Adaptation Development Program. To date, the program has provided insurance against the consequences of severe drought for poor villages in Kenya, Mali, and Ethiopia.

In most major insurance companies, there seems to be a complete disconnect between the risk underwriting side of the business on the one hand and its asset management activities on the other. In the case of climate change, this represents an enormous lost opportunity for insurers; no one knows more about both global trends and company-specific risk exposures than insurance underwriters, and this knowledge could be of real value to the investment team. To its credit, Swiss Re has recognized this potential and begun to leverage its climate risk knowledge on *both* sides of the house. In 1996 the company began to assemble a portfolio of investments for its own account in alternative energy, water, waste, and recycling companies that stand to benefit directly from providing climate solutions. In 2007 it consolidated and expanded that effort, launching the European Clean Energy Fund, which has now grown to over EUR 350 million in assets under management. The fund invests in clean energy projects across western, central, and eastern Europe. It also has the flexibility to invest directly in carbon credits, and Swiss Re itself has a trading desk active in the carbon markets.

In addition, in 2008, Swiss Re was selected by a consortium of European development banks to be the investment manager for an innovative, EUR 125 million carbon credit fund that will be focused on the *post*-2012, post-Kyoto carbon market. Even more recently, Swiss Re became the largest investor in a new "climate solutions" fund introduced by Generation Investment Management, a relatively new asset management firm that we shall profile in Chapter 10. In both its risk underwriting and its asset management activities, Swiss Re's focus on the transformational potential of climate change makes it another company for sustainability investors to watch carefully.

The Coming Revolution in "Green" Real Estate: Investa

The financial case for "green" real estate is becoming increasingly compelling. The investment logic is straightforward and is a simple extension of the fundamental thesis of this book. Energy costs typically comprise

30 percent of the total operating costs of commercial real estate. Buildings with energy and environmental efficiency superior to those of competing alternatives have, therefore, a substantial financial advantage. Such companies are generally well managed in other respects as well.

"Green" real estate can create a number of important strategic and financial benefits for builder/developer/managers *and* investors:

- Marketing differentiation: there is a strong trend toward higher rent premiums and higher tenant retention rates in green buildings.
- Significant gains in operating profit, through reductions in operating costs at the individual building level.
- A financial premium associated with the trend toward enhanced green property valuations upon sales of the property.
- Emerging recognition of "high-performance" building design as an indicator of quality. Green is rapidly becoming the new de facto standard for a "Class A" building.
- A hedge against unpredictable energy price increases.
- Superior risk-adjusted financial returns at the portfolio/REIT level.
- First-mover and "thought-leader" advantage, including substantial free public relations and marketing benefits.

From an investor's perspective, real estate companies whose overall *portfolios* are "greener" than their competitors' portfolios also have a similar competitive and financial advantage at an aggregate level. The sustainable investment hypothesis suggests that such companies are quite simply better managed and more far-sighted in general. In short, they are likely to be superior *investment* candidates as well.

Sydney-headquartered Investa has understood all of this better and earlier than most of its competitors. Investa was one of the first major real estate companies in the world to recognize the saliency of sustainability issues to its core business, and it has placed the concept at the very center of both its competitive strategy and its operations.

Investa, purchased by Morgan Stanley Real Estate in September 2007, has a real estate portfolio of approximately $8.3 billion of assets under management. This includes an Australian commercial office portfolio valued at nearly $5 billion, as well as external funds managed on behalf of both retail and institutional investors of $2.4 billion. Investa is also engaged in the direct construction of residential and commercial real estate.

Committed to procuring 10 percent of its energy from approved "green" energy sources, Investa has already begun to generate "carbon credits" in the Australian state of New South Wales, which includes Sydney. Investa has also reduced the energy intensity of its entire real estate portfolio to 116 kilowatt hours per square meter—the lowest intensity of any of the real estate companies in its sector.

Water efficiency is another hugely important issue in Australia, where an unprecedented 10-year drought has elevated both its commercial importance and political profile. Global investors would do well to regard Australia as the "canary in the mine shaft" in this regard; over the next decade, water efficiency is likely to become an increasingly pressing issue for business in other countries as well. Investa has also demonstrated strong performance in this area, having achieved a 40 percent reduction in water consumption across its entire portfolio over the past 5 years.

Since 2004 Investa has saved nearly $2 million per year from its energy and water conservation initiatives. The total cost of the programs that provide these savings was only $2.8 million, so the financial return on investment has already been an excellent one. Interestingly, these efficiency improvements have been derived from quite modest capital expenditures on "smart" meters and other energy "demand-side" management projects. In all cases, the payback period has been less than 3 years.

Overall, Investa's ecoefficiency performance has been outstanding. Under the Australian green building rating system, a score of 2.5 is "average" and 3.0 represents "best practice." Investa's entire portfolio currently has an average rating of 3.53! In an era—and a country—increasingly dominated by concerns about climate change, Investa's initiatives to reduce energy use provide the company with an important "hedge" against increased and unpredictable operating costs due to volatile and skyrocketing energy prices.

Unlike many of its competitors, Investa has also decided to pass along many of these operational cost savings to its tenants through innovative lease structures. These efforts will inevitably result in greater tenant loyalty and "stickiness," lower turnover costs, and higher market valuation premiums.

Beyond the purely monetary benefits, however, lie a number of intangible benefits, the most important of which is reputational capital. Investa's high occupancy rates and superior access to government tenants who have committed to lease highly rated "green" buildings are two of the immediate dividends from this. Given that government agencies represent approximately 20 percent of the total real estate tenancy market in Australia, the competitive advantage to Investa is an extremely valuable and strategic one. Moreover, if and when Investa actually sells any of its green buildings, it can expect a premium price in the marketplace.

The business case for greener real estate operations is clear. Investa has achieved higher tenant retention rates, lower operating costs, and the ability to charge premium rents. All of this adds up to a much stronger financial and competitive position. We are convinced that in 10 years Investa's competitors will either be emulating its "green" initiatives or their profitability—and even their very survival—will be at serious risk.

Tackling the "Access to Medicines" Challenge: GlaxoSmithKline

We have argued throughout this book that far-sighted investors should seek out companies that are sustainability leaders, in part because they tend to be better managed, more strategic, and more agile companies. Such companies are likely to have increasingly powerful competitive positions in a world where environmental and social issues are assuming ever greater importance.

No issue on the *social* side of the sustainability ledger provides a better illustration of this than the vexed question of providing access to affordable medicines in emerging markets. At present, roughly two *billion* people in such areas lack access to affordable medicines, vaccines, and drugs. In Guatemala, for example, Kaletra, an antiretroviral drug used to combat HIV/AIDS, costs $2000 per person per year, but the average per capita annual income in Guatemala is only $2400. Improving affordable access to these types of medicines could save an estimated 10 million lives each year.[11] Tackling this problem, while clearly important from a humanitarian perspective, has historically fallen well outside of the remit—and the comfort zone—of most major, profit-seeking pharmaceutical companies. Yet doing so can confer significant strategic benefits for those companies willing and able to figure out how to do it effectively.

The access to medicines (ATM) challenge provides companies with a supreme test of both strategic management and execution capabilities. Any large global pharmaceutical player that can pull it off is, almost by definition, an extremely well-managed one. It is likely to build new reputational capital with key stakeholders, which should in turn help it attract, retain, and motivate the best talent. In an increasingly "meaning-oriented" world of thirty- and forty-something professionals, "solving" the access to medicines question is a huge attraction. Of all of the "Big Pharma" players, GlaxoSmithKline (GSK) stands out in this regard.

GSK's principal activity is creating, discovering, developing, manufacturing, and marketing pharmaceutical products and consumer health-related products. In 2007 GSK had revenues of over $32 billion.

GSK has recognized that supplying medicines and vaccines at highly discounted prices in the world's poorest countries can be commercially sustainable only if it can also continue to make adequate financial returns in the wealthier markets. The growing wealth of countries such as Brazil, China, India, Indonesia, Mexico, Russia, and Turkey means they could well account for as much as 20 percent of the global pharmaceutical market by 2020. Creating and maintaining a "social license to do business" in these future growth markets will depend primarily on how GSK navigates the tricky shoals of ATM issues in the lower-income countries in Africa and elsewhere.

GSK has a wide range of relevant ATM programs, including R&D investment into neglected diseases, an equitable pricing policy, voluntary licensing of its drugs to generic drug distributors, drug donations, and philanthropic activities. GSK clearly (and correctly) believes that addressing ATM issues will help it attract, retain, and motivate highly skilled employees and secure both credibility and long-term business opportunities in the developing world. The company has not only laid out its long-term objectives clearly, it has defined a wide range of relevant key performance indicators to measure the impact of its ATM activities and report on progress. GSK even uses an independent third party, Bureau Veritas, to certify the accuracy of the information disclosed in the ATM section of its corporate social responsibility report.

Strategic partnerships are an important part of GSK's R&D strategy in general and its ATM strategy in particular. Some of its most successful relationships are with academic institutions, public–private partnerships, and international agencies, such as the World Health Organization. GSK is a particular leader in R&D for what are called "neglected diseases." It has a dedicated R&D center called The Diseases of the Developing World Drug Discovery Centre in Spain. The R&D center employs over 100 scientists who are solely dedicated to the discovery of new medicines for neglected diseases, with a special focus on malaria and tuberculosis. GSK does not expect to make a profit on the new treatments for neglected diseases; it therefore works in partnerships to share the R&D costs and ensure affordable prices of new treatments for poor patients in the developing world.

Of the 20 vaccines still in GSK's drug pipeline, fully one-third target diseases particularly prevalent in the developing world. In March 2008, GSK announced a new price cut for its antiretroviral HIV/AIDS drugs in the developing world, stating that it would offer a further price reduction on 14 antiretroviral drugs that are already offered on a not-for-profit basis. By offering a new price cut for its HIV drugs, GSK actually increases the likelihood that it can sustain premium pricing in *industrialized* countries. At an even more strategic, "big-picture" level, this may also have a direct impact on the maintenance of the current patent system and limit the potential for emerging markets to opt out of or weaken the international intellectual property rights system on which GSK depends.

Since 2001 GSK has entered into eight voluntary licenses with local companies in Africa for antiretroviral drugs, such as Epivir and Combivir. GSK also granted a voluntary license to Simcere, a Chinese manufacturer, giving it the right to manufacture and sell Zanamivir in China and a number of other countries, including all 50 of the so-called "least developed countries." GSK has also signed a technology transfer agreement with the Brazilian government to produce HIV drugs for the domestic market, as well as for export to other developing countries. A similar agreement exists in Brazil for GSK's oral polio, measles, mumps, and rubella vaccines. In addition, GSK shares technologies with local generic companies such as Ranbaxy in India.

GSK's handling of the increasingly critical access to medicines issue in emerging markets stands in sharp contrast to that of many of its rivals, most of whom have failed to appreciate the issue's long-term strategic importance to pharmaceutical companies' "license to do business," both in emerging markets and in the developed world. Investors should pay close attention to GSK; the company's handling of this difficult and controversial issue also augurs well for its ability to manage the *next* competitive challenge, whatever it may turn out to be.

Creating Value and Wealth at the "Base of the Pyramid": Unilever

The roughly four billion people in the world currently living on incomes of $2 a day or less have been described as the "base of the pyramid" (BoP). The concept was first popularized by two U.S.-based business academics, Stuart Hart and C. K. Prahalad, in their seminal 2002 article, "The Fortune at the Bottom of the Pyramid."[12]

The basic thesis of the initial BoP concept was that contrary to popular misconceptions, poor people *do* in fact have real purchasing power and *are* responsible borrowers. They therefore represent a potentially viable and attractive market for companies innovative and flexible enough to find the new ways and business models necessary to capture it. The most celebrated success story from the BoP is, of course, Bangladesh's Grameen Bank and its multiple corporate offshoots, including the billion dollar per year Grameen Phone.

Founded in 1983, the Grameen (meaning "village") Bank was predicated on two basic theses: first, that even very small amounts of capital could make an enormous difference to the economic capabilities and potential of the very poor, and second, that contrary to what might seem intuitively logical, the poor could actually be very *good* credit risks. Since then, Grameen has provided $6 *billion* in loans, with an average loan size of less than $100. Its repayment rate has been an astonishing 99 percent —far better than that of even the leading commercial banks. Today, the Bank has over seven *million* customers, 97 percent of them women, in over 70,000 villages in Bangladesh. Over half of the Grameen borrowers have been lifted above the poverty line. Grameen's founder, former economics professor Dr. Muhammud Yunus, won the Nobel Peace Prize in 2006 in an eminently well-deserved recognition of his outstanding contribution to the alleviation of poverty and to economic and social development.

The importance of the BoP to sustainability and sustainable investment is two-fold, quite apart from the fact that social justice and humanitarianism alone dictate that the incomes and lifestyle of the denizens of the BoP must improve. First, any economic and social system in which the talents and potential contribution of nearly 70 percent of its members are wasted is self-evidently massively suboptimal and unsustainable on many levels. Second, from a purely ecological perspective, in the absence of new approaches, should Western-style consumption patterns be adopted by an additional four billion people, the earth's ecosystems and carrying capacity would quite simply be overwhelmed. And this is to say nothing of the billions of *new* people who are expected to be born over the next 20 years, most of them in emerging markets.

Hence, the planetary stakes are high indeed. The BoP must be developed, but it must be done "right." Current best practice might be called "BoP version 2.0." Its predecessor, BoP 1.0, has been justly criticized as simply a new form of corporate imperialism—merely "selling to the poor," with most of the benefits accruing to the vendor.[13] BoP 2.0 envisions a much more egalitarian approach of "cocreation" in which the unique knowledge and skills of both a major corporation and an impoverished local community are combined to develop entirely new, locally embedded enterprises. Under the BoP 2.0 model, local communities get much more than simply new products or services; they develop new entrepreneurial skills, economic and social development, and dignity.

Needless to say, the challenges of creating, managing, and sustaining such innovative, frame-breaking initiatives along these lines are prodigious. Only a handful of companies worldwide have so far attempted it successfully. The sustainable investment maxim states that companies capable of managing the risks and capitalizing on the opportunities of such a complex challenge are better managed, more agile, "future-proof" companies and are *precisely* the sorts of companies that sustainable investors should be looking for.

Unilever is one such company, and it is a prototype of the "sustainability leaders" that will become the Holy Grail for twenty-first century investors.

The Unilever Story So Far

If any multinational giant has come even close to "cracking the code" for penetrating the BoP, it is Unilever.

Unilever, which has 180,000 employees worldwide in over 100 countries and annual revenues of over $50 billion, has two principal lines of business: foods and home and personal care. Its brands hold strong market positions, with 13 individual brands (including Lipton, Knorr, Dove, Lifebuoy, and Vaseline) generating over $1 billion each in sales per year. Those brands are unquestionably one of Unilever's most valuable assets; how well or poorly the company plays the sustainability "game" will have an enormous impact on that value—either for good or for ill. So far, it has been mostly good.

Unilever has had a long-standing presence in most emerging markets around the globe, an asset that will become even more valuable as the world's economic center of gravity continues its inexplorable shift there. This positioning has helped the firm gain a competitive advantage over newcomers, and today more than 44 percent of its revenues come from developing and emerging markets. Unilever expects to see an even larger share of its sales come from emerging markets in the future. As the populations and purchasing power of countries such as China and India continue to grow, Unilever's early engagement in these regions positions the company well to take advantage of growing business opportunities. The group has a lengthy pedigree in both countries, having been in India since 1888 and China since 1911.

Whereas most companies aim to cultivate the wealthy consumer segment, Unilever, through its various subsidiaries, sells a significant number of products to and employs a large number of people at the bottom of the wealth pyramid. The group categorizes its consumer group into "have lots," "haves," and "have nots" and tries to design products that suit each group's lifestyle *and* ability to pay. Its approach is not limited to simply "selling to the poor"; it also attempts to create sustainable wealth at the BoP so as to create improved economic conditions and purchasing power among this largest segment of the global population.

One good example is Unilever's "Shakti" (translated as "power" or "strength") program, a direct-to-consumer sales distribution network established by Hindustan Lever (a Unilever subsidiary) to reach millions of consumers in remote villages in India. In those areas, there is no retail distribution network, no advertising coverage, and poor roads and transport. The key to Shakti's success, as is the case with the Grameen Bank, is women. Women are invited to become direct-to-consumer sales distributors for Hindustan Lever's soaps and shampoos. The company provides training in selling, business management, and bookkeeping to help them become microentrepreneurs. After an initial investment in stock—usually borrowing from self-help groups or microfinance banks facilitated by Hindustan Lever—most Shakti entrepreneurs net a monthly profit of 700–1000 rupees ($15–22). This is a far cry from the few rupees single mothers had earned before, and for those with husbands who work in the fields, this typically doubles the household income. Shakti taps into women's self-help groups and has proved highly successful for both Hindustan Lever and the women entrepreneurs. Unilever has gained in terms of an extended consumer network, which was heretofore almost impenetrable due to lack of communication media, such as television and radio. In turn, the women entrepreneurs have gained financial independence, self-confidence, and a chance to provide a decent education for their families. By the end of 2006, the Shakti network had grown to over 30,000 microentrepreneurs selling products in 100,000 villages across 15 states in India.

The Shakti model is now being adapted and is gaining momentum in Bangladesh, where an estimated 3000 women entrepreneurs are already participating. Through an agreement with CARE Bangladesh, this initiative (called Project Aparajita) will empower another 2000 rural women. In addition to recruiting and training women, CARE will also monitor and evaluate the program to obtain a better understanding of its impact.

Today, Unilever is at the forefront of efforts at what must surely be "ground zero" in the battle for sustainability—the BoP in emerging markets. It is too early to describe its efforts as an unqualified success, and Unilever itself would be the first to agree that it is still in its early days. Nonetheless, as the developed markets become increasingly competitive and saturated, major companies that can succeed in expanding both their potential markets and their purchasing power will have an increasingly critical competitive advantage. From a sustainability investor's perspective, Unilever is precisely the kind of far-sighted, adaptable, well-managed company they should be looking for. While I cannot predict what the next over-the-horizon business issue will be, I would have a high level of confidence that a company such as Unilever will be able to confront it successfully.

A Winning Formula for Investors

In this chapter, we have profiled a wide variety of large, publicly traded companies from many different countries, with businesses across a broad spectrum of industry sectors. What all of them have in common, however, is this: each of them has explicitly recognized the power of the Sustainability Revolution to disrupt and transform both markets and the very basis of competitive advantage. What's more, they have not merely identified and tried to manage the downside risks for their businesses created by this Revolution; they have also discerned and seized opportunities on the *upside*.

It is hoped that these real-world examples will help convince the reader that superior sustainability performance *can* indeed translate directly into a competitive advantage for companies. It should, therefore, follow logically that these are precisely the sorts of companies for which twenty-first century investors and their advisors should be on the lookout.

In Chapter 8, we return to the *investors'* side of the table. Fortunately, as we shall see, growing numbers of institutional investors are beginning to awaken to both the importance *and* the staying power of the Sustainability Revolution. The more they do so, the more companies such as those we have profiled here will become attractive to and rewarded by investors. And the more frequently this occurs, the more often will the leaders be financially rewarded and reinforced and the laggards have significant incentives to catch up. A virtuous, worldwide circle will have begun in earnest.

The beginning of it all, however, is investor *awareness*. In Chapter 8, we discuss a number of innovative initiatives by *groups* of investors designed to do precisely that. Those collaborations have arguably done more than any other factor to raise and broaden awareness about sustainability issues within the investor community. Until recently, as we have seen, that community has been virtually impervious to the logic of the Sustainable Investment Revolution. The good news, however, as we shall soon see, is that this is all about to change. The journey is far from finished, but at least it has clearly now begun!

Chapter 8

The Game-Changers

Part I: Collective Initiatives

*Over the longer term, investments based on sustainability
criteria are expected to outperform those based on
traditional performance resources.*

—RODERICK MUSTERS, CHIEF INVESTMENT OFFICER, APG,
NETHERLANDS (SECOND-LARGEST PENSION FUND IN THE WORLD)

In Chapter 2 we explored the powerful cognitive forces that have, historically at least, militated so effectively *against* the acceptance of the sustainable investment hypothesis by the mainstream community. Chief among them was the unquestioned—and, as it turns out, totally unfounded—belief that sustainability factors were either irrelevant or even harmful to financial returns. It followed "logically" from this that addressing them explicitly in any investment strategy was completely antithetical to the notion of fiduciary responsibility.

In Chapter 3 we examined some of the perverse, real-world consequences and lost opportunities triggered by this largely unthinking rejection. One of the many examples of the unfortunate consequences of this myopia was the spectre of the $40 billion Gates Foundation steadfastly refusing to even *consider* sustainability investing or research, even if its own investment activities might well be significantly undermining all of its good work on the grant-giving side. It would at the very least be nice to *know*.

The next three chapters, however, make for much more encouraging and uplifting reading. Here, we focus on a set of *countervailing* forces —those leading-edge organizations and individuals whose pioneering efforts will, ultimately, make the Sustainable Investment Revolution all but inevitable. These are the game-changers; they are currently the exceptions to the dominant paradigm, but their path-breaking initiatives are paving the way for the eventual thorough-going mainstreaming of sustainable investing.

In the next three chapters we shall focus on three different sets of actors from different parts of the investment value chain. Each group has been instrumental in catalyzing and accelerating the Sustainable Investment Revolution:

- Collective initiatives, usually led by the owners of capital.
- Initiatives undertaken by owners of capital as *individual* organizations.
- A series of innovative service providers—the asset managers who are charged with investing the capital of others and the consultants, advisors, and research houses that assist both the owners and the managers of capital.

Each group provides a number of examples, which should amply demonstrate to the organizations' peers that it *is* indeed possible—and indeed advantageous—to overcome the lethargy and inertia of conventional investment approaches. One final caution to the reader, however: while these examples are encouraging and even inspiring, they must still be regarded very much as the *exceptions,* not the rule. We shall devote the rest of this chapter to the path-breaking *collective* initiatives.

Schopenhauer's Iron Law

The Danish philosopher Arthur Schopenhauer, early in the nineteenth century, made the astute observation that there were at least three distinct and inevitable stages in the revelation of new "truths": first, they are ridiculed, then resisted, and finally considered as perfectly self-evident and unremarkable.

So it was with the Copernican revolution, which ultimately established that the earth was *not* in fact the center of the universe and indeed revolved around the sun and not the reverse, as was then commonly believed. I am firmly convinced that we are already embarked on a similar path with regard to sustainable investing. In my own view, we are currently still lodged somewhere in the resistance phase, with the odd bit of ridicule thrown in for good measure.

The good news, however, is that there are now also occasional glimpses of sustainable investing becoming considered simply matter of fact and normal. Ten years hence, I hope and believe that this approach will be thoroughly mainstream, and people will have difficulty remembering or believing that it was ever otherwise. Sustainability factors will become as common central investment criteria as price/earnings ratios are today. (They will arguably also be considerably more useful!)

In the meantime, however, there is money to be made by those investors astute enough to avail themselves of what is still at this point a major information advantage that sustainability "deniers"—still firmly in the majority—do not have.

The Collective Initiatives

The United Nations Environment Program's Finance Initiative (UNEP-FI)

In many ways UNEP-FI was the seminal and remains the quintessential example of a collective, multiorganizational initiative that helped launch the Sustainable Investment Revolution. Today it is a dynamic partnership between the UN Environment Program and nearly 180 financial institutions from over 40 countries. This includes commercial banks, investment banks, insurers, asset managers, and financial advisors. It was the first major collaboration among *investors* to focus on environmental and social (ES) challenges, and thus should really be considered the "father" of sustainable investing.

UNEP-FI began back in 1991 in New York City when 28 commercial banks agreed to team up with the UN Environment Program to promote better awareness of environmental issues within the banking sector. Much of the credit for the initiative should properly go to two people: Dr. Mustafa Tolba, the then head of the UN Environment Program, and

Scott Vaughan, a UNEP staffer with a particular interest in the potential role of the capital markets in promoting sustainability. The founding banks at the meeting included global giants such as HSBC and Deutsche Bank, which together controlled an impressive $2 trillion. Two years later a parallel initiative was launched in the insurance sector, which included Swiss Re, Gerling, and Sumitomo Marine and Fire. Quite sensibly, the two streams of activity were subsequently merged together in 2003, and today UNEP-FI subsumes all of the different branches of the financial services industry under one conceptual and organizational roof.

Without question, UNEP-FI's greatest contribution has been to raise awareness, and its unambiguous focus on the finance sector has made it both unique and extraordinarily broad in its impact. Since this sector provides the "financial oxygen" for companies in every other industrial sector, its influence is virtually ubiquitous and absolutely critical. Yet, perhaps because its most important environmental and social impact is "only" indirect, the financial services industry has arguably been the very last one to awaken to both the risks and the opportunities created by the Sustainable Investment Revolution. (I distinctly recall the chairman of a world top 10 bank declining to join the World Business Council for Sustainable Development in 1990 for the stated reason that "we don't cut down any trees here at the bank!") In fairness to him, he wasn't alone; all three of the top 10 bank chairmen we approached declined, despite the opportunity to mingle with dozens of Fortune global 100 CEOs and the WBCSD's multibillionaire founder and then chairman Stefan Schmidheiny. The combination of the financial sector's absolute centrality to almost all economic activity *and* its lagging awareness levels made UNEP-FI's role all the more indispensable.

Much of the credit for UNEP-FI's impact is the result of its dynamic if unorthodox leader Paul Clements-Hunt. Operating with little if any assistance (and, indeed, at times, considerable hindrance) from the rest of the UN Environment Program, Clements-Hunt positively epitomized the "entrepreneurial bureaucrat"—far more concerned with achieving concrete results than with the niceties of the sometimes suffocating UN procedures—or the ultraconservative organizational culture that spawned them.

For our purposes, the most relevant and influential component of UNEP-FI has been the Asset Management Working Group, an assemblage of nearly 20 money management firms from a dozen countries, with a combined $2 trillion under management. Since its inception in 2003, this group has commissioned, written, and published dozens of influential reports.[1] The common thread linking all of the reports was their strong focus on the materiality of ES factors to *investment* performance. The fact that several of the briefs were authored by Goldman Sachs, JP Morgan, Morgan Stanley, Merrill Lynch, and UBS gave them infinitely more credibility and impact in the investment world than anything authored by a UN agency by itself could possibly have achieved.

Another report commissioned by UNEP-FI that had a major impact was written by the international law firm Freshfields, Bruckhaus, Deringer, one of the very largest law firms in the world. The report, which came to be known simply as "the Freshfields Report," examined fiduciary legislation and case law in 10 Organisation for Economic Cooperation and Development (OECD) countries. It concluded that it was not only legally permissible for pension fund trustees and other fiduciaries to integrate ES factors into their investment strategies and mandates, but it was arguably *mandatory* in cases in which they could reasonably be expected to be financially material.[2]

This report, from one of the largest and most respected law firms in the world, which was a direct repudiation of the fiduciary mythology we examined in Chapter 2, was a pivotal intellectual event. Conventional wisdom and practice had always dictated that precisely because they were presumed to be financially *im*material, if not injurious, ES factors were completely incompatible with fiduciary responsibility. An entire belief system grew up accordingly, implying potentially serious legal consequences for any trustee foolhardy enough to ignore the custom. The Freshfields report effectively demolished this argument—or at least on pure merit it should have done so. Regrettably, however, despite its compelling arguments and documentation, the report has yet to change either the attitudes or the practices of 95 percent of pension fund trustees. The seed has definitely been planted, though, and it continues to grow and change behavior today.

Continuing its theme of examining the materiality of ES for investors, the Asset Management Working Group (AWG) also published a summary of the results of both academic and investment bank research on investment performance and ES factors.[3] Consistent with the evidence that we presented and that was discussed in Chapter 5, that report concluded that the balance of the evidence did indeed support the materiality argument. In another important and even more recent report, UNEP-FI published a summary of what leading pension funds around the world were doing to integrate ES factors.[4] One of UNEP-FI's most potent weapons has always been the peer pressure and competitiveness among the financial institutions. Clements-Hunt and his staff expend considerable energy in providing evidence of global best practice and then encouraging a "race to the top" among the laggards.

Over the past two years the AWG has made another important contribution—broadening the integration of ES factors into other asset classes. Until very recently, the overwhelming majority of ES integration work had focused on the most obvious asset class—equities. To a much lesser degree, some analysts had also been looking at corporate bonds. But in 2007 the AWG spawned a new working group on real estate. An important but neglected asset class is the real estate sector, which has major ES impact and risks, but also presents some intriguing ES-driven investment opportunities. As we have seen, "green" real estate has become a dynamic and attractive asset class and has also created business and investment opportunities in providing its "infrastructure"—most notably products and services promoting improved energy, water, and materials efficiency.

The new working group was co-chaired by senior representatives from three real estate heavyweights—Axa Real Estate, France's Caisse de Depots, and the U.K.'s Prudential Property group. This work marks an important intellectual expansion, and undoubtedly presages UNEP-FI's future growth into other important asset classes such as infrastructure and private equity.

From its inception in 1991, but particularly over the past few years, the UNEP-FI collaboration has made a major contribution to the growing legitimation of the sustainable investment thesis. It was the first of the major collaborations among international institutional investors, but fortunately it would not be the last.

Ceres

Ceres—more formally known as the Coalition for Environmentally Responsible Economies—is a bit of a hybrid organization. Part advocacy group, part large-scale convener and animator, and part think-tank, Ceres today has developed enough of a profile and organizational infrastructure in its own right (it now has a full-time staff of roughly 40 people) that it is sometimes easy to forget that it is, above all, really a collective undertaking by *dozens* of different member organizations. Since its inception nearly two decades ago, but particularly over the past 10 years, Ceres has been a critically important actor in advancing the sustainable investment agenda—and it has done so in the comparatively barren ideological soil of the United States.

A not-for-profit nongovernmental organization (NGO), Ceres was founded in 1989 by Joan Bavaria, one of the pioneers of SRI in America and the long-time leader and president of Trillium Asset Management, a prominent U.S. SRI investment house. The initial impetus for Ceres was actually the notorious Exxon Valdez oil spill in Alaska. Members of the organization were originally challenged to sign the "Valdez Principles" of environmental stewardship; fairly early in the organization's life, they were rechristened the "Ceres Principles." The Principles were a 10-point code of environmental conduct for companies emphasizing themes such as energy conservation, waste minimization, senior management commitment, and communication with stakeholders.

Ceres' membership is a diverse collection of over 150 institutional investors, environmentalists, labor groups, and other public interest groups. The original game plan was to engage leading, high-profile companies, such as General Motors, to have a "dialog" with Ceres, agree to sign and follow the Principles, and remain on a path of continuous improvement and ongoing engagement with the Ceres staff. Over time, Ceres' focus has shifted somewhat, expanding to include a strong focus on *investors;* hence its inclusion in this book!

The organization has been blessed throughout its life by three long-serving heads, each a visionary and each with prodigious coalition-building and political skills. After Joan Bavaria came Bob Massie, a gifted academic, ordained minister, and charismatic leader. When health problems forced Massie to step back from his day-to-day role in 2005, his successor became Mindy Lubber, the current head and a multitalented "quadruple threat"—MBA and lawyer, former senior federal environmental regulator, former head of several public interest environmental law organizations, and founder of one of America's first "green" investment houses, Green Century Capital Management.

Two of Ceres' major contributions have been of particular importance to the progress of the Sustainable Investment Revolution. The first was its creation and initial leadership of the Global Reporting Initiative (GRI), the de facto international standard for corporate environmental, social, and economic reporting. The second was its role as catalyst and secretariat for the Investor Network on Climate Risk (INCR), a network of more than 60 leading U.S. institutional investors and financial institutions with assets of over $5 *trillion* that promotes better understanding of the financial risks and investment opportunities posed by climate change.

The GRI, established in 1997 by Ceres, had the mission of developing globally applicable guidelines for reporting on the economic, environmental, and social performance of corporations, governments, and NGOs. Originally spearheaded by Ceres in partnership with the United Nations Environment Programme, the GRI in 2002 was spun off as a permanent, independent, international body with its own multistakeholder governance structure. In 2006, the GRI published the third generation of its widely influential standards.

The GRI Guidelines are expressly designed to provide corporations with a way to report clear, measurable, and comparable information. Conceptually, the GRI is not unlike efforts in any other industry to define a common standard—the Generally Accepted Accounting Principles in conventional accounting of the United States would be one example. In principle, this simplifies the reporting process for companies and also makes it easier for investors to make "apples-to-apples" comparisons, at least among companies in the same sectors. Simply put, GRI was and remains all about information transparency. The GRI standards have unquestionably been a significant factor in improving both the quantity and quality of sustainability reporting by companies, which in turn has improved the ability of investors to make sustainability-conscious decisions. Although not without their critics, the GRI Guidelines are currently the most frequently used, credible, and trusted sustainability reporting framework in the world, largely because they were created through a herculean multistakeholder, consensus-seeking approach that involved industry, NGOs, and a myriad of other stakeholders. To date more than 1500 companies, including many of the world's leading brands, have declared their voluntary adoption of the Guidelines worldwide, making them today's de facto gold standard for reporting.

INCR is the second monumental contribution by Ceres. INCR is a network of U.S. institutional investors and financial institutions that promotes improved understanding of the financial risks and investment opportunities posed by climate change. Equally, if not more importantly, INCR is also actively involved in promoting and organizing *action* by its members once a sufficient level of understanding has been reached. Launched at the first Institutional Investor Summit on Climate Risk at the United Nations in November 2003, INCR's membership now includes more than 60 investors managing in excess of $5 trillion of assets. Members include U.S. state and city treasurers and comptrollers, public and labor pension funds, foundations, asset managers, and other institutional investors. INCR uses the collective power of its members to encourage improved disclosure and better management of the business risks and opportunities being created by climate change. INCR's remit and mission are virtually identical to those of its global predecessor, the Carbon Disclosure Project (CDP), which we shall discuss later in this chapter. While INCR came later and is largely confined to the United States, its tighter geographic focus may have actually allowed it to galvanize more concrete action than the CDP, despite the latter's seminal role in consciousness raising on a global scale.

In May 2005 INCR signatories adopted a 10-point "Call to Action" at the second Institutional Investor Summit on Climate Risk at UN headquarters. At that event INCR members publicly pledged to do the following:

- Invest capital, individually or collectively, in companies developing and deploying clean technologies, which we believe will enhance and sustain the long-term viability of corporate assets and shareholder value.
- Support appropriate shareholder resolutions and company engagement to improve corporate disclosure and governance on climate risk.
- Adopt a reliable and generally accepted global standard for disclosure of climate risk.
- Promote information sharing among the growing number of institutional investors and organizations around the world concerned with climate risk.
- Improve the capacity to assess climate risk.
- Improve mutual fund engagement in addressing climate risk.
- Encourage all publicly held companies in the auto, electric power, and oil and gas sectors to follow the lead of some companies and report within a year on how likely scenarios for climate change, future greenhouse gas limits, and dwindling access to inexpensive energy will affect their businesses and competitiveness; in addition, identify steps they are taking to reduce the impact of those financial factors and seize emerging new market opportunities.
- Renew the dialog between investors and all companies that have already disclosed their climate risk to focus on steps that investors and companies can take to address this risk.
- Help investors assess climate risk.

- Request the U.S. Securities and Exchange Commission (SEC) to require that companies disclose the risk associated with climate change as part of their securities filings.

1NCR's advocacy work has already paid dividends in the form of observable changes in corporate behavior. The organization can point to over two dozen Fortune 500 companies that have already made significant improvements to their climate risk management practices and disclosure, at least in part in direct response to Ceres/INCR's interventions. Executives from major electric utility companies, such as Duke Energy and AEP, credit INCR with helping improve their awareness, policies, and disclosure regarding climate risk. In addition, INCR has been actively lobbying the U.S. SEC to strengthen (actually, more accurately, to *create* in the first place) regulations requiring companies to disclose their exposure to climate risk.

And INCR's members are already beginning to put their investment capital where their mouths are. Its members have invested over $1.5 billion of their assets in renewable energy and other clean technology ventures in 2006 and 2007 in areas including hydrogen fuel cells and geothermal energy. Boldly going where no one has gone before, Ceres' work on the GRI and INCR has helped make it one of the leading catalysts for improving the capital market's understanding of sustainability issues.

In February 2008, during the most recent Investor Summit on Climate Risk at the United Nations (which it organized), the INCR released a "climate change action plan." Noting that climate change presents both material risks and significant opportunities, the investors pledged to do the following:

- Collectively invest $10 billion in clean technology opportunities over the next 2 years.
- Require that asset managers, consultants, and financial advisors consider climate risks and opportunities.
- Incorporate green building standards into real estate portfolios and investment decisions.
- Reduce energy use in core real estate holdings by 20 percent over the next 3 years.
- In addition, the plan calls for policy actions aimed at the SEC and Congress, engagement with companies to improve their disclosure and responses to climate change, and encouraging others in the

industry—such as analysts, ratings agencies, and investment banks —to consider climate investment risks and opportunities.

All of this work has not gone unnoticed: in 2006 Ceres won the coveted Skoll Foundation Award for Social Entrepreneurship and was also named one of the 100 most influential players in the corporate governance movement by *Directorship Magazine.* Its convening and attention-getting/ focusing power is almost without peer. And here's the best part: knowing some of the principals involved, it's a pretty safe bet that Ceres will *not* be resting on its laurels; we'll hear much more from Ceres in the months and years to come.

The Carbon Disclosure Project: The "Mother of All" Investor Collaborations

The CDP, currently in its sixth annual incarnation, is arguably the largest investor collaboration in history. In 2008, the project has brought together over 380 major investors with combined assets under management of over $55 *trillion.* The CDP itself is a not-for-profit NGO, raising its operating funding from philanthropic and corporate contributions as well as from a modest but growing income stream from fees for services provided to its members.

Current signatories supporting the project include financial heavyweights, such as Goldman Sachs, Merrill Lynch, and Morgan Stanley, as well as leading international pension funds, such as ABP from the Netherlands, CalPERS and CalSTRS from the United States, the Canadian Pension Plan Investment Board, and national pension plans from France, Sweden, New Zealand, Thailand, Korea, and elsewhere.

The CDP's mission is two-fold: to inform investors regarding the significant risks and opportunities presented by climate change and to inform—and put pressure on—the management of companies regarding the serious concerns of shareholders relative to the impact of these issues on company value. On the risk side of the ledger, among many other things, climate change can do the following:

- Reduce company profits through new regulations and taxes.
- Require multihundred million dollar capital expenditures to achieve mandated reductions in CO_2 emissions.
- Threaten key inputs, such as industrial water supplies, and even core businesses, such as agriculture and tourism.

- Render previous technology investments inadequate or even irrelevant.
- Create reputational and competitive risks if companies are perceived to be laggards.

On the positive *opportunities* side of the ledger, as we have seen, climate change is already creating a myriad of interesting options for investors, ranging from clean technologies to the trading of CO_2 emission permits.

In our own view, the CDP has been one of the three most powerful global forces elevating investor awareness of the financial consequences of climate risk. (The other two on our list would be the work of Nobel Laureate and former U.S. Vice President Al Gore, and that of Sir Nicholas Stern, who wrote a highly influential, eponymous study for the U.K. government.)

The CDP, founded in London, England in 2001, was essentially the brainchild of Tessa Tennant and Paul Dickenson. Ms. Tennant was already one of the most dynamic, visionary, and accomplished figures in the "green investment" movement in the U.K. (Indeed, once the CDP was well established, she went on to found and chair the first NGO promoting responsible investment in Asia, called AsRia—The Asian Socially Responsible Investment Association.) Paul Dickinson, who has been the CDP's chief executive for the past five years, is another superbright sustainability campaigner.

While today the CDP is well established, well funded, and a success on multiple levels, the early years were extraordinarily difficult and required almost superhuman dedication from the two primary cofounders. Fortunately, they had several key "coconspirators" from the outset. The first was world-class environmental lawyer James Cameron, who went on to cofound the innovative finance boutique Climate Change Capital[5] and who today chairs the CDP. Others included Jeremy Smith, an investment banker, and Craig Mackenzie, who then headed the socially responsible investment team at U.K. asset manager Insight. In later years Paul Simpson joined the team and became a key factor in its growth and success. Today he serves as the CDP's chief operating officer.

Visionary initiatives almost invariably require financial support and resources as well, and the CDP was no different. In the beginning, it took three committed and courageous initial funders to launch the project: the family foundation of British financiers and environmentalists Teddy and Zac Goldsmith, American media pioneer and sustainability philanthropist Ted Turner, and the U.S.-based W. Alton Jones Foundation. While by 2008 the CDP had attracted a huge institutional investor support base, in the early years it took a significant level of organizational courage for the first signatories to step forward. The first group of intrepid signatories included the following:

- Asset managers, including Credit Suisse, UBS, Merrill Lynch, Allianz Dresdner, and Société Générale.
- Insurers, such as Swiss Re, Munich Re, and the U.K.'s Cooperative Insurance Society (CIS).
- Asset owners, including the U.K.'s University Superannuation Scheme (USS) pension fund.

Careful readers will notice a distinct Eurocentric bias in the initial cast of CDP characters. This was partly a function of the project's initial base of operations in London, but more importantly it was also due to the much more highly developed awareness of climate risk in Europe than in North America at that time—and, arguably, even today.

The two principal objectives of the CDP have remained the same since its inception: first, to increase awareness about climate change among both major corporations and the large institutional investors who tend to own the majority of their shares and, second, to encourage them to *act*. The logic behind the project is simple but compelling: if it can be made clear to company executives and boards that their institutional owners are both concerned about climate risk *and* watching their investee companies carefully, the performance of those companies in managing and minimizing their "carbon footprint" should improve. (As the old business school bromide correctly observes: "what gets measured, gets managed.") And since industrial corporations are, in aggregate, huge contributors to the worldwide climate change problematic, the CDP should be able to help make major inroads in helping to ameliorate it.

The focal point for the project is the CDP Secretariat, headquartered in London, which organizes and coordinates what has now become an enormously complex, multistakeholder, multicountry process. Over time, the Secretariat has grown from its initial two hardy souls to today's group of over 20. The CDP's chief strategic weapon is information transparency, and its principal instrument in generating that transparency is a questionnaire sent annually to company chief executives.

Initially, the recipients were the CEOs of the Financial Times 500—the 500 largest publicly traded companies in the world. In subsequent years, the CDP has been able to reach further down the market capitalization food chain and to broaden the project's geographic reach.

By 2008 over 3000 information requests were being sent out. The letter that the CDP sends to company CEOs was described (perhaps somewhat breathlessly, but you get the point) by *Fortune* magazine this way in 2008: "Each February, perhaps the most important letter on Earth is sent to the CEOs of the world's largest companies."[6]

The information requested focuses on four primary areas: climate change risks, opportunities, and strategy; greenhouse gas emissions management; climate change governance; and greenhouse gas emissions accounting. Based on the answers to its questionnaire, CDP creates a major report for the investment community with detailed information about corporations' greenhouse gas emissions and climate change management strategies.[7]

The history of the CDP demonstrates the growing interest by investors and companies in the issue of climate change: in 2003 CDP1 attracted 35 investors with $4.5 trillion in assets under management; today CDP is supported by 385 investors with collective assets under management of $57 trillion. Only the most oblivious or foolhardy of CEOs would ignore an information request with that kind of financial firepower behind it, and although a few actually continue to do so, their numbers are dwindling rapidly.

Today, the CDP Web site[8] represents the largest single repository of corporate greenhouse gas (GHG) emissions data in the world; the total GHG emissions reported to the CDP in 2007 were 6,977,346,712 tons of CO_2e (CO_2e = carbon dioxide equivalent) in 2005. This represented approximately 14 percent of all global GHG emissions attributed to human activity and a 109 percent increase from CDP4.

More important than the mere reporting of information, however, is the fact that there is at least anecdotal evidence that the CDP has indeed helped catalyze concrete *action*. Among the financial institutions themselves, several firms, including HSBC, Merrill Lynch, Citigroup, and Bank of America, have developed major climate-related initiatives during the period since the CDP's launch. In addition, other finance houses, such as Lehman Brothers, UBS, JP Morgan, and ABN Amro, have all issued substantial equity research reports analyzing the risks and opportunities associated with climate change. At least *some* of that flurry of activity can be fairly ascribed to the CDP. High-profile report launches in New York City with former U.S. Vice President Al Gore in 2006 and former President Bill Clinton in 2007 and the explicit endorsement of then U.K. Prime Minister Tony Blair and Germany's Chancellor Angela

Merkel were also instrumental in extending the CDP's reach, credibility, and impact.

Each year, the project has expanded, both geographically and in terms of reaching smaller public companies. In 2007, however, the project took another step that promises to take it to another level altogether. That year the CDP entered into an innovative partnership with Walmart Stores to extend the reach of the CDP by sending the information request to a subset of their *suppliers*. The goal is to measure the major companies' entire global supply chain footprint and to encourage suppliers to reduce their own greenhouse gas emissions as well.

The initiative is now being extended to cover companies with $350 billion in annual sales and 60,000 suppliers. Hewlett Packard, L'Oréal, PepsiCo, Reckitt Benckiser, Tesco, Nestlé, Unilever, Procter & Gamble, Cadbury Schweppes, and Imperial Tobacco have joined the initiative during its first year. Each company, in turn, has selected up to 50 suppliers to work with it and to respond to the CDP pilot information request, which went out in the first quarter of 2008.

For its most recent (sixth) edition, the CDP once again extended its geographic reach, sending information requests to China's 100 largest companies by market capitalization for the first time and launching new collaborations with local partners in Korea, Latin America, Spain, and the Netherlands. Partner organizations already existed in the United States, Japan, Germany, China, the United Kingdom, France, Canada, Brazil, Australia, and New Zealand, among others.

The CDP has also recently announced another major strategic triumph: a three-year global partnership and funding agreement with longtime supporter Merrill Lynch. This augurs well both for the project's continuing stability and for the likelihood of its having even greater impact going forward.

The Enhanced Analytics Initiative

The Enhanced Analytics Initiative (EAI), another collective, not-for-profit investor sustainability initiative, was established a few years after the CDP in October 2004. The EAI's founding premises were both ingenious and difficult to dispute:

- The investment banks, such as Morgan Stanley, Merrill Lynch, and Goldman Sachs, which issued research opinions on companies (the "sell" side), had enormous influence on the investment choices and patterns of the actual asset *owners* (the "buy" side).

- At that time, the sell-side investment banks were displaying very little interest in ES/sustainability issues ("extrafinancial," as the EAI termed them), regarding them as largely immaterial financially.
- If they could actually be induced to do so, however, it would have a major catalytic and accelerating impact on the mainstreaming of sustainability investing.
- Sell-side investment banks respond, above all, to direct *financial* incentives.
- In the wake of the then recent Wall Street research conflict of interest scandals being exposed and prosecuted by then New York State Attorney General Elliott Spitzer (not to mention $1.4 billion in fines), the Wall Street investment banks could use all the good PR they could get, and the EAI could give it to them.

And thus was born the EAI, a concerted effort to stimulate the sell-side research houses to take sustainability issues seriously. The bait was trading commissions—the fees investment banks are paid for buying and selling securities on behalf of their buy-side clients.

As with most such initiatives, it was really just a handful of committed institutions and individuals that got the ball rolling. Key players at the outset were the major U.K. pension fund USS (through Dr. Raj Thamotheram), the Dutch health-care workers pension fund PGGM (Gerritt Musselman), leading French bank BNP Paribas (Eric Borremans), and German asset manager RCM, a member of the huge Allianz group (Bozena Jankowska)

EAI members[9] have agreed to allocate a minimum of 5 percent of their broker commissions on the basis of how well brokers integrate the analysis of extrafinancial issues and intangibles into their mainstream (sell-side) research. Some of the nontraditional, "extrafinancial" issues that have been addressed to date include climate change, human capital management, supply chain risk from human rights issues, and corporate governance. The 5 percent commitment is a minimum, however; some participants have already started allocating as much as 10 percent and expect to review this figure in light of the nature, scope, and quality of what brokers actually deliver. In 2005 total commissions for this project, at 5 percent of the total brokerage spend by current EAI members, were in the order of EUR 8 million.

Today, there are 27 EAI members with combined assets under management of some $2.4 trillion. EAI members make their own decisions on how to allocate the 5 percent. These decisions are informed by an independent evaluation conducted on 6-month cycles by an independent specialist consultancy based in Zurich called onValues.[10] A criteria-based framework has been developed to assess research in a consistent, rules-based process. The criteria used for the evaluation are designed to reward both high-quality research and also to encourage a broad research universe.

Research reports are evaluated by EAI on the basis of the following key guidelines:

- Scope of the extrafinancial issues (EFIs) covered:
  - Coverage of relevant EFIs
- Overall presentation and originality:
  - Includes an assessment of the user friendliness, originality, and transparency of research outputs
- Investment relevance of sector and issue analysis:
  - Thoroughness of top-down analysis
  - Quantitative modeling of sector impacts
  - Allocation to both long- and short-term horizons
- Comparative company analysis:
  - Analysis of EFI impact on company-specific investment value drivers
  - Integration into stock valuation
  - Ranking of companies and integration of EFI analysis in stock recommendations
- Coverage of research universe:
  - Coverage of relevant sectors
  - Coverage of global investible universes

The results of the evaluation are aggregated at the level of individual corporate research providers to identify the highest ranked organizations. These institutions are then commended for EAI commission allocation for the ensuing six-month period.

The credibility and impact of the EAI have unquestionably been enhanced by the caliber, stature, profile, and, above all, *mainstream* credentials of its chairmen, which have included David Blood, cofounder and partner with Al Gore in Generation Investment Management and, in his previous life, CEO of Goldman Sachs Asset Management in the U.K. Goldman Sachs had not—and indeed has not since—ever been accused of sloppy, misty-eyed, granola-chomping, Birkenstock-wearing, sentimentalism about the environment, so Blood's role as chair was critical to enhancing the EAI's credibility and impact with a tough, skeptical mainstream investor audience.

While it is still too early to deliver a final verdict on the EAI, it has unquestionably already produced some concrete, positive results. Since its inception, over 500 reports have been submitted by over 40 research providers. (By our guesstimate, that is roughly 490 more reports than would have been prepared *without* the EAI!) Of that total, over 70 have been selected and widely disseminated. For many of the investment banks submitting reports, such as Goldman Sachs and JP Morgan, it was their first real foray into sustainability research; and since both have continued to do subsequent sustainability research, it is difficult to argue that the EAI has had no impact.

Whether the EAI effort will ultimately prove sufficiently powerful and durable to catalyze a real change in the capital markets remains to be seen. Without question, however, it has been a step in the right direction and has achieved at least some of the ambitious goals of its founders.

The UN Principles for Responsible Investment

The most recent investor collaboration may ultimately prove to be the most influential of all; without question it is the one that is taking place amid the most favorable "tipping point" conditions. In April 2006, at the New York Stock Exchange, then UN Secretary General Kofi Annan rang the opening bell and officially launched the UN Principles for Responsible Investment (PRI). The PRI were the product of a two-year collaboration between UNEP-FI and the UN Global Compact, another major Annan initiative focused on encouraging major global corporations to become more socially responsible. The Principles themselves were hammered out over 15 months by representatives of 20 major institutional investors, with input and advice from a 70-person, multidisciplinary "expert group."[11] The key driving forces among the asset owners were Knut Kjaer, the then head of the 340+ billion Norwegian "petroleum fund," and Colin Melvin, the then head of the responsible investment group at Hermes. Two skilled and entrepreneurial UNEP-FI officials were also instrumental: James Gifford, a bright and personable Australian who was later to become the UN PRI's first Executive Director, and Gordon Haggert, an equally bright and incisive young Scot with previous capital markets experience who subsequently rejoined the private sector. When the dust had settled, the following six principles were agreed to and adopted, and signatories were committed to implement them:

1. We will incorporate environmental, social, and governance (ESG) issues into investment analysis and decision-making processes.
2. We will be active owners and incorporate ESG issues into our ownership policies and practices.
3. We will seek appropriate disclosure on ESG issues by the entities in which we invest.
4. We will promote acceptance and implementation of the Principles within the investment industry.
5. We will work together to enhance our effectiveness in implementing the Principles.
6. We will each report on our activities and progress toward implementing the Principles.

While the Principles themselves may seem both modest and rather obvious, it has to be conceded that they represented (and still represent) a *considerable* advance on the status quo and provided some real "stretch targets" for the signatories. As of late 2008 there were over 380 signatories, with combined assets under management of over $14 trillion. The PRI is governed by a board composed of 12 asset owners representatives and two representatives from the UN. The board and membership are served by a small but dynamic and capable secretariat, headed by James Gifford.

While it would be the height of naiveté to equate signing up to the UN Principles with actually *implementing* them,[12] it would also be a mistake to dismiss them as a mere public relations exercise. Each of the signatories has stakeholders and constituencies to whom they must be at least moderately responsive. The mere act of signing the Principles in a highly visible way sets the "accountability clock" ticking, and at some point a complete disjunction between rhetoric and reality becomes untenable —if not to the stakeholders themselves then certainly to the media. There is even some talk within the organization about expelling signatories who simply sign and do nothing. This step already has been taken by the PRI's sister organization, the Global Compact, with a predictably positive impact on the Compact's credibility.

The UN Principles also have another major advantage: unlike all previous generations of pious declarations, we are finally now at a point when the entire *zeitgeist* should make the PRI's actual implementation much less of an uphill battle than would have been the case even a year or two previously. This combination of timeliness, peer pressure, and accountability to external stakeholders and media strongly suggests that the UN PRI will have a lasting and positive impact.

In Chapter 9, we shall turn from these path-breaking collective initiatives to examine a number of innovative steps taken by *individual* asset owners. In almost all cases, the intellectual momentum for their work can be traced back to one or more of the breakthrough collaborations that we have discussed in this chapter.

Chapter 9

The Game-Changers
Part II: The *Individual* Owners of Capital

*Increasingly, our organization assesses investment opportunities
not only in terms of expected financial return, but also from a
social and environmental perspective. . . . Businesses that
acknowledge their responsibilities in relation to human rights,
the environment and social policy are generally managed by
people who are quick to recognize and respond to changes
in society. . . . Evidence indicates that the best-performing
businesses are those that promote sustainable development.*

—PGGM, NETHERLANDS

The Collective initiatives that we examined in Chapter 8 [UNEP-FI
(United Nations Environment Program's Finance Initiative), Carbon
Disclosure Project, Enhanced Analytics Initiative, and UN PRI (Principles
for Responsible Investment)] have been enormously useful as awareness
builders and accountability enhancers. Any real *investment* action, *however*, almost always takes place at the level of an *individual* institution.
And, inevitably, some of the organizations involved in those collective
efforts have taken the messages from those efforts more closely to heart
than others. In this chapter we profile a number of exceptional institutions, each of which has "pushed the envelope" and blazed a trail that
other, similarly situated organizations can and should now follow.

APG in the Netherlands

The Dutch pension fund Stichting Pensioenfonds APG is currently the third largest in the world. It manages the pensions of over 2.5 million current and former Dutch government employees and workers in the education sector.[1] It has over $300 billion in assets and has been a significant thought leader and opinion shaper in the world of sophisticated pension fund investors for some time. Therefore, any actions—or, for that matter, inactions—APG takes in the field of sustainable investment can and do have a powerful "demonstration effect" on APG's peers.

APG takes its role as a long-term "universal owner"—and one of the largest in the world at that—very seriously. Because of its size, APG also has the advantage of having the resources to manage roughly 80 percent of its assets itself, in house. This minimizes the likelihood that any of its investment policy initiatives could be subverted or imperfectly executed by an external money manager, whether intentionally or otherwise.

Under the leadership of its then Chief Investment Officer Jean Frijns, APG began exploring the potential utility of integrating environmental and social (ES) factors in its investment strategies as early as 2002. It began cautiously, commissioning company research on ES factors from an external provider, Innovest Strategic Value Advisors. The next step was to construct and manage two trial investment portfolios explicitly integrating ES research into the stock selection and portfolio construction processes. Roughly $200 million was invested in the two portfolios, one with European equities and the other with North American equities. The combination of the portfolios' performance and a growing comfort level with ES factor integration at a board level persuaded Frijns and his team that a broader use of sustainability research was both desirable and possible.[2] When he retired in 2005, his role as Chief Investment Officer was taken up by Roderick Munsters, who had formerly held the same position at the second largest Dutch pension fund PGGM (more about them later). Munsters had been a strong proponent of sustainability investment at PGGM, and his arrival at APG served only to accelerate its adoption there as well.

APG's strategic investment plan for 2007–2009 explicitly states as one of its major objectives the extension of ES considerations across its entire investment portfolio. This will entail, for starters, the use of ES research throughout its entire equity portfolio, not simply in its one, stand-alone sustainability fund. The next step will be the inclusion of ES factors in other asset classes, such as fixed income, real estate, private equity, and infrastructure.

APG's achievements in sustainable investment have already been considerable:

- Continuing to manage a dedicated, stand-alone global equities sustainability fund, which was begun in 2004 and currently has roughly $200 million.
- Integrating ES research systematically into two internally managed equity portfolios totaling EUR 22 billion.
- A $600 million investment in innovative carbon trading funds including a $360 commitment to a fund created by specialist boutique Climate Change Capital.
- A $300 million commitment to private equity investments in clean technology companies through Alpinvest, a joint venture with PGGM.
- A $140 million investment in a renewable energy infrastructure fund, the Ampère Equity Fund. The fund invests in wind farms, biomass power stations, and similar projects.
- A $75 million investment in sustainable forestry in Mozambique, Angola, and elsewhere in sub-Saharan Africa.
- A $50 million investment in microcredit, including participation in a $125 million fund run by Catalyst Microfinance Investors.
- A $20 million founding investment in the world's first emerging markets sustainability fund managed by Rexiter Capital Management and Innovest.
- A strategic investment in the specialist Dutch "green" bank Triodos.
- Taking strategic equity ownership stakes in two leading environmental, social, and corporate governance (ESG) research providers: Innovest Strategic Value Advisors and Governance Metrics International.

In addition to its direct investment activity in the sustainability space, APG provides financial support to the European Centre for Corporate Engagement, a new and high-powered sustainability research think tank based in the Netherlands and led by former APG research chief Dr. Rob Bauer. It is also an active participant in each of the major collective investor initiatives discussed in Chapter 8. In addition, it has supported innovative "engagement" exercises, such as the Pharma Futures and Access to Medicines Index projects, both of which were designed to improve the performance of global pharmaceutical companies in providing better access to medicines for low-income people in emerging markets.

As the third largest pension fund in the world, APG's commitment to sustainable investment has begun to have a powerful demonstration effect among its smaller peers in legitimizing the entire approach. Perhaps, most importantly, for APG it is not primarily a matter of ethics or "social responsibility"; rather it is an increasingly important ingredient in maximizing long-term, risk-adjusted financial returns for its beneficiaries. Rob Lake, senior portfolio manager with lead responsibility for ES issues, puts it well:

> APG exists to make investments and pay people's pensions, and we can't simply abandon that objective. Our interest in sustainability is seen very much in the context of that overriding financial obligation that we have in law.[3]

The U.K. Environment Agency

The U.K. Environment Agency is the environmental regulator for England and Wales, with an obvious institutional interest in environmental quality and improvement. What is exceptional about the Agency, however, is the lengths to which it has gone to leverage the economic power of its staff pension fund to complement and enhance the effectiveness of its core mandate—or, at the very least, to avoid actively undermining it.

The Environmental Agency Pension Fund (EAPF) is one of the 100 largest pension funds in the U.K., with assets of over $2.7 billion and over 18,000 members. It is difficult to dispute the logic of the man who has been the principal driving force behind the efforts—the Agency's head of Environmental Finance and Pension Fund Management Howard Pearce:

> What's the point of retiring in a dirty, filthy, degraded environment? We saw that there was a direct link with how we could be managing our pension fund—that we could be using our own fund to help deliver an environment for future generations that is clean and safe.[4]

This is disarmingly simple logic, but the EAPF's work in sustainability investment is, regrettably, virtually unique among environmental agencies around the world. It is a quintessential example of an organization putting its money where its mouth is and provides a pleasant contrast to each of the organizations profiled in Chapter 3.

As with many positive developments, it took negative publicity to jolt the Agency out of its previous patterns of behavior and to catalyze change. The stimulus came in June 2003, when the Agency was suddenly attacked in both print and electronic media for the environmental failings of some of the equity holdings of its pension fund. (Alert readers may recall that a very similar provocation has conspicuously *failed* to stimulate any comparable initiatives at the Gates Foundation.)

At the same time, the Agency's investment strategy was overdue for a complete overhaul. Its financial performance was indifferent, its concentrated exposure to large cap U.K. equities was excessive, and it lacked the diversification benefits of exposure to asset classes such as real estate and private equity.

In late 2003 Pearce was mandated to help rethink the entire strategy. Perhaps fortuitously, he did *not* have an investment background; this arguably sheltered him from many of the pernicious conventional "wisdoms" that we examined in Chapter 2. One of his first tasks was to commission research on two key topics: the fiduciary implications of including companies' environmental performance as an investment consideration and the link between environmental and financial performance. Reassured on both counts, Pearce proposed a more aggressive, environmentally sensitive investment strategy to his board, led by Lady Barbara Young. The board approved it.

In some respects, the EAPF is even further ahead than APG in its integration of ES factors across multiple asset classes. To begin with, fully 10 percent of its overall portfolio is invested in dedicated sustainability strategies run by a variety of external managers. The first of these was launched as far back as 2003. Over and above this, however, the EAPF requires all of its other equity managers to undertake or acquire—and then actually *use*—ES research when building their more conventional portfolios. (This is a difference of degree, I believe, rather than one of kind.) Thus, at least in theory, 100 percent of the Agency's equity portfolio is now sensitized to ES issues—and the Agency does indeed check, question its managers, and weed out those whose commitment and/or performance on sustainability issues is judged to be wanting.

Beyond equities, though, the Agency also screens its fixed-income portfolios for ES risk, invests in clean technology companies through a private equity fund of funds, and invests in a real estate fund of funds, which includes a specialist sustainability and urban regeneration mandate.

Perhaps most remarkably, the EAPF has also taken the trouble to determine whether all these efforts were actually paying any "environmental dividends." It commissioned and published a benchmarking analysis of its portfolio holdings in 2007 and found that its environmental footprint was 14 percent smaller than that of its investment benchmarks and was improving each year.

The Agency's efforts are beginning to pay off. In addition to the environmental dividend, it has received extraordinary external recognition, winning over a dozen awards of excellence, including *Investments and Pensions Europe* magazine's 2007 award for "best investor in ES," that same magazine's Fund of the Year award in 2006, and another 2006 award, this one from *Global Money Management,* as Public Pension Fund of the Year. The fact that these are resolutely mainstream publications should not be lost on the reader.

One final measuring stick is *financial* performance. While it would be disingenuous to ascribe that performance entirely or even primarily to ES integration, the fact is that the Agency outperformed its composite benchmark by 80 basis points (0.8 percent) in 2006 and an improved 120 basis points in 2007.

A number of critical success factors seem to be involved: a supportive board, Pearce's skillful and determined leadership, the conscious avoidance of reliance on a single investment consultant, the rigor of the manager selection process, and, just perhaps, the dearth of investment banking and money management "experts" on the board to cast aspersions on the efforts.

The last word here goes to Howard Pearce:

> We are not doing this for ethical reasons. We are doing this for financial reasons. We're concerned about the environmental risk that could hit our investments, and we also believe that there are material, environmentally-driven opportunities on the upside. We aren't just doing this for 1 percent of our fund; we're doing it across the entire fund.[5]

The "California Sisters"

CalPERS

The California Public Employees Retirement System (CalPERS), with over $230 billion in managed assets, is the largest public pension fund in North America and the fourth largest in the world. The scheme has long enjoyed an international reputation for its efforts to improve standards of corporate governance and management, both in the companies in which it invests and more broadly. Like APG and PGGM in the Netherlands, CalPERS is acutely conscious of its status as a long-term investor and "universal owner," with interests transcending individual companies, industry sectors, and even entire countries.

Historically, CalPERS' activities in that regard had been focused almost entirely on the traditional staples of the corporate governance movement: maximizing shareholder rights, access to information, and accountability, promoting the independence of board directors and the separation of the chairman's and CEO's roles, and combating excessive executive compensation.

One of the most visible features of CalPERS' corporate governance work has been its celebrated "focus list"—an annual list of 15–20 companies in which CalPERS' investment staff believe that governance improvements could translate directly and relatively quickly into increased shareholder value. Indeed, there is some academic evidence to suggest that this approach can indeed work: one report on the so-called "CalPERS effect" by the fund's investment consultants Wilshire Associates found that companies on the focus list outperformed their peers by 12.2 percent over the 5 years following their inclusion on the list.[6] A second study by University of California finance professor Brad Barber found that the 115 companies on the focus list between 1992 and 2005 had generated over $3 billion in excess returns for the fund.[7]

Much of CalPERS' work in the sustainability space is simply a logical extension and expansion of its corporate governance activism into new areas. To that end, CalPERS has

- Been a leading supporter and participant in the global Carbon Disclosure Project since 2005.
- Been an active participant in the North America-focused Investor Network on Climate Risk, pushing for improved regulatory requirements for company disclosure and engaging with companies directly.
- Pursued specific initiatives and engagement with individual companies in the electric utilities, insurance, and automobile sectors.

CalPERS' size, sophistication, and credibility all imbue these efforts with much greater impact than would otherwise be the case; the fund has long been the U.S. bellwether and opinion leader for investor activism on emerging issues. The extension of its activism and advocacy into the ES aspects of corporate governance may prove less transformational in the long run, however, than the steps it has taken recently in actually allocating its *capital* to promote ES improvement. We have long believed that *how an institution actually invests its assets is a far more telling and influential indicator of its commitment to sustainability than any rhetoric,* no matter how well intentioned and sincere.

In CalPERS' case these concrete asset allocations began in earnest in 2004, with the impetus, appropriately enough, coming from its board of directors. Then State Treasurer Phil Angelides (an elected official and a board member of both CalPERS and its "sister" fund, the $170 billion California State Teachers Pension Fund, CalSTRS) announced an ambitious "Green Wave" initiative, with four major components:

- An explicit allocation of $1 billion to "sustainability-enhanced" public equities.
- A specific asset allocation of $500 million to clean technology private equity companies.
- A comprehensive effort to "green" the two pension funds' $16 billion real estate portfolios by improving its energy efficiency by 20 percent over 5 years.
- Using the funds' financial muscle to improve company disclosure of environmental risks and performance, with an explicit objective of improving the latter.

The financial commitments were to be shared by the two giant funds roughly equally. Both of the big California funds have made significant progress in integrating ES factors.

Grand pronouncements by politicians are, of course, one thing; concrete actions are quite another. In CalPERS' case, progress from the former to the latter was due in part to an inspired appointment by the fund's then CEO Fred Buenrostro. Buenrostro fully appreciated that the Green Wave represented a significant challenge to the inertia of existing processes, practices, and investment staff attitudes. Such a challenge would be much more likely to succeed with fresh resources from the outside, specifically a "change agent" as a coordinating focal point with the responsibility, authority, and credibility to move things forward. He hired an experienced, dynamic, and committed individual—Winston Hickox— with a mandate to translate the lofty rhetoric of the Green Wave into concrete action "on the ground"—across at least four different divisions within CalPERS' investment staff. Hickox proved an excellent choice: he had impeccable environmental credentials as the former cabinet Secretary for the Environment for the State of California. In addition, however, he was a seasoned executive from the private sector and understood what would actually be required to mix environmental objectives with commercial imperatives.

The results were neither quick nor easily achieved, nor were they even remotely all the personal handiwork of Hickox. Having said that, however, as a close but outside observer of CalPERS' efforts in this area, I am absolutely persuaded that he was the one individual most responsible for moving the sustainability agenda forward. As of 2008, CalPERS had accomplished the following:

- It allocated $500 million to five "sustainability" funds managed by credible mainstream managers, such as Axa Rosenberg and State Street Global Advisors. Three of the five funds focus on domestic U.S. equities; the other two include international stocks.
- It created a special, $200 million private equity program to make investments in privately held environmental technology companies via a number of specialized funds.
- It began an aggressive effort to maximize energy efficiency throughout its $5 billion core real estate portfolio, including office, retail, residential, and industrial properties.
- It created a focused, $120 million "green" real estate fund with the Hines Corporation, an experienced and innovative real estate developer/manager. All of the fund's investments must be in buildings eligible for the rigorous LEED silver accreditation.
- It designed and constructed its own new office headquarters building to LEED silver status.
- It explicitly and routinely integrated ES considerations into the determination of its "permitted countries" list for its emerging markets investment portfolios. (This last initiative as well as CalPERS' $475 million program for "economically targeted" investments in California's inner cities and other underserved markets both predate the Green Wave Initiative, but reflect a similar attempt to include sustainability considerations explicitly in its investment strategies.)
- In May 2008 CalPERS' Investment Committee adopted a new policy to include in its formal criteria for evaluating external money managers an assessment of their ability to identify and manage climate risk in their investment portfolios. This latest initiative is potentially extremely important, and could have far-reaching "ripple

effects" in a country that has historically been one of the last bastions of "climate denial."

CalPERS' achievements in sustainability investment must be put in their proper perspective. While they are perhaps less impressive and thoroughgoing than some of their European counterparts, such as APG and PGGM, relative to their North American peers, CalPERS is and has been clearly in the vanguard. The mythologies that we examined in Chapter 2, all of them militating against the integration of ES factors, have long been more powerful in North America than in Europe. By North American standards, CalPERS' performance has been exemplary, and it has already begun to catalyze similar initiatives by other major North American public pension funds, including the New York City employees' (NYCERS) funds in the United States and the Canada Pension Plan Investment Board (CPPIB) in that country. The size, prominence, and credibility of these major funds should, over time, spawn similar actions by their more cautious peers.

CalSTRS

The California State Teachers' Retirement System, better known as Cal-STRS (pronounced "Cal-stirs"), is the second largest U.S. public pension fund with roughly $170 billion in assets and more than 810,000 members. CalSTRS' primary responsibility is to provide retirement, disability, and survivor benefits to teachers from the public schools and community colleges of California.

CalSTRS was one of the first public pension funds in the world to adopt an explicit sustainable investment strategy; its first Statement of Investment Responsibility was drafted and adopted over 30 years ago. Revised half a dozen times since, most recently in 2005, this document was one of the first of its kind. Today, it lays out CalSTRS' current understanding of responsible investment. In part it states the following:

> In addition to its fiduciary responsibilities to its members, the Board has the social and ethical obligation to require that corporations in which securities are held meet a high standard of conduct in their operations.
>
> The act of investment in the securities of a corporation predominantly reflects a judgment that the ownership will produce a rate of return which will make it an attractive investment. While

not outwardly signifying approval of all of a company's policies and products, it is possible however that such investment may be interpreted as an indication of the shareholders approval or support of all of a company's policies and products.

The System is a large investor and as such is in a position to exert influence on the corporations in which it has invested.[8]

CalSTRS has actually gone beyond its Statement of Investment Responsibility in many respects. In 2006, it adopted a Policy Regarding Geopolitical and Social Risks designed to ensure that the "CalSTRS 20 Risk Factors" adopted by the Board were systematically addressed by both CalSTRS' in-house portfolio managers and their external ones as well.[9] While the 20 risk factors include traditional topics such as accounting principles, fiscal transparency, auditing, and OECD principles on corporate governance, they also addressed sustainability factors including human rights, civil liberties and political rights, workers' rights, and environmental issues (air quality, water quality, climate change, and land protection).

CalSTRS actively votes it proxies and is remarkably transparent about its voting record. It also actively engages with companies on environmental and social issues and divests as a last resort, "when there is little or no possibility of obtaining from a company a commitment to pursue activities designed to correct practices or policies involving grave social injury." During the 2006–2007 proxy season, for example, CalSTRS staff voted on 108 company ballots. Sustainability/environmental issues were on 47 percent of the ballots; CalSTRS voted in favor of the proposal issues at a rate of 80 percent.[10]

CalSTRS' commitment to examining the risks of global warming began with its participation in the 2003 U.N. Institutional Investor Summit on Climate Risk in New York City. In 2004 CalSTRS' sustainability initiatives took a quantum leap forward when then State Treasurer Phil Angelides introduced his high-profile "Green Wave" initiative. State Controller Steve Westley, another strong proponent of environmental change and fellow board member for both funds, was also instrumental. As with CalSTRS, for CalPERS the Green Wave meant four things:

- Structure an environmentally focused program of investment in public equities.
- Demand environmental accountability and disclosure.

- Target private investment in clean technologies.
- Audit real estate portfolios to boost long-term value.

In December 2005 the CalSTRS Board voted to explore the creation of a specific investment program to make sustainable investments. CalSTRS then hired leading pension fund advisors Pension Consulting Alliance (PCA) to provide an overview of sustainable investment opportunities with an environmental focus—a report that concluded that so-called "double bottom line" expectations were indeed achievable in the market. Indeed, it concluded that an environmentally oriented public securities investment program could achieve reasonable financial *and* environmental returns.

CalSTRS' sustainability initiatives could easily have been stillborn without the consistent and aggressive leadership of the Fund's two top executives: CEO Jack Ehnes and Chief Investment Officer Chris Ailman. In 2007 they formed a multidepartmental Green Initiative Task Force and tasked it with coordinating the efforts of all of CalSTRS' "Green Wave" efforts.

Under this program, in 2007 CalSTRS hired four outside money asset management firms to manage environmentally focused Sustainable Investment strategies, committing $225 million to the mandates. They were managed by Acuity, Generation, New Amsterdam, and a joint venture between Light Green Advisors and Rhumbline. On the private equity side, the System's Alternative Investments division has already invested over $280 million in investments and coinvestments in the clean technology and environmental sustainability sector in funds including the US Renewables Group, the Hg Renewable Power Fund, NGEN, and Craton Equity Partners.

CalSTRS has also been a major proponent of improving corporate environmental disclosure. In 2004 it was one of the first public pension funds to write to the U.S. Securities and Exchange Commission (SEC) requesting that the agency review its disclosure requirements in this area. It is a member of both the Carbon Disclosure Project and the Investor Network on Climate Risk and was the first U.S. pension fund to join the Enhanced Analytics Initiative. It has systematically researched climate risk exposures of companies in the electric utility sector and engaged with individual companies directly where concerns had surfaced. In 2007 it became a signatory to the UN Principles for Responsible Investment. Most recently, CalSTRS was also a signatory to a Ceres-led petition calling on the SEC to require full corporate climate risk disclosure, and is actively involved in the Global Warming Shareholder Campaign.

When business as usual doesn't achieve satisfactory results, CalSTRS has been known to get both aggressive and creative in its efforts to change company behavior. In the lead-up to the May 2008 shareholder meeting of the gas pipeline utility OneOK Inc., for example, CalSTRS launched a public relations campaign that included a full-page ad in the *New York Times* pressuring the company to report its greenhouse gas emissions. CalSTRS threatened to propose the same resolution for Dynegy Inc., another major utility, but under pressure Dynegy agreed to report its emissions and the resolution was withdrawn before the shareholder meeting.

Although best known for its actions as an investor, CalSTRS also recognizes that with over 800 employees, its own direct operations also have social and environmental impact. Partly for that reason, CalSTRS has designed its new 14-storey, $280 million headquarters building as an environmental showcase and example to others. The building has state-of-the-art environmental design and technology (and a LEED Silver certification), which is expected to save up to $2 million per year in operating costs. In addition, the building is also a critical element in a broader urban revitalization effort on the banks of the Sacramento River.

CalSTRS, like its sister pension fund CalPERS, is a world leader in translating the high-minded rhetoric of sustainability investing into concrete action on the ground. (That said, there is plenty left to do for *both* organizations—and their peers.) CalSTRS' CEO Jack Ehnes summarizes his organization's rationale for sustainable investment this way:

> As a "forever" investor, we have to look at the impact environmental problems have on the long-term profitability of our holdings. Environmental responsibility simply makes sense for the future growth and stability of our portfolio.[11]

PGGM in the Netherlands

With nearly $100 billion in assets, PGGM is the third largest pension fund in Europe and one of the 25 largest in the world. It provides pension benefits to over two million former and current employees in the healthcare and social work sectors in the Netherlands. Like its friendly rival and sometimes partner ABP, PGGM is one of the leading exemplars of sustainable investment in action.

Like ABP, PGGM is an active participant in a number of the collective sustainable investment initiatives that were described in Chapter 8:

the UN Principles for Responsible Investment, the Carbon Disclosure Project, and the Enhanced Analytics Initiative.

One striking aspect of PGGM's own approach to sustainable investment is its explicit recognition of the *positive* impact that can be achieved, over and above the benefits of avoiding risks on the downside:

> PGGM believes that financial and social returns can be compatible objectives, and in the development and implementation of our investment policy we take account on a structural basis of how investments may affect—*and, where possible, improve*—environmental and social conditions.[12]

Perhaps even more importantly, PGGM has also put its money where its mouth is through a number of initiatives:

- Investing $300 million in the FTSE 4 Good Europe index via Barclays Global Investors.
- Investing $270 million in an emerging markets sustainability fund created by Albright Capital, headed by former U.S. Secretary of State Madeleine Albright.
- Investing $250 million in Climate Change Capital's innovative carbon trading fund.
- Cofounding and funding (with Triodos Bank) Dutch Sustainability Research, a specialist provider of ES research.
- Creating and funding two ES-enhanced portfolios, one for European equities and the other for U.S. stocks.
- Investing $200 million in the Hermes European Focus Fund, which uses company engagement on corporate governance to attempt to generate superior returns.
- Investing in clean technology private equity through Alpinvest, its joint venture with APG.
- Investing $140 million in renewable energy infrastructure through the Ampere Equity Fund.
- Investing in Hg Renewable Power Partners, a fund focused on onshore wind farms in Western Europe hiring U.K. asset managers F.C. to conduct a broad program of company engagement on its behalf around ES issues.
- Investing $200 million in a long-horizon international timberland fund managed by the well-regarded Boston-based firm GMO.
- Investing $270 million for microfinance into the Dexia Microcredit Fund. This investment, announced in March 2008, represents one

of the largest single institutional investor commitments to the micro-finance space.

Despite these numerous initiatives, PGGM's Chief Investment Officer Els Bos regards the fund as still in its early days of sustainability investing. Like APG, PGGM has announced its intention to expand the integration of ES research across its entire portfolio of different asset classes, a process that it hopes to complete by 2009. In late 2006, it created a formal focal and coordinating point for these efforts by hiring Marcel Jeucken as its first head of sustainable investments. Jeucken arrived with excellent knowledge of both the sustainability field and his new employer; his previous job had been as a senior executive with Dutch Sustainability Research, the specialist research boutique cofounded and partially owned by PGGM.

France's FRR

France's Fonds de Réserve Pour les Retraites (FRR) is the country's principal public pension fund vehicle. Set up relatively recently (in early 2003), the FRR began its investment operations only in mid-2004. With assets of over EUR 32 billion it is one of the most rapidly growing pension funds in the world—by 2020 it is expected to grow to EUR 150 billion. The Fund is publicly owned and is supervised by both the French Minister of the Economy and Budget and the Minister of Social Security in Paris. The fact that it will not need to make any pension payouts until 2020 gives the FRR even more ability to think—and act—like a long-term, universal owner.

The FRR's governance structure is very "French"; its 20-person Supervisory Board includes legislators, labor and management representatives, and civil servants. The board's general policy direction and the day-to-day management of the FRR are carried out by a three-person Executive Board. A small three-person unit reporting to the Board coordinates all of the FRR's SI initiatives.

The FRR's approach to sustainability investing has been unique in several respects. As a recent creation, it was free of the institutional/ideological baggage that we have seen at work in Chapters 2 and 3. Indeed, the FRR's own charter *requires* its Executive Board to report regularly to the more senior Supervisory Board on how it takes ES factors into account in its investment strategy. Influenced by some general British pension legislation several years previously, the FRR is nonetheless unique in having sustainability "hard wired" into its founding legislation. Two uniquely French factors allowed this to happen. The first was the strong influence of both the trade unions and civil service at the Supervisory Board level. Both of these groups understood the importance of ES issues much better than France's corporate sector at the time. The second factor was the importance to the process of a single key individual—Antoine de Salins. As is so frequently the case when innovations and social progress occur, in his absence it is quite likely that the outcome would have been markedly different. A graduate of France's elite Ecole Nationale d'Administration (ENA), de Salins had been a senior official in the French Treasury and a French representative to the European Union (EU) in Brussels prior to joining FRR. Experienced, highly intelligent, and strongly motivated, he was the perfect choice to navigate the tricky shoals of French governmental and senior business circles and help set the new institution on a solid and credible, yet intellectually ambitious, footing.

In a relatively short space of time the FRR has designed *and* begun to execute a remarkably sophisticated SI strategy. The FRR was one of the very first public asset owners to make a conscious, strategic commitment to the integration of ES factors across its *entire* investment portfolio. (The U.K. Environment Agency Pension Fund was another.) This was accomplished in a rather ingenious way: in addition to creating specialized stand-alone SI mandates, FRR staff made it clear to those who sought to manage its assets that although it did not expect them to be ES experts on day 1, they *were* absolutely expected to acquire "ES literacy" and research capabilities over time as an explicit condition of retaining mandates and obtaining any future ones. This too, in my experience, is extremely rare among institutional asset owners.

In 2005 the FRR adopted an explicit statement of responsible investment principles. While perhaps unremarkable at first blush, the principles too are very "French," with their strong emphasis on employment, workers' rights, and social issues:

- Respect for international law and basic workers' rights.
- Job development through better management of human resources.
- Corporate environmental responsibility.
- Respect for consumers and fair trade practices in local markets.
- Promotion of best corporate governance principles and practice.

To date, the actual execution of the FRR's sustainable investment strategy has consisted of the following:

- Drafting and publishing a detailed set of ES performance criteria.[13]
- Instituting an active program of proxy voting and shareholder engagement.
- Participating actively in collaborative investor initiatives including the Carbon Disclosure Project, the UN Principles for Responsible Investment, and the UN Global Compact.
- Tendering five dedicated SI mandates to external money managers, with a combined value of approximately EUR 700 million. World-class sustainability investment managers AGF, Dexia, Morley, Pictet, and Sarasin were hired under that program.
- Promoting closer integration of ES research across its entire EUR 6 billion European equities portfolio.
- Commissioning external reviews assessing both its Eurozone and global equity portfolios to assess both their environmental footprint and their conformity to international norms such as the Global Compact.
- Creating a dedicated "responsible investment" committee of the Supervisory Board in 2008.

As of mid-2008 the two key drivers of ES integration at the FRR remain Antoine de Salins, a key member of the three-person Executive Board and chair of the asset manager selection committee, and Nada Villermain-Lécolier, a bright and committed investment director. They and their colleagues have accomplished an impressive amount in a remarkably short period of time, and they look set to continue.

Sweden's MISTRA

MISTRA, the Swedish Foundation for Strategic Environmental Research, is a textbook example—albeit a regrettably *rare* one—of a strategic, long-term, foundation investor that both recognizes *and* exploits the power of its capital to reinforce and enhance its program mission. Its approach stands in sharp contrast to North American endowments and foundations such as the Nature Conservancy and the Gates, Ford, and Rockefeller foundations.

MISTRA was established in 1993 by the Swedish Foundations Act, which states the following:

- The aim of the foundation is to support research of strategic importance for a good living environment.
- The foundation shall promote the development of robust research environments of the highest international class that will have a positive impact on Sweden's future competitiveness. The research shall play a significant role in solving major environmental problems and contribute to the development of a sustainable society. Opportunities for achieving industrial applications shall be taken advantage of.

These are noble words and aspirations indeed. But most environmentally oriented foundations and nongovernmental organizations (NGOs) produce similar rhetoric. What sets MISTRA apart is the extent to which it actually "walks the talk" and puts its money where its mouth is. MISTRA is perhaps the only environmental foundation in the world to have completely aligned its investment strategy with its mission.

Founded with initial capital of $393 million, MISTRA's endowment now stands at over $570 million, despite distributing approximately $345 million in grants over that period, with $30 million in 2006 alone. Since 2005 the Foundation's Swedish fixed-income securities, valued at almost $205 million, and its entire Swedish and European share portfolios have been subject to positive environmental and ethical screening. In the United States, another $67 million has been managed on a negative screening basis.

According to the foundation's investment policy, "MISTRA's approach to asset management seeks to serve as a model for efforts to secure sustainable development." Furthermore, "the management of MISTRA's assets will promote sustainable development when investments are made in companies which (i) can be expected to provide high value growth and at the same time (ii) actively comply with international social conventions and (iii) consciously seek to work proactively with regard to global environmental issues such as climate, chemicals, and protection of particularly vulnerable ecosystems."

As early as 1995 MISTRA began to consider the possibilities of sustainability investment under the direction of Göran Persson, MISTRA's first managing director. In 1998 Swedish journalists examined the investments of public foundations, and the issue immediately acquired an additional dimension: organizational reputational risk. This led to the adoption of negative screens to eliminate tobacco stocks. However, it wasn't until 2000 when MISTRA staff brought the issue back to the boardroom table that things really took off. By then a new board was in place that was more open to such ideas, yet still primarily concerned with reputational risk. They had one overriding concern: would they lose money?

In early 2001 MISTRA decided to investigate the impact on financial performance of including environmental and social criteria in its investments. The Foundation commissioned an external appraisal of the economic implications of shifting its portfolio into "socially responsible" investments. The report concluded that "although existing literature is limited, it nevertheless indicates that the financial returns and risk levels are not affected negatively by adding SRI-criteria." MISTRA commissioned additional research and began its progression to where its policy stands today:

> Our investment policy makes clear our determination to set a
> good example in terms of working towards sustainable develop-
> ment. As an owner of capital, we take a long-term view. It isn't
> just a matter of cleaning up our own backyard—we want to work
> with others to ensure that what we do has a greater impact.

When asked in 2002 why the foundation was progressing down this path, Eva Thörnelöf, MISTRA's deputy director for asset management and administration, said simply:

> since we support environmental research for sustainability, our
> board decided last year that we should have a vision that our
> assets should work in the same direction.

In April 2007, MISTRA announced that it had met its goal of having 100 percent of its assets invested on the basis of sustainability criteria. According to Märtha Josefsson, who chairs MISTRA's Committee for Asset Management, "we now feel fairly confident that sustainable investments actually provide a better financial return." According to MISTRA, in the 2 years since it has entrusted its capital to managers who apply sustainability criteria (State Street Global Advisors, Generation Investment Management, and Robur), all of the investments in question have outperformed their goals. By contrast, interestingly, several of their *traditional* managers failed to meet their benchmarks and have actually been dropped!

MISTRA initially chose to work with negative screening criteria based on UN resolutions and international agreements signed by the

Swedish government. Since then, however, their model has evolved into putting an emphasis on investing in "best in class" companies. Each of MISTRA's asset managers has different methodologies and degree of environmental and ethical information in their mandates, but all are closely monitored by MISTRA to ensure conformity with its overall sustainability objectives. MISTRA closely follows the work of the external managers in order to learn more about the processes and also influence the future asset management.

But what is the actual *impact* of such an investment policy based on sustainability criteria? MISTRA is setting out to answer that question with one of its funded programs, Sustainable Investment, a SEK 42 million program housed at the Göteborg School of Economics. This program is examining both the conceptual and empirical case for sustainable investment and its relative profitability. The research is also seeking to understand how sustainable investment could best be promoted within an investment organization and, finally, incorporated among its internal investment criteria. The program involves applied research into the value chain of financial markets, covering areas such as equity valuation, the behavior of financial analysts and other players, and portfolio selection based on sustainability criteria. Currently, MISTRA funds 20 major research initiatives, with average time spans of between 6 and 8 years—an unusually patient and long-term approach.

MISTRA clearly believes that "sustainable development is dependent on a critical mass of market players taking a long-term view" and that "short-term return requirements must not be allowed to stand in the way of long-term development." MISTRA, like the other organizations we profile in this chapter, wants to be a leader in creating that critical mass, and has already made an impressive contribution.

Australia's VicSuper

Today, Australia is one of the unquestioned leaders in sustainable investment. My own suspicion is that this is directly linked to the unusually high level of awareness and concern in that country about the "mother of all" sustainability issues—climate change. There is nothing like an unprecedented 10-year drought to focus the mind on climate change! Whatever the cause, Australia is a world leader in this space today. Indeed, the very first official action taken by the new Rudd government in 2008 was to sign the Kyoto Protocol, which had languished under its predecessors. And within Australia, the pioneer and leader among the investors has been the principal pension fund in the State of Victoria—VicSuper.

Founded in 1994, VicSuper's leaders believe that

> companies that display superior standards of corporate governance through the integration of social, environmental and economic principles into all decision support systems are more likely to increase their long-term shareowner value through better management of risks and opportunities.

As is so often the case in this business, VicSuper's leadership in this space was due in large part to the convictions, skills, and advocacy of a single individual. In this case that individual was the fund's dynamic and charismatic chief executive Bob Welsh. Not entirely coincidentally, one of Welsh's favorite hobbies happens to be "bush-walking"—a singularly Australian pastime that involves hiking, often alone and often for days at a time, in pristine, isolated, and frequently dangerous back country and wilderness. In speaking with Welsh, I get the unmistakable impression that his hobby has imbued him with two attributes critical to the success of his sustainability initiatives at work—an acute appreciation for nature and wilderness, and a top-notch set of survival skills necessary for working alone in a harsh and dangerous environment.

In November 2001, VicSuper became the first Australian pension fund to create a specific allocation to sustainability funds. Fully 10 percent of its listed equity portfolios' assets were invested in large Australian and international companies rated as having the best sustainability business strategies in their industry sectors. The majority of the fund's $580 million in sustainable investments is managed by Vanguard Investments in two specialized Sustainable Asset Management (SAM) funds: SAM Sustainability Leaders Australia Fund and its Sustainability Leaders International Fund.[14] In addition, the fund holds an additional $66 million in a Generation Investment Management fund with a concentrated global portfolio of 30 to 50 companies that Generation considers to be sustainability leaders and therefore long-term financial outperformers.

In the private equity space, VicSuper has committed 10 percent of its international allocation to early-stage and expansion stage companies through the Emerald Technology Ventures Sustainability Fund, a fund devoted to companies "whose products or services contribute towards and/or assist in using resources more efficiently, and reduce the ecological impact of economic development." VicSuper has also committed $46 million to Australian private equity through Cleantech Ventures' Cleantech Australia Fund and Starfish Ventures' Cleantech Companion Fund. In addition, VicSuper works with its external real estate asset managers such as Colonial First State, Investa Property Group, and Eureka to improve the energy efficiency and sustainability performance of its real estate portfolios.

VicSuper has not just taken the issue of sustainability into account in its investments—it is also integrating it into its own daily operations. The fund's headquarters office building in Melbourne has adopted strict energy conservation measures and is now 100 percent powered by renewable energy. Its fleet of cars are hybrids, it uses only recycled paper, and it involves staff actively in community and environmental programs. VicSuper has also commissioned an external audit of the "carbon footprint" of its equity investments and is working on reducing that footprint.

VicSuper is also a leader in establishing new industry standards for *communicating* about its sustainability performance and challenges; it was the first superannuation or pension fund in the world to release its own sustainability report, and is one of only 25 financial institutions worldwide to have done so. VicSuper is also active on the collective advocacy front; it is a member of both the Australian Investor Group on Climate Change and the Carbon Disclosure Project, and is a signatory to the UN PRI.

All of this pioneering work has not gone unnoticed; VicSuper has won over half a dozen awards for its sustainability work. In 2003 it won both the Banksia Environmental Award for Business Environmental Responsibility and Leadership and one for Leadership in Socially Responsible Investment. In 2007 Bob Welsh won the UNEP FI Carbon Leadership Recognition for Executives in Financial Markets award for his contribution within the pension funds sector. In 2007 Ethical Investor Australia also presented VicSuper with the "Sustainable Super Fund of the Year" award.

VicSuper has been a real leader and catalyst in introducing both the philosophy and practice of sustainability investing to Australia. We would judge that its catalytic work is now done; Australia is arguably the most active and dynamic market for sustainable investment solutions in the entire world today.

The Forgotten Players: Corporate Pension Funds

One potentially major set of players in the Sustainable Investment Revolution has, for the most part, been conspicuous by its absence—the *cor-*

porate pension funds. With only a handful of exceptions—virtually none of them, notably, in the United States—corporate funds have avoided sustainable investment like the plague. Given the arguments and evidence presented throughout this book, this is somewhat difficult to fathom. Perhaps more to the point, however, is the enormous waste of both financial and sustainability impact: in the United States alone corporate pension plans have combined assets of roughly $4 *trillion;* in the U.K. they represent an additional $1.8 trillion and in Asia Pacific some $2 trillion.[15] That's an awful lot of economic firepower that is essentially ignoring altogether at least the *possibility* of earning better risk-adjusted returns, not to mention having a positive environmental and/or social impact.

Not all is bleak, however; after an exhaustive worldwide search, we have managed to unearth at least a few corporate pension funds that *have* enhanced the Sustainable Investment Revolution.

In Britain, the company pension fund for British Telecom (BT) is a conspicuous exception to the general role. The only corporate pension fund to receive a "Platinum" rating in an October 2007 report on Sustainable Pensions by the U.K. Social Investment Forum, the British Telecom Pension Scheme (BTPS) has made social, ethical, environmental, and governance issues a centerpiece of both its investment and engagement activities.

The BTPS's responsible investment policy is implemented through aggressively exercising its shareholder voting rights, direct engagement with companies to encourage better performance, investing its assets in specialist sustainability mandates, and participation in collaborative initiatives, such as the EAI and the UN PRI, of which it is a founder member and provides the founding and current chairman in Donald MacDonald, a BTPS Trustee.

A pension plan with over 350,000 members and assets worth over $80 billion, BTPS took a bold and innovative step in 1990. It created Hermes Pensions Management Limited, a wholly owned subsidiary, to manage its assets and provide other services to its funds and to others as well. As of January 2008, the Hermes Group itself managed directly 59.4 percent of the Scheme's total investments.

In July 2004 Hermes went one step further and created a new division, Hermes Equity Ownership Services (HEOS). Led by Colin Melvin, HEOS assists clients with voting at general meetings at over 4000 companies worldwide, and represents their interests in direct engagements with the companies in which they invest on strategic, environmental, social, and governance matters. With a team of 20, Hermes now has one of the largest and most highly regarded company "engagement" teams in the world. According to BTPS, Hermes' approach is to focus on those issues that are likely to have a significant impact on shareholder value, thereby connecting the Scheme's interests as a long-term investor with the sustainability of its portfolio companies' activities.

Hermes has also been a pioneer and global leader in "activist investing." The logic behind activist investing is both straightforward and compelling: invest in undervalued companies in which governance and management problems are believed to have been critical impediments to performance and growth, use your leverage as an owner to push executives and board directors of the companies to make governance changes— including ES ones—and hope that those interventions will improve the performance and share prices of the companies.

Where Hermes believes that those circumstances apply, it may make an investment in the company through whichever of its activist "Focus Funds" is most appropriate. Hermes has three in-house Focus Funds—for U.K. large companies, for continental European companies, and for U.K. smaller companies—as well as a Japanese fund, the Nissay Hermes Stewardship Fund, launched in 2005 in partnership with Nissay Asset Management Corporation.

The investment logic certainly seems to work well enough; under the leadership of Peter Butler and David Pitt-Watson, the Hermes funds have performed well. The original U.K. Focus Fund has outperformed the FTSE All Share Total Return Index by 3.1 percent on an annualized basis (net of fees) since its inception in 1998 (to 30 June 2006). Similarly, since its inception in 2002, the European Focus Fund has outperformed its benchmark by 3.9 percent on an annualized basis (net of fees) (to 30 June 2006).

Hermes, which now manages in excess of $5 billion in this area, is a leader in shareholder engagement, investing on behalf of over 40 institutional investors from 10 countries now investing alongside BTPS in these funds. Hermes has estimated that significant incremental value— several tens of millions of pounds—has been added to the value of the Scheme's investment in such companies above and beyond what might have been expected if the companies had merely performed in line with their sector peers.

Colin Hartridge-Price, Secretary and Chief Pensions Officer for the BTPS, captures the scheme's investment logic nicely:

> BTPS invests for the long-term and believes that monitoring and improving ESG issues is in the long-term interest of investors and society as a whole.

If only more company pension funds would adopt even a *fraction* of British Telecom's approach!

Each of the organizations profiled in this chapter has made remarkable strides in advancing the Sustainable Investment Revolution. Perhaps their greatest contribution, however, will lie in their "demonstration effect" on other more timorous asset owners, both in their home markets and internationally. They have demonstrated that it *can* be done and that it *is* being done. The only remaining question is this: What's holding back the *other* 95+ percent of investors?

In Chapter 10 we shift gears from looking at the organizations that own the capital to those that help them actually invest it. As a group, these service providers are an absolutely critical link in the investment value chain. Historically, as we saw in Chapter 2, the asset managers, consultants, and other advisors have generally acted as a *retardant* to the advance of the Sustainable Investment Revolution. The organizations we shall profile in Chapter 10, however, are radically different: they have *accelerated* its progress and will be indispensable to its future.

Chapter 10

The Game-Changers

Part III: The Service Providers

We believe that sustainability performance is a good overall proxy for the management quality of companies relative to their peers and, as such, provides insight into their ability to succeed on a sustainable basis.

—ANTHONY LING, MANAGING DIRECTOR, GOLDMAN SACHS

In Chapter 9 we reviewed some of the impressive leadership displayed by individual institutional owners of capital on three continents. In the world of institutional investment, however, very little actually happens without the input and guidance of a whole cadre of advisors—pension fund consultants, research providers, strategy consultancies, and, perhaps most important of all, money managers (see Chapter 1 for a refresher on the investment management value chain). Although for the most part the consultants and money managers have been at best reluctant participants in the Sustainable Investment Revolution—and quite belated ones at that, there *have* been a number of pioneering organizations that have done an enormous amount to advance it. Without their contributions it is virtually certain that today's "tipping point" conditions for sustainable investment could not have been reached. We shall profile a number of these pioneering contributions in this chapter.

The Money Managers

Sustainable Asset Management (SAM)—Switzerland

Sustainable Asset Management, or the SAM Group, was founded in Zurich in 1995 by Reto Ringger, who had previously worked at "brand name" mainstream Swiss financial institutions such as Bank Vontobel, Bank Sarasin, and Swiss Re (that we profiled in Chapter 7).

SAM was the first international asset manager dedicated solely to sustainability-enhanced strategies and as such was a true pioneer. Today it is an autonomous subsidiary of the major Netherlands-based investment management firm Robeco Group (with a 64 percent ownership stake), which is in turn wholly owned by the financial services group Rabobank. With 75 employees and clients that include institutional investors such as banks, insurance companies, pension funds, foundations, as well as private clients, SAM is one of a tiny handful of "pure play" asset management companies specializing in sustainable investment strategies.

SAM's core investment thesis is almost identical to that propounded throughout this book:

- Sustainability factors are becoming increasingly important to the long-term competitiveness and profitability of companies in virtually every industry sector.
- Companies that excel in managing the risks and capturing the opportunities created by global sustainability trends are quite likely to be better managed and therefore more financially successful, at least over the long term.
- In general, sustainability performance has historically been under-recognized by the market, so identifying top performers can give investors a major advantage as this market recognition begins to increase.

SAM is perhaps best known for launching the Dow Jones Sustainability Index (DJSI) in 1999 in partnership with Dow Jones Indexes. The DJSI, which was the first major global index tracking the financial performance of the leading sustainability-driven companies worldwide, retains an extremely high profile in the marketplace to this day. Currently 60 DJSI licenses are held by asset managers in 15 countries. They are used to manage a variety of financial products, including active and passive funds, structured products, and segregated accounts. In total, these licensees collectively manage over $5 billion based on the DJSI today. Now *that's* mobilizing capital!

The DJSI indexes are based on company responses to a detailed, proprietary SAM questionnaire. The company also uses external documents, as well as personal contacts between the analysts and companies, to complete its analysis. PricewaterhouseCoopers has been retained to ensure that the corporate sustainability assessments are completed in accordance with the defined procedures and to provide an assurance report. Companies are ranked within their industry groups and selected for the Indexes if they are among the sustainability leaders in their respective industry sectors. The flagship DJSI global index is composed of the top 10 percent of responding companies from the 2500 companies in the Dow Jones Global Index.

The DJSI family now includes World, European, and North American indexes as well as smaller funds covering the largest 40 in each. Of the three major indexes each in turn has another version that excludes stocks involved with controversial activities such as tobacco and alcohol. More recently, the company has also launched the Dow Jones Islamic Market Sustainability Index for investors who want to apply stringent Islamic screens in addition to sustainability criteria.[1]

SAM currently offers 12 investment products based on these indexes, as well as specialized private equity funds focusing on specific sustainability factors. One is a "smart energy" fund focusing on new technologies; a second is a "sustainable water" fund based on the upside potential of companies able to take advantage of trends in the market, including greater demand for water distribution and management, advanced water treatment, demand-side efficiency, and water and nutrition. A third is a "smart materials" fund focused on the more efficient use of materials, recycling and disposal, and innovative materials and technologies.

In addition to its own direct pioneering contributions, SAM has also contributed a number of "alumni" who have gone on to make significant contributions to the Sustainable Investment Revolution elsewhere. Alois Flatz, SAM's original head of research, is today a managing director at Zouk Ventures, a London-based cleantech private equity firm. Ivo Knoepfel, his successor as research head, had joined from Swiss Re, where he was head of corporate environmental management, with a special focus on climate change. After leaving SAM, Knoepfel founded the small but influential Swiss consultancy onValues, which, among many other things, is the principal advisor to the Enhanced Analytics Initiative. The third distinguished alumnus was Knoepfel's successor as head of research at SAM, Colin le Duc. le Duc was a cofounder and head of sustainability research at Generation Investment Management, an innovative firm that is discussed next.

All in all, both in its own right and as an incubator and developer of talent for other firms, SAM can rightly be regarded as one of—if not *the*—founding father of the Sustainable Investment Revolution on the asset management side.

Generation Investment Management

Investing in high-quality businesses, with highly competent and well-motivated management teams, at the right price, and with a long-term horizon is a philosophy adhered to by many of the investment greats—including the "father" of fundamental securities analysis himself, Benjamin Graham. One of today's most interesting—and increasingly influential—exemplars of this approach is the London-based sustainable investment management boutique Generation Investment Management. The two highest profile founders of Generation were Nobel Prize (*and* Academy Award) winner and former U.S. Vice President Al Gore and former Goldman Sachs Asset Management CEO David Blood. (The two last names, inevitably, caused journalistic wags to dub the firm "Blood and Gore"—much to the amusement of both principals.)

On the face of it, the two seemed an odd couple: Gore is a passionate long-time environmental crusader and Blood is the hard-nosed CEO of the asset management arm of the profit-seeking missile that is Goldman Sachs. But that really is the whole *point:* sustainable investing, properly conceived, is *all about* integrating the best of what had previously been two disciplinary solitudes: hard-headed investment analysis on the one hand and a broader, deeper understanding of global environmental and social megatrends on the other. Generation is, at this moment, arguably the quintessential practitioner of the investment philosophies proposed in this book. And they *do* seem to work. Generation has just passed the magic three-year track record milestone—and with a top-decile financial performance.

Generation, created in 2004, was, like many worthwhile innovations, the product of a serendipitous confluence of both events and interpersonal networks. At that time Al Gore was looking around for an asset management company in which to invest, one that shared his deep convictions about both the environment and its eminent compatibility with profitable business enterprise. Through a mutual friend he was introduced to David Blood at Goldman Sachs, who had begun to be intrigued by his colleague Mark Ferguson's frequent musings about the relevancy of sustainability factors to investment results. Ferguson was at the time cohead of European equities research and a global portfolio manager at Goldman Sachs. After several rounds of conversations, Blood and Gore reached the same conclusion: the best solution to what they were both looking for was to build their *own* asset management company—from scratch. And thus Generation was born.

There were six founding partners: Blood, Gore, Ferguson, and three others. One was Peter Harris, former global operations chief at GSAM. Another was Peter Knight, a lawyer, Gore's long-time chief-of-staff and the campaign manager for Bill Clinton's successful reelection as President of the United States in 1996. The key *sustainability* piece of the puzzle, however, was cofounder Colin le Duc. As we have just seen, le Duc, who had previously been head of research at SAM in Zurich, was deeply knowledgeable about both sustainability issues and how to research them. He would be the head of sustainability research for the new firm.

Today, Generation is on course to having $5 billion under management in its flagship fund—a concentrated portfolio of 30–40 "high-conviction" stocks judged to be long-term winners on *both* sustainability and financial grounds. The firm's client list includes some of the world's most prestigious and sophisticated institutional investors, and there is even a waiting list!

At the outset, Generation had one enormous advantage denied to most less prominent start-ups: the founders could—and did—pony up enough cash to allow the new firm to attract top talent and exist comfortably for several years without worrying about mundane trappings of the asset management business such as clients, assets to manage, or revenues! This enabled it to build the kinds of investment products its founders actually *wanted* to build. The normal client-driven compromises were not a factor; nor was the need to chase short-term returns while sacrificing their longer-term vision or investment strategy. In the event, the firm has attracted all three in spades: clients, assets, and revenues.

The one conventional Wall Street nostrum with which Generation does concur is that management quality is the principal determinant of the financial performance of companies. For Generation, a high-quality management team has a culture of integrity, a focus on the long term, and a strategic appreciation of how major global megatrends are likely to affect its business. As we have argued throughout this book, Generation believes that companies capable of managing environmental and social (ES) challenges better than their competitors are quite likely to be better managed companies overall.

One example of this logical link between sustainability factors and the quality of company management often cited publicly by David Blood was Generation's investment in T. Rowe Price, an American fund-management group. Generation's decision to invest was significantly affected by Blood's convictions about the high level of personal integrity of the company's executives and their success in motivating the staff to adhere to those same high standards. Blood reasoned that this "soft" attribute would enable T. Rowe Price to avoid the types of mutual fund scandals and other landmines that have plagued other companies in the industry. Blood's reasoning proved to be spot on, and so far T. Rowe has one of the most exemplary records in the industry in this regard. Avoiding such mishaps has, in turn, enabled the company to increase its market share by gaining the trust of its clients, avoiding costly fines and legal proceedings, and ultimately boosting its shareholder returns—as well as Generation's own in the bargain.

In the competitive and highly lucrative world of managing money, Generation has successfully differentiated itself from the rest of the pack by, as Gore puts it, "integrating rigorous, traditional fundamental equity analysis with sustainability research to create a new approach to long-term investing."

Generation's next forays promise to be equally rewarding—and sustainability driven. The firm is now in the early stages of leveraging its investment philosophy and knowledge of macro sustainability trends into the private equity (unlisted, privately held companies) space. In November 2007, it announced that it has teamed up with Kleiner Perkins Caufield & Byers—arguably the most highly regarded private equity firm in the United States, if not in the entire world. Kleiner Perkins' managing partner and private equity demigod John Doerr has famously pronounced the environment to be the single greatest economic opportunity of the twenty-first century. He will get no argument on that from Al Gore, who recently became a partner in Doerr's firm.

Most recently, in May 2008, Generation announced that it was launching its second product—a "Climate Solutions" fund. As the name implies, the fund will focus on (typically smaller, early-stage) companies poised to capitalize on their ability to provide solutions to the global climate challenge. The new fund will focus on early-stage companies, both publicly traded and privately held, in areas such as renewable energy, cleaner fossil energy, energy-efficient buildings and manufacturing facilities, and the carbon markets. Clearly there will be both financial and intellectual synergy between Generation's new fund and its partnership with Kleiner Perkins.

Climate Change Capital[2]

When a cement factory in China is provided with the technology to reduce its CO_2 emissions and does so, it is awarded carbon credits that can be sold to other companies that have yet to reduce their own carbon emissions.[3] This is the market-based approach that exists to take pollutants out of the air as part of a so-called "cap-and-trade" mechanism. As we have seen earlier, the basis of such a system is this: overall emission limits are set by government, and companies that can reduce their emissions below these limits are given (or sometimes sold) "carbon credits" by the public regulatory authorities. Those credits can then in turn be sold to companies anticipating difficulties in meeting their own targets or for whom the cost of the credits would be less than the capital and other costs of achieving the reductions directly themselves.

The objective of such systems is straightforward—they attempt to deliver the biggest emissions reductions "bang for the buck." They are intended to direct financial and intellectual resources to the interventions that promise the greatest emission reductions at the lowest cost, that is, with the greatest economic efficiency. Such "cap-and-trade" systems have already proved extremely effective in reducing acid rain-causing sulfur and nitrogen dioxide emissions in the United States. Essentially, they put a price on what had previously been a "free good" or externality—the ability to emit pollutants into the atmosphere without limit. In economic theory (and, to a considerable extent, also in practice) this creates a new scarcity value as well as a financial incentive to reduce those emissions.

This market mechanism is now being applied to the even more formidable challenge of climate change. This time, instead of SO_2 and NO_2, the pollutants being addressed are the greenhouse gases responsible for climate change. At present, by far the most highly evolved "carbon market" is the one created by the European Union called the European Trading System, or ETS. The EU ETS has effectively converted greenhouse gases into a commodity and, equally important, created the supply and demand machinery with which to create a *price* for it. The EU ETS in essence creates penalties for excessive carbon emissions and corresponding financial incentives for "carbon efficiency" and reductions.

The ETS has also provided the launching pad and "home court" for one of the most innovative drivers of the Sustainable Investment Revolution—Climate Change Capital (CCC). CCC is a London-based niche investment and merchant bank specializing in capitalizing upon the commercial opportunities created by this incipient "commoditization" of carbon. It advises and invests in companies that recognize that combating global warming is both a necessity and an economic opportunity. CCC's activities also include investment management and financing emission reductions. With over $1.6 billion under management today, CCC has already had a significant impact in the marketplace.

Founded in 2005, CCC currently employs over 130 people from a wide variety of backgrounds including international lawyers, commodity traders, corporate financiers, international policy experts, carbon finance experts, investment advisors, and fund managers. Members of the team have worked for organizations as diverse as major investment banks, specialist merchant banks, private equity funds, The World Bank, international energy companies, governments, and nongovernmental organizations (NGOs). CCC is today arguably the greatest single repository of "carbon finance" knowledge, expertise, and experience in the world.

Four of the key founders and driving forces of CCC were James Cameron, Gareth Hughes, Mark Woodall, and Tony White. Cameron, a British/Australian environmental lawyer, was and remains a towering figure in carbon finance. (Towering in *both* senses of the term: Cameron is well above average in height!) He had founded and led the world's first climate change legal practice at Baker & Mackenzie, one of the largest law firms in the world. Perhaps even more important, he had been intimately involved in negotiating the landmark Kyoto Protocol as a senior advisor to a group of small island states that were (understandably) concerned about the climate-driven rise in sea levels. A former professor of environmental law, he also serves today as chairman of the Carbon Disclosure Project, which we discussed in Chapter 8. Hughes, an Englishman, left the major insurance broker Marsh and McLennan to cofound CCC. At Marsh, he had been a managing director, with a special focus on the energy sector. Woodall, another Englishman, came to CCC from Impax Capital, a niche investment bank focused on environmental technology companies that he had helped create in 1993. White had been managing director and head of the European utilities sector teams at two major investment banks: Kleinwort Benson and Citigroup. Together, they made a formidable team, and have built a game-changing, world-class company in the astonishingly short space of only 3 years.

CCC has advised and raised capital for numerous low-carbon projects, including destroying industrial gases in India and China, financing renewable energy installations in the United Kingdom, facilitating waste-to-energy projects in China and Hungary, and advising on acquisition and divestiture strategies for private equity funds and carbon-intensive industries in Europe. CCC also has a EUR 200 million private equity fund (CPE) that targets the high-growth clean technology areas of clean power, clean transport, energy efficiency, waste recovery, and water across Europe. CPE, which invests its funds in expansion and later-stage companies, is one of the largest vehicles of its kind in Europe. It has already attracted investment from "A-list" outfits, including HSBC, Alliance Trust, and Harcourt.

Carbon funds are not unlike traditional investment funds: they invest in projects to generate returns. The major difference is that the return a carbon fund seeks is the generation of carbon credits. By 2007 (according to New Carbon Finance, a specialist research company), carbon funds worth $11.8 billion had been raised. CCC raised $130 million for its first carbon fund launched in July 2005. The company's second fund launched only a year later was over 10 times its size, at roughly $1.5 billion. Apart from the tremendous growth and size of such a fund, what is even more interesting is the change in the composition of the investors attracted to it. According to Tony White, all of the money for the first fund came from hedge funds, which tend to like risk and short-term speculative investments. However, by the time the second fund was established, more cautious investors with a longer time horizon, such as pension funds and banks, were among those participating. Two of the largest investors in CCC's second carbon fund were two of the most sophisticated—*and* sustainability-savvy—institutional investors around: APG and PGGM from the Netherlands (both were discussed briefly in Chapter 9). Their participation in the CCC carbon fund was a *huge* vote of confidence that conferred virtually instantaneous credibility on both CCC itself and the potential of the broader carbon finance market.

A case that nicely illustrates the potential financial margins and tremendous profits that can be realized in the carbon market is provided by one of the most potent greenhouse gases, HFC-23. HFC-23's global-warming effect is, ton for ton, close to 12,000 times greater than that of carbon dioxide! Although HFC-23 is today only rarely found in the developed world, it is still common in many emerging markets, particularly China. Although harmful, HFC-23 is relatively inexpensive to get rid of, with a disposal cost of less than EUR 1 for the equivalent of 1 ton of carbon dioxide. China, the major producer of most of the world's HFC-23, is also the one benefiting most from its disposal. Credits obtained via the disposal of HFC-23 have been sold on the market for up to EUR 11. As a result of such attractive margins, several Chinese factories have found that their most damaging by-product, HFC-23, has actually become more valuable than their primary output!

In 2008 CCC began to diversify its portfolio of activities substantially. In addition to its core offerings of carbon credit funds and clean tech venture capital, it has added two additional arrows to its quiver. It began to leverage its specialized knowledge and contacts into the publicly traded markets for the first time by creating a long/short public equities fund. CCC also began a major push into the real estate sector. As a contributor of some 30–40 percent of total worldwide greenhouse gas emissions, the sector was a logical target for CCC's core competence: solving climate-related environmental problems and making money in the bargain. As CCC's Chief Executive Mark Woodall aptly put it:

> The value of commercial property will increasingly be driven by sustainability and climate change issues. The move to create low-carbon buildings will accelerate, and both occupiers and investors will drive this shift, motivated by the desire to reduce energy costs, corporate social responsibility, brand-value, and the need to future-proof their properties.[4]

In May 2008 CCC was rewarded with yet another vote of confidence from the marketplace. It raised over $110 million in fresh equity capital from four major institutional investors. Both the stature and geographic diversity of the new investors—Alliance Trust and the University Super-annuation Scheme from the U.K., SNS Real from the Netherlands, and Japan's Mitsui & Co.—augur extremely well for both CCC's future as a company and the carbon markets in general.

The Advisors

SustainAbility

London-based SustainAbility is perhaps the most venerable of the thought-leading advisory firms that have paved the way for the Sustainable Investment Revolution. The firm SustainAbility is a bit of an oddity in our pantheon of game-changing service providers: neither asset manager nor direct advisor, it is instead a hybrid of a dynamic strategy consultancy, think-tank, and campaigning organization. Established in the earliest days of the Sustainability Revolution in 1987, SustainAbility advises clients in all three sectors: corporates, governments, and NGOs. A leader in sustainability research, the company has contributed the terms and concepts "Green Consumer," "People, Planet, Profit," and the regularly used phrase "Triple Bottom Line" to the sustainability discourse. It has tackled issues from HIV/AIDs to microfinance, the business case for sustainability, and what's next for SRI funds. It has been honored by *Fast Company Magazine* and Ethisphere, and its cofounder and CEO John Elkington was named one of the 100 most influential people in *Business Ethics* (2007).

Elkington, described by *BusinessWeek* in 2004 as "a dean of the corporate-responsibility movement for three decades," cofounded SustainAbility in 1986 after the foundation he was working with at the time, Earthlife, ran into a series of financial troubles. His team had a few projects underway at the time and, with the failing of Earthlife, Elkington was faced with the choice of abandoning the projects altogether or carrying them forward. SustainAbility was duly created and moved them forward. Involved in sustainability since 1961, when at age 11 he raised pocket money from schoolboys for the recently founded WWF, Elkington also founded Environmental Data Services in 1978 and John Elkington Associates in 1983, which he rolled into SustainAbility in 1989.

In 1989 SustainAbility began work on *The Environmental Audit* report with WWF, which was instrumental in spurring rapid growth in both the quantity and quality of company environmental reporting and auditing. In 1994 it launched its first survey of company reporting with UNEP and helped establish its "Engaging Stakeholders" program. In 2000 it published its first of four biannual Global Environmental Reporters benchmarking surveys. In 2004 SustainAbility published *Values for Money* with the MISTRA Foundation, the leading foundation practicing SRI, looking at the future of SRI funds and their global advisors and re-searchers. In 2006 SustainAbility began an innovative 3-year partnership project with the Skoll Foundation, looking at social entrepreneurship and its relevance to mainstream business. Over the past 20 years Sustain-Ability has published over 50 reports. Collectively, they have changed the way we think about business and sustainability, and they have done a great deal to elevate sustainability to a more visible and urgent part of the corporate agenda.

SustainAbility's work is divided into two major divisions: its con-sultancy and its think-tank. Its consultancy offers consulting services on corporate reporting, stakeholder engagement, strategy development, corporate governance, and nonfinancial risk management and trend analysis, among others. Its list of past and current clients reads like a who's-who of companies practicing strong environmental, social, and corporate governance (ESG) management: ABN-AMRO, BASF, Baxter Healthcare, Ben & Jerry's, MISTRA, Nike, Novo Nordisk, Starbucks, and Toyota. SustainAbility was also instrumental in helping Royal Dutch Shell improve both its practices and its reputation for sustainability after major stakeholder relations challenges created by the Brent Spar North Sea oil platform incident as well as its human rights problems in Nigeria. SustainAbility has also worked with leading NGOs such as UNEP, the UN Global Compact, Greenpeace, and the World Resources Institute.

As a think-tank, SustainAbility has been a part of some of the most significant independent and agenda-shaping reports in the field of sus-tainable business. It has been a tireless advocate of improved corporate reporting on sustainability issues. Without the improvements that Sus-tainAbility has been instrumental in catalyzing, investors today would be experiencing much more difficulty in accessing the information and research analysis that they need to invest sustainably. In particular, on the investment side, the company has written three main reports: *A Re-sponsible Investment (2000), Screening of Screening Companies (2001),* and *Values for Money: Reviewing the Quality of SRI Research (2006).*

For most of its life, SustainAbility's driving force and public face was the remarkable John Elkington. In recent years, in a reflection of his changing role in the firm, he changed his title from "Chairman and Chief Executive" to the apt "Chief Entrepreneur." He has published no fewer than 17 books, the most recent of which is the coauthored *The Power of Unreasonable People* (Harvard Business School Press, 2008).

In a reflection on its 20 years in existence, SustainAbility says that

> We are an integrated organization, for profit but not solely profit-driven, combining consulting, research and advocacy. Our Articles of Association specify that we pursue value right across the triple bottom line. As a result, many companies think of us as an NGO, while many NGOs think of us as a company: in a sense, both are right.

Going forward, Elkington intends to keep his hand in SustainAbility; however, he has also started a new venture called Volans Ventures ("volans" is the Latin word for "flying"). Still in its early days, Volans is intended to be something of an incubator and accelerator for new socially and environmentally beneficial companies, organizations, and projects. With typical Elkingtonian ambition, Volans is intended to be "an increasingly powerful magnet for talent, a world-class incubator of new thinking and initiatives, and a strongly preferred partner for people and organizations committed to deep-running political, economic, social, and environmental change." Whew! Worthy objectives all, and don't bet against the man.

Whatever the impact of his newest venture will turn out to be, Elkington and his colleagues at SustainAbility can take justifiable pride in building and growing a company that has truly been one of the handmaidens of the Sustainable Investment Revolution.

Mercer Investment Consultants

We have argued previously that investment and pension fund consultants have done more than any other single actor in the investment "food chain" to *retard* the growth of sustainable investing. As an industry, the consultants' advice to their clients has taken the terms "conservative" and "change-resistant" to new levels. That mind set, coupled with their enormous influence, particularly in the English-speaking pension markets, has been a potent recipe for inertia and an avoidance of innovative investment approaches of many kinds, including sustainability investing. Indeed, in our darker—and private—moments we have sometimes despairingly and only half-jokingly referred to the pension fund consultants as the "Axis of Evil." Perhaps that is unduly harsh; "Axis of Inertia" would probably be fairer and more accurate. Happily, however, as we will see, there have been a number of recent and encouraging developments within the consulting community. The Axis of Inertia may actually be on its way to becoming an Axis of Progress.

Also, in fairness, most of the consultants' pension fund clients are, quite properly, highly conservative themselves. After all, they are trustees and fiduciaries for *other* people's money. They are the consultants' clients, and their wishes must be respected. Moreover, there is little or nothing in the consulting industry's traditional compensation model to encourage risk taking. Failed experiments are punished savagely by clients, whereas there are really no exceptional "merit points" or financial rewards for bold innovations that succeed. The herd mentality is at least as well ensconced in the consulting fraternity as it is among asset owners and their money managers. "Maverick risk"—the risk of being different from the herd—is apparently to be avoided at all costs. As discussed earlier, it is seemingly much better to fail conventionally than to risk succeeding by trying something unprecedented. The head of one major consulting firm displayed remarkable candor—and accuracy—in a recent remark to an investor conference in California which I attended:

We consultants are not leaders; we are *followers.*

Against this rather bleak backdrop, Mercer's bold innovations in the sustainability space become all the more remarkable. They stand out markedly from their competitors and, if our diagnosis of global megatrends in Chapter 1 is even remotely accurate, they stand to be handsomely rewarded commercially over the next decade. Even more important, given the absolutely pivotal role that consultants play in influencing investor behavior, Mercer promises to be a harbinger and an accelerator of major changes *throughout* the investment world.

The Mercer sustainability story really began in earnest in 2002. Tim Gardener, the London-based global head of Mercer's investment consulting practice, began hearing more consistently from clients about the potential relevance of ES issues to their investment strategies. Gardener's interest was further piqued by one of his senior consultants in Toronto, Jane Ambachtscheer, who began lobbying for a proactive, firm-wide response.

It is worth recalling that at the time, the conventional "wisdom" in the investment consulting world was unequivocal: ES factors were irrelevant at best and harmful at worst to clients' investment strategies and the responsibilities of the prudent fiduciary. As we noted earlier, this view has been remarkably persistent and continues to dominate most consultants' thinking and behavior to this day. Mercer, to its infinite credit, made a conscious strategic choice to break from the pack and to provide some leadership to its clients.

This is *not* to imply that Mercer had abandoned its focus on fiduciary responsibility; quite the contrary. Mercer embraced the same "new fiduciary paradigm" advocated earlier in the Freshfields report—and throughout this book. Far from being incompatible with fiduciary responsibility, sustainability analysis is often *required* by it. Fiduciaries have *always* been obligated to pursue the best risk-adjusted returns for their beneficiaries. All that has changed is that Mercer has begun to use and promote a *twenty-first century* definition of "risk."

Mercer is a classic case of a firm making a strategic bet—and investment—*before* there was any clear market demand. This takes both vision and organizational courage, and Mercer had both.

In 2004 Tim Gardener pulled the trigger; he created a new, specialist ES unit and chose Jane Ambachtsheer to lead it. It proved an excellent choice; today the one-person unit has grown to 17 professionals in six offices worldwide. To put that number in perspective, Mercer's closest rival currently has a grand total of *one* sustainability specialist. Watch for this situation to change very soon as more and more asset owners demand "sustainability literacy" from their consultants and advisors.

But what does Mercer's ES specialist team actually *do?* The answer is simple: they do precisely what all investment consultants do—they help institutional investors craft an appropriate mix of investment strategies and then help them find and hire the best money managers to carry these strategies out. The one major difference is this: the Mercer team tries to inject "sustainability DNA" into its advice.

One of the core competencies of any investment consultant is to have an intimate understanding of the products, strategies, and capabilities of money managers. Logically enough, in 2005 Mercer began to do extensive research into the ES capabilities of the various asset management houses and then began to feed the results of that research to its clients. Today they have an industry-leading level of knowledge in that regard; as a result their clients are beginning to ask an entirely different set of questions of their current and potential money managers. Because of Mercer, an appreciation of sustainability issues is becoming an increasingly common and important criterion when asset owners evaluate external candidates to manage their assets. And, better still, those same clients are becoming increasingly sophisticated in evaluating the answers—*and* acting accordingly.

Mercer has become a strong and effective proselytizer for what it terms "responsible investment." It encourages its clients to consider the appropriateness of incorporating ES considerations into the design of their investment mandates, their selection of money managers, and their use of proxy voting and engagement with portfolio companies. At a macro level, on the theory that "a rising tide raises all boats," the Mercer team also does extensive speaking at investment conferences, and Ambachtsheer was instrumental in the "expert group" that drafted the influential UN Principles for Responsible Investment.[5]

Mercer currently enjoys the enviable and strategic status as *the* global "go-to" consulting firm in the sustainability space. The firm is having a growing and demonstrable effect on the thinking and behavior of its clients and has even begun to trigger competitive responses from other consulting firms. Given the almost hegemonic grip that the consulting industry has over its investor clients, I fully expect Mercer's "multiplier effect" to be large, growing, and strategic.

Innovest Strategic Value Advisors

Including your own company in a chapter on exceptional innovators hardly qualifies as the epitome of journalistic objectivity. However, I believe that sufficient independent third-party commentary on Innovest's work makes us more comfortable in doing so than would otherwise have been the case.[6] Indeed, it could plausibly be argued that the story of the Sustainable Investment Revolution would be at least modestly incomplete if the company were omitted.

As noted in the Introduction to this book, Innovest was first established in 1992, shortly after the historic Earth Summit in Rio de Janeiro. Its mission seems even more audacious today with the benefit of hindsight than it did at the time: to attempt to help "reengineer the DNA" of investment analysis and financial markets. This would entail trying to bring sustainability factors from their current status entirely beyond Wall Street's radar screens—*and* its Bloomberg terminals—to a much more central position in the investment process, in essence moving them from the margin to the mainstream. The initial logic behind the establishment of Innovest was quite simple:

- *If* the substantial variations in the performance and positioning of companies on sustainability issues could be credibly demonstrated to "the market" and
- *If* a compelling case could be made that those differences could be *financially* material, then

- "The markets" would do what they've always done with relentless effectiveness: reward the leaders, punish the laggards, and create incentives for the laggards to improve. "Creative destruction" at its finest!

This should, in turn, create powerful, tangible incentives for both leadership and improvement and, hopefully can help trigger a "race to the top." Companies would make the effort and investments necessary to improve, with a salutary impact on both environmental and social conditions as well as investor returns.

This all seemed logical enough at the time; indeed, it still does. The sheer magnitude and difficulty of *both* of the two "ifs," however, have proved to be an enormous intellectual and practical challenge. It is one that Innovest, the other firms profiled in this chapter, and many others continue to pursue to this day. In 1992 I had—generously, I had naively thought—allowed a full 36 to 48 months to complete the "reengineering of capitalism"—after all, how difficult could it possibly *be?* Well, 16 years later the job is admittedly slightly behind schedule, but I firmly believe that we are now making discernible and accelerating progress.

Innovest's early years were excruciatingly difficult and were spent flying in the face of what seemed to be a 250 mile per hour intellectual and ideological headwind. Four important milestones along the way, however, proved invaluable in gaining market traction for the firm and its then heretical investment thesis.

The first was the arrival of Hewson Baltzell in 1995. Innovest's current president, Baltzell, held an MBA in finance from the prestigious Wharton School of Business. Better still, he also had previous experience at both JP Morgan Chase and Lehman Brothers, two of the absolute pillars of Wall Street. His skills, credibility, perspective, determination, and contributions over the subsequent 13 years would prove invaluable.

The second catalyst was the creation of what we believe was a world-class initial board of directors for the firm. In addition to business guidance and direction, the board was invaluable in providing credibility to the fledgling enterprise *and* in positioning it as a *mainstream* investment player. Innovest's first chairman was Jim Martin, the former chief investment officer for TIAA-CREF, one of the largest and most respected institutional investors in the United States, with over $400 billion under management. The vice-chairman was David van Pelt, formerly one of the top executives at Citigroup. The board also included luminaries such as Lord Nigel Lawson, former Chancellor of the Exchequer in Margaret

Thatcher's U.K. government, and Sir Mark Moody-Stuart, former chairman and CEO of Royal Dutch/Shell. All in all, the board was much more high powered and distinguished than would normally be warranted by a mere start-up, particularly one with a counterorthodox business premise.

The third critical development was a major, founding investment from the Wallace Global Fund (WGF) in 1998. Actually a U.S. foundation, WGF made a so-called "program-related investment" on the logic that Innovest's work could reinforce the foundation's regular program activities and have an impact on ES areas. The foundation's patriarch, the late Bob Wallace, was the key visionary who made it happen. This critical funding finally allowed Innovest to hire enough professional staff to provide global clients with both the breadth and the depth of research coverage that they demanded.

The fourth transformational event occurred in 2003. It came in the form of a strategic equity investment from a joint venture formed by two Innovest clients. One was APG (formerly ABP), a $ 300+ billion Dutch pension fund that is the second or third largest in the world, depending on who's counting. The other partner was State Street Global Advisors, the world's second largest money manager with over $2 trillion under management. Needless to say, that investment brought more than "mere" financial capital to Innovest; it conferred a significant level of legitimacy and credibility on a young firm and its unconventional investment thesis.

Today, Innovest provides sustainability and other "intangible" investment research and investment products to clients in over 20 countries. Its clients include resolutely mainstream financial houses, such as JP Morgan, Goldman Sachs, and HSBC, as well as major pension funds and foundations, governments, and NGOs. Its professional staff of over 80 people works from eight offices in seven countries on four continents. My Innovest colleagues and I fervently hope that we have had and are having a significant and positive impact on the capital markets. Whether that is true is best left to others to judge.

Up to this point in the book we have attempted to make a logical, conceptual, and financial case for sustainable investment. We have also tried to provide brief portraits of a number of catalytic initiatives and organizations that have been critical in bringing us to where we stand today. The Sustainable Investment Revolution is far from completed, however. Indeed, even its eventual success cannot be fully ensured. To continue to move forward, literally thousands of new adherents—and, more importantly, *practitioners*—will need to become mobilized. We fervently hope that by this point in the book the reader has become persuaded to join the groundswell, if only for purely financial reasons. If so, terrific! If not, well . . . we're not quite sure what it would take to convince you.

But even the most ardent convert to the sustainable investment thesis will need *tools* to turn intellectual commitment into *action*. It is to the task of providing some of those tools that we now turn.

Chapter 11

Making It Happen

*Investors need to be able to construct scenarios that are better
suited to anticipating possible future states of a company.
Integrating "extra-financial" factors in their analysis allows
them to think differently from the market, which enhances
their prospects for out-performing it.*

—ENHANCED ANALYTICS FOR A NEW GENERATION OF INVESTORS
UNIVERSITIES SUPERANNUATION SCHEME, U.K.

Outperforming the market is the Holy Grail for investors! And, from
a purely hard-nosed financial perspective, that's the whole *point* of
sustainability-enhanced strategies. And that outperformance can be
achieved in precisely the manner suggested by the opening quotation
above: *by providing a different, more comprehensive, and more forward-
looking perspective on companies.*

It is to be hoped that by now the reader has found the sustainable
investment thesis compelling and, ultimately, persuasive. The combination of logic, empirical and academic evidence, and the seriousness—
and financial materiality—of global environmental and social issues (ES)
should, in principle, provide a powerful impetus for investors to act.

On the optimistic assumption that readers would *like* to incorporate sustainability research into their investment strategies and practices, the question then becomes *how* best to do so. This chapter will attempt to provide some specific guidance and concrete examples in this regard.

The approach ultimately taken by the investor will depend very heavily on what *kind* of investor is involved. "Investors" can be individuals selecting and trading their own securities online. More commonly, they will have outside advisors investing their savings in mutual funds. At the institutional level, investors may be pension funds, insurance companies, endowments and foundations, or asset management firms such as Fidelity or Vanguard. If the institution is large and sophisticated enough, like a CalPERS, an APG, or a Yale Endowment, it will have in-house professional staffs managing the majority of the assets; typically it will hire outside money managers only to deal with the more esoteric asset classes such as real estate, infrastructure, commodities, or perhaps hedge funds. Some even have *those* skills in house.

The 10 Commandments of Sustainable Investment

Whatever the circumstances, whether the investor is an individual managing his own retirement account or a $200 billion pension fund, we would argue that certain key principles and disciplines *must* be followed:

1. Make *sure* that you or your money managers have access to top-quality, company-specific research on sustainability risks and opportunities. Money managers are constantly increasing their capacity to do sustainability research in house. If the ones working for you have that capability, great! (Although we'd strongly recommend a "trust, but verify" policy.)
2. Make sure that they actually *use* it. (This, sadly, does not always result from following Commandment 1). If your money managers cannot explain exactly how they are doing so, it's almost certain that they *aren't*.
3. Do *not* use sustainability research in isolation; always combine it with more traditional fundamental and/or quantitative investment research. Being a sustainability leader does not mean that a company is worth investing in at any price, at any particular time.
4. Do *not* expect perfection from your investee companies. Remember, with 150,000 employees in 100 countries, a major multinational com-

pany is unlikely to have a sustainability track record that is completely beyond reproach. Investors (at least the "long-only" ones) should instead look for at least two qualities in "their" companies: best-in-class performance and positioning, and a genuine ethos of continuous improvement. Find those two attributes and you're well on your way.

5. Do *not* presume that all sustainability factors—or even *any* of them—are relevant to all investment decisions, in all industry sectors, all of the time. They're not.

6. Do *not* assume that each of the "Four Pillars" (Environment, Human Capital, Stakeholder Capital, and Strategic Governance) is equally relevant to a particular company. As we shall soon see, they probably aren't.

7. Do *not* assume that the relative financial importance of each of the Four Pillars will remain constant over time. It won't.

8. Do *not* apply a double standard to the financial performance of your "sustainability-enhanced" portfolios. Remember, fully 80 percent of *traditional* active money managers underperform their benchmarks every year; fortunately it's not the *same* 80 percent every year! *No* investment factor or style "works" all the time in all market conditions; it is unreasonable to hold your sustainability portfolios and managers to standards that your conventional managers could not possibly meet either.

9. *Do* adopt a long-term investment horizon. (That would also be good advice for just about *every* investor, sustainability oriented or otherwise.) Sustainability factors, by their very nature, tend to be longer term in nature and relatively slow to play themselves out in stock prices. Our own multiyear stock market research at Innovest suggests that the "incubation period" before sustainability factors manifest themselves in stock price changes can often be 2–3 years or even more. (Bear Stearns' implosion in only 12 months was a conspicuous exception.) Patience is indeed a virtue; don't look for spectacular outperformance from your sustainability portfolios after the first 48 hours!

10. *Do* challenge your advisors and money managers. If managers are recommending an investment in a coal company, for example, the onus should be on *them* to make a convincing financial case for doing so despite all the "big picture" sustainability indicators pointing in the opposite direction. (It is not entirely beyond imagination to think that they may very well be able to do so, but the discipline of explaining and defending their recommendations to you will do them a world of good—and you too!)

In principle, it is immaterial whether the sustainability research is generated internally by an institution's professional investment staff or is secured from specialist outside providers.[1] In practice, the latter course is probably a more realistic and effective option for all but the largest, most heavily staffed institutions or investment advisors. Regardless of which route is chosen, one thing should not be negotiable: the research must be done by *somebody*—*and* must be used.

This would seem to be self-evident. Yet it is truly remarkable that many of the otherwise sophisticated institutional investors who today claim to be "on top of" sustainability trends, issues, and risks frequently have no access to any research whatsoever! (Most of the organizations profiled in Chapter 3, such as the Gates Foundation and the UN staff pension fund, would currently fall into that category.) I have often wondered precisely *how* sustainability factors could possibly be "integrated" by investors if the *means* to do so are utterly lacking. Research is needed at the company-specific level, but also, preferably, at a level that addresses cross-cutting sustainability issues and themes such as climate change, water scarcity, and acute income disparities in emerging markets.

Even for investors who have accepted that ES issues may indeed be relevant to their returns, excuses for inaction remain. Two common ones are frequently encountered:

- "It's too expensive; we can't justify the cost."
- "Even if we *had* the research, we wouldn't know how to incorporate it into our investment process."

The first objection is generally a smoke screen for the fact that the investor actually *hasn't* in fact accepted the sustainable investment hypothesis. Otherwise, the "cost" argument is very difficult to defend, *particularly* in the current investment environment, replete as it is with volatility and hidden risks. Indeed, it is richly ironic that some of the *loudest* complaints about the cost of sustainability research come from the very institutions that have recently taken multi*billion* dollar losses because of the subprime mortgage crisis. As we saw in Chapter 4, top-flight ES research just might have actually *helped* those very same investors detect and mitigate their subprime risk exposures *before* they blew up! In the increasingly complex and unpredictable investment climate of today, the question investors and fiduciaries *should* be asking themselves is can we afford *not* to have the most comprehensive, 360-degree "risk radar" possible?

The second objection—"But we don't know how to go about *using* ES research"—is much more valid and substantial, and answering it will be the focus of much of the balance of this chapter.

Three important points need to be made at the outset. The first is that there is no universally applicable, one-size-fits-all approach for integrating sustainability research; searching for the "one right answer" is a misguided and quixotic effort. That leads us directly to the second point: sustainability factors are *not* a set of occult, bizarre considerations requiring some sort of special treatment. They are, quite simply, just another group of potentially material factors to be considered alongside the dozen-plus factors professional investors consider today as a matter of course—price/earnings ratios,[2] consensus analyst expectations, balance sheet strength, and so on. As with "normal" factors, the precise way in which they are combined—and *weighed*—will vary widely. They will vary based on the risk/return objectives and expectations of the investors, the investment beliefs, styles, and skills of the asset managers, and a myriad of other factors. *Sustainability factors by themselves are no panacea; they are, however, an essential building block.*

The third point is this: contrary to the widespread misconception among traditional investors, sustainability investing does *not* require the invention of some radically new, arcane analytical tools and techniques. It is, instead, a relatively straightforward matter of *adapting* the investment tools they already have by integrating sustainability factors and research. What is essential—and far too frequently missing—is the *will* to do so.

As an example let's take one of the tools most widely used used by investors today—discounted cash flow (DCF) analysis. Analysts first attempt to predict and project companies' earnings and cash flows into the future, year by year. They then "discount" those figures back to create a single "present value" equivalent of all of those future earnings. They are discounted for the simple and valid reason that a $1 million profit 5 years hence is much less certain—and therefore less valuable—than an identical amount today. Moreover, $1 million today, at the very least, could be earning some interest going forward; therefore there is such a thing as the "time value of money," which discounting should try to reflect.

Like all investment analysis, DCF techniques are rife with assumptions, and not all of them are always clearly articulated. What discount rate should be used in a particular circumstance and why? What assumptions are being made about the length of time a company can sustain a competitive advantage over its rivals and maintain premium pricing?

Although the numbers that are ultimately spat out the other end of the DCF calculations usually have the patina of scientific accuracy and inevitability, they are nothing more than an elegantly packaged product of a set of assumptions—and often completely arbitrary ones at that.

So investors who were actually persuaded by the sustainable investment thesis need only *modify* their modeling assumptions accordingly. A top-quintile sustainability performer, for example, might have its future cash flows discounted less heavily and its "fade rate"—the period over which its competitive advantage is assumed to decline—also decreased accordingly. By how much? That's up to the investor/analyst. Just remember, though: the *initial* assumptions were not exactly derived from some incontrovertible physics experiment; they were simply *assumptions.* And the assumption of a "sustainability premium" for a top-quartile company (or a corresponding discount for a laggard) of, say, 25 percent is certainly no more arbitrary than the original ones. The central argument of this book is that adding these sustainability factors—where they are judged to be relevant and material—simply creates a richer, more complete investment analysis.

Thus, just as there is no universal "operating manual" telling investors which *traditional* factors to use and how much weight to give to each one, so it is with sustainability-enhanced investing. Readers should therefore *not* expect some sort of foolproof formula; *the important point is simply that sustainability factors should automatically be considered.* Whether, and to what degree, the various sustainability issues will be relevant to a particular company at any given time will depend on a multiplicity of factors, such as the company's industry sector, its competitive environment, and the geographic locations of its operations and customer base. Even I would never attempt to argue that *all* sustainability factors are relevant all of the time, in every industry sector, and for every company.

Let us return briefly to the four-factor sustainability taxonomy we proposed in Chapter 1—Environment, Human Capital, Stakeholder Capital, and Strategic Governance.[3] If we take the example of a company such as Microsoft, only the most rabid environmentalist would argue that Microsoft's competitive prospects are directly dependent on its *environmental* risks, positioning, or performance. In contrast, those prospects *are* directly dependent on Microsoft's relationships with its regulators—notably the European Union officials prosecuting it for anticompetitive practices, to take but one example—that is, its *stakeholder* capital. Microsoft is currently appealing a $1.4 *billion* fine levied by those same regulators. Whatever the legal outcome of the proceedings, the damage to

Microsoft's reputation has already been substantial. This leads us directly to the second of our "four pillars" of sustainability. Microsoft's ability to continue to attract, retain, and motivate top talent—i.e., its *human capital*—is absolutely critical to its ongoing success. The European legal proceedings have done nothing to enhance the perception of Microsoft as the "employer of choice" in the hypercompetitive software industry, where labor is exceptionally mobile.

So Microsoft *is* absolutely affected by sustainability factors—at least as we define them here. Having said that, however, anyone who pretends that by some miracle all sustainability factors are relevant all of the time do themselves, their clients, and the entire sustainability investment thesis an enormous disservice.

Let us turn now to a concrete example of how investors can integrate sustainability research into their security selection and portfolio construction processes.

Building a "Sustainability-Enhanced" Portfolio

As we noted earlier in this chapter, sustainability research, properly utilized, should be just *one* set of factors in the decision calculus when assessing companies for their suitability for an investor's portfolio. Ideally, they will form one-third (albeit a critically *important* one-third) of a "holy trinity" of analytical tools; the other two-thirds include traditional quantitative and fundamental analysis (Figure 11.1)

Quantitative analysis is often helpful in narrowing down the total investable universe to a more manageable number requiring and justifying deeper investigation. Quantitative tools can process an enormous amount of financial information quickly. They can rapidly narrow down a universe of, say, 3000 securities to a much smaller "focus list." For example, suppose that an investor wanted to focus only on high-growth stocks. Quantitative models can be used to narrow the eligible universe down to, say, only those global stocks that have generated at least 20 percent annual earnings growth in each of the past 4 years. Presto! The investors have a starting point. (It is also possible to screen for all companies with names beginning with the letter "T," but we wouldn't necessarily recommend it as an investment strategy!) At this point the *real* fun begins, and a smaller universe of, say, 300 companies needs to be narrowed down to a choice of 50 to 60. At this stage, *both* fundamental *and* sustainability analysis come into play.

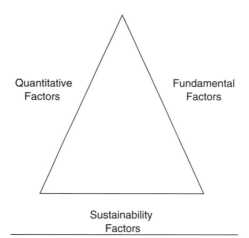

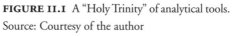

FIGURE II.I A "Holy Trinity" of analytical tools.
Source: Courtesy of the author

Fundamental factors that would typically be examined include the following:

- Valuation (Is the stock overpriced?)
- Earnings quality (How confident are we in the ability of the company to deliver earnings consistently?)
- Momentum (What is the recent trajectory of its share price?)
- Analyst "sentiment" (What is the consensus forecast of the sell-side analysts?)
- Capital efficiency (Has the company been able to consistently earn more than the cost of its capital?)

To that traditional fundamental analysis the sustainable investor would then add research and insight about the company's performance and strategic position with respect to the "Four Pillars" of sustainability:

1. Human Capital
   Labor relations
   Recruitment/retention strategies
   Employee motivation
   Innovation capacity
   Knowledge development and dissemination
   Progressive workplace practices

2. Environment
    Board and executive oversight
    Risk management systems
    Disclosure/verification
    Process efficiencies—"ecoefficiency"
    Health and safety
    New product development
3. Stakeholder Capital
    Regulators and policymakers
    Local communities/nongovernmental organizations (NGOs)
    Customer relationships
    Alliance partners
    Emerging markets
4. Strategic Governance
    Strategic scanning capability
    Agility/adaptation
    Performance indicators/monitoring
    Traditional governance concerns
    International "best practice"

How much *weight* is actually allocated to any individual pillar—and indeed to the entire group of four sustainability meta-factors together, depends on a myriad of factors: What industry sector is the company in? What is the geographic layout of its supply chain? Who are its competitors? The list can be a long one, and its application is at least as much art as it is science—*just as, by the way, is invariably the case with choosing and weighting the traditional investment factors!*

It should also be emphasized that the different factor weights can and usually do vary significantly from one industry sector to the next, from region to region, and over time. Figures 11.2 and 11.3 illustrate this clearly.

Factor weights vary by both industry sector and geographic region[4] as well as over time.

Pulling all three strands of the analysis together, a sustainability-enhanced investment process might look something like that shown in Figure 11.4.

Ideally, companies that are candidates for the sustainability portfolio must excel across *all three* dimensions: quantitative, fundamental, and sustainability. We are loath to propose specific names in a market as

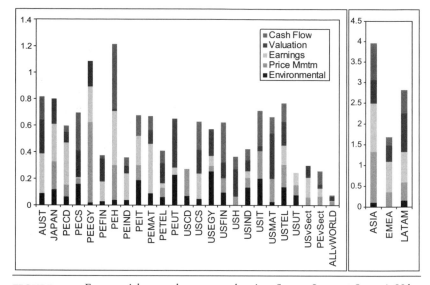

FIGURE II.2 Factor weights vary by sector and region. Source: Innovest Strategic Value Advisors

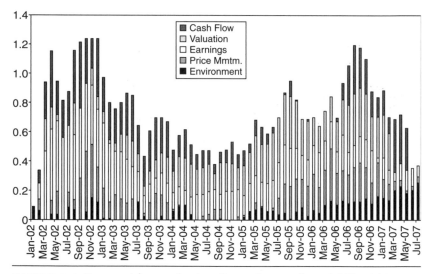

FIGURE II.3 Factor weights vary by time. Source: Innovest Strategic Value Advisors

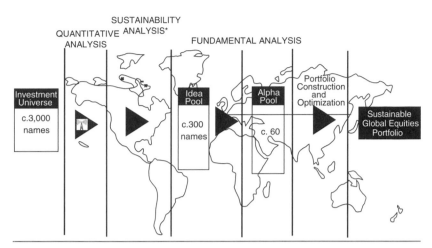

FIGURE 11.4 A sustainability-enhanced investment process. *Environment, human capital, stakeholder capital, strategic governance. Source: Innovest Strategic Value Advisors

volatile as the one in which we find ourselves in 2008. Let us therefore confine ourselves to saying that *at present* the types of companies that we believe to be superior across all three sets of criteria include the following:

- Rio Tinto (mining)
- Lufthansa (airlines; industrials)
- Swiss Re (financial)
- Old Mutual (financials)
- Norsk Hydro (Industrials)
- Pinnacle West (Utilities)
- Royal Dutch Shell (energy)
- Westpac (financials)
- Halifax Bank of Scotland (financials)
- Intel (information technology)

This list is simply intended to provide the reader with a sample of the kind of companies that this type of investment process selects. Purists [i.e., traditional socially responsible investing (SRI) advocates] would likely be either dubious about or steadfastly opposed to holding companies with substantial environmental impact, such as Rio Tinto, Royal Dutch Shell, and Norsk Hydro. As a matter of personal philosophy, however, I would argue instead that it is possible to make a much more significant contribution to planetary sustainability by actually *investing* in high-impact companies and using that leverage and access to help *improve* their performance. Financially boycotting one of these companies—or even worse, their entire industry sector—may make us feel better and morally superior, but it certainly does *not* take a single ton of CO_2 out of the atmosphere or provide a single dose of affordable medicine to people in emerging markets. In addition, I would challenge anyone who opposes the inclusion of these companies in an investment portfolio to survive for even a week without using at least one of their products!

For a second concrete example of how sustainability factors can be integrated directly into the stock selection and portfolio construction process, let us focus more narrowly on one single sustainability factor—albeit a big one.

Climate Change: The "Mother" of All Sustainability Issues

Few environmental issues pose as real, significant, and widespread a financial threat to investors as climate change. International policy responses aimed at cutting greenhouse gas emissions, together with the direct physical impact of climate change, will require investors and money managers to take a much closer look at how their portfolios might be affected by company "carbon" risks and opportunities.

Since there is now growing and incontrovertible evidence that superior overall environmental performance can in fact improve the risk level, profitability, and stock performance of publicly traded companies,[5] and given the emergence of climate change as arguably *the* preeminent environmental issue of our time, fiduciaries can now be considered to be derelict in their duties if they do *not* consider climate-driven risks and opportunities where they may be material.

Investors and other fiduciaries would be well advised to assess their portfolios for carbon risk for at least four reasons:

- There is increasing evidence that superior performance in managing climate risk is a useful proxy for superior, more strategic corporate management, and therefore for superior financial performance and shareholder value creation.
- The considerable variations in net carbon risk among same-sector industry competitors are currently neither transparent to nor systematically analyzed by mainstream Wall Street and City of London

analysts (or analysts anywhere else on earth, as near as we can determine!). As a result, carbon-driven risks and value potential remain, for the present at least, almost entirely hidden from view. This creates an enormous potential information advantage for those sustainability investors willing and able to make the effort to find out.

- In the longer term, the outperformance potential will become even greater as the capital markets become more fully sensitized to the financial and competitive consequences of environmental and climate change considerations.

- International fiduciary best practice now demands it.

Historically, however, institutional investors—even foundations active in combating climate change on the program side—have been inordinately slow in responding to climate risk. As we saw in Chapter 2, there have been a number of reasons for this:

- Investment professionals have long believed that company resources devoted to environmental issues are either wasteful or actually injurious to their competitive and financial performance and therefore to investor returns.

- As a direct result, money managers, investment consultants, and even pension fund trustees have historically regarded explicitly addressing environmental factors in their investment strategies as incompatible with the proper discharge of their fiduciary responsibilities.

- Until recently, there has been a dearth of robust, credible research evidence and analytical tools linking the environmental performance of companies directly with their financial performance. Today, however, a number of the specialist sustainability research providers referenced in Appendix 4 have added climate risk research to their offerings.

All of this, however, is changing rapidly. In many parts of the world, such as the U.K., Australia, and France, fiduciaries are already legally *required* to address environmental risks in their investment strategies, precisely because these "nontraditional" risk factors demonstrably *can* affect the financial performance of companies.

It is now increasingly recognized by leading-edge financial analysts and investors that there is a strong, positive, and growing correlation between the "sustainability" performance (on climate change in particular) of industrial companies and their competitiveness and financial performance.

"Carbon risk" is, today, arguably the most salient of these sustainability factors for investors, at least in high-impact sectors such as electric utilities, oil and gas, mining, and chemicals.

As we have seen earlier in this book, unbeknownst to most investors, the variation in climate risk exposure, even within the same industry sector, can be enormous—up to *30 times* or even more! Investors and/or their advisors simply *must* be able to identify those companies at greatest risk.

Capturing the "Carbon Beta™" Premium: Don't Take the Easy Way Out!

Most of the discussion about climate risk among large institutional investors occurs at a lofty "40,000 foot" level; very rarely are they equipped with the *company-specific* research necessary to make informed investment decisions on the ground. And, for individual companies the analysis is typically focused on two things: information voluntarily disclosed by the companies themselves, and the size of their "carbon footprints." While certainly relevant, these two pieces of information have serious limitations that sophisticated sustainability investors need to appreciate:

- At this stage, disclosed information on carbon risk is notoriously unreliable, inconsistently reported across companies and over time, and only rarely validated by independent third parties.
- In today's regulatory environment—and for the foreseeable future—CO_2 emissions have very different financial and strategic implications depending on where they occur. All emissions are *not* created equal. Carbon footprints need to be analyzed on a granular, geographically sensitive basis.
- Independent empirical research suggests that if any relationship exists between the carbon footprints of companies and their financial performance, it may actually be a counterintuitive one—that is, the larger the carbon footprint, the *better* the financial returns often are.
- Emissions data alone, if it is available at all and even when it has been analyzed properly, provides less than 25 percent of the information a sophisticated investor requires.

We believe that much more comprehensive robust models and analysis are required. At a minimum, such a model should in our view address the following for companies:

- Their overall carbon footprint or *potential* risk exposure, but adjusted to reflect the vastly differing regulatory and taxation circumstances in different countries and regions.
- Their ability to manage and reduce that risk exposure.
- Their ability to recognize and seize climate-driven opportunities on the upside, including cost efficiencies, new products and services, and carbon trading.
- Their dynamic rate of improvement or regression over time.

Other factors to consider on a company-specific basis include the following:

- Energy intensity and energy source mix and consumption patterns.
- Geographic locations of production facilities relative to specific regulatory and tax liabilities and compliance schedules in different countries.
- Product mix: the level of both direct and indirect carbon emissions created by the manufacture and use of different products—e.g., automobiles versus furniture.
- Company-specific "marginal abatement" cost structures: some companies can reduce emissions at much less cost than others.
- Technology trajectory—the level of progress that a company has already made in adapting/replacing its production technologies for a carbon-constrained environment.
- Industry competitive dynamics—the ability/inability of companies to pass on new costs to consumers

The *bad* news for investors about climate risk is twofold. First, there is a real dearth of the sorts of granular, company-specific research that investors absolutely need in order to make concrete decisions. With same-sector risk variances among companies of 30 times or more, this poses a real challenge for investors wishing to "climate-proof" their portfolios, or at the very least to be aware of where the greatest risk exposures actually lie.

Second, what little company-specific research *is* available tends to focus on the readily available: the size of companies' "carbon footprints," and using only company-disclosed data at that. Unfortunately, this is a bit like a drunk looking for his keys under a light pole because the light's better there. (Remember our highlighting of "availability bias" as part of our discussion of behavioral finance in Chapter 4. Just because data are

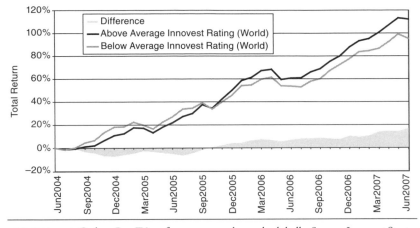

FIGURE II.5 Carbon Beta™ performers versus laggards globally. Source: Innovest Strategic Value Advisors

readily available doesn't mean that the data are *useful!*) Our own research at Innovest suggests that reliance on gross carbon footprint data can actually be financially *counter*productive for investors, and voluntarily disclosed company data are often of limited use at best. Deeper, more fundamental research is required.

The *good* news, however, is also twofold. First, both the quantity and quality of company-level climate risk research are improving markedly. In addition to the growing number of independent research houses now producing climate risk research, increasing numbers of investment banks (such as HSBC, Lehman Brothers, UBS, and JP Morgan) are now producing high-quality research themselves. And the Carbon Disclosure Project, the "grandfather" of all climate risk company research, is providing more and more useful information with each of its annual iterations. Second, if investors *can* in fact access good, fundamental research addressing the factors we've discussed in this chapter, there *is* an outperformance premium available based on the results of a recent three-year study undertaken by our firm.

In that study the group of companies rated as top "carbon performers" surpassed the returns of the group of those companies rated as below average from June 2004 to June 2007 by an annualized rate of return of 3.06 percent (a cumulative total return of 81.85 percent compared to 72.67 percent).[6] This is shown in Figure 11.5.

The even *better* news for investors is that given the political, economic, and regulatory forces acting in concert to increase the financial saliency of climate risk, this "Carbon Beta premium" will only become *larger* with time.

So how might these climate risk factors play themselves out in the real world of investing? How, concretely, could this research be used and integrated? Figure 11.6 illustrates one approach. We focus on the example of the high-profile U.S. tool-maker Black and Decker. When this analysis was carried out (mid-2008), the company rated very strongly on a traditional fundamental and quantitative investment basis. It had strong earnings growth and momentum, had a healthy balance sheet, and appeared attractively priced relative to both its competitors and its own historical performance. So far, so good. When we examine the far right-hand column, however, we see that Black and Decker's rating on climate risk is *below* average—a BBB rating. In other words, the company has *greater* risk exposure to climate change than its same-sector peers. This higher risk level is largely driven by the company's apparent lack of understanding of either the threats or the opportunities that climate change can potentially create for its business. And whatever the company's level of understanding, it certainly has not taken the appropriate organizational *actions* necessary to identify and deal with those possibilities. In short, we would consider the company to be a risky investment from a sustainability perspective.

						Strong Rating by Global Multifactor model	Strong Rating on Capital Efficiency		Above-Average Carbon Risk
EQUITY RADAR					Aggregate MultiFac GL	Holt Price 2 Best	Aggregate MultiFac Loc	ISVA EcoValue	ISVA IVA	ISVA Carbon
DATE: 12-Jun-07										
Universe: NewGlobal		Mcap($m)	In Portfolio							
2637785	NVP INC	NORTHAMIConsDiscretion	3,199.7		1	1	1	CCC	CCC	CCC
2250687	D R HORTON INC	NORTHAMIConsDiscretion	6,191.3		1	3	4	CCC	CCC	CCC
2101503	BLACK & DECKER CORP	NORTHAMIConsDiscretion	5,855.3		1	1	1	BBB	BBB	BBB
2896092	TOLL BROTHERS INC	NORTHAMIConsDiscretion	3,160.9		1	3	5	CCC	CCC	CCC
2960384	WHIRLPOOL CORP	NORTHAMIConsDiscretion	8,736.6		1	1	2	A	A	A
2598699	MOHAWK INDUSTRIES INC	NORTHAMIConsDiscretion	5,505.1		1	2	1	BBB	BBB	BBB
2485070	KB HOME	NORTHAMIConsDiscretion	3,350.7		1	4	2	BBB	BB	BB
2414580	HASBRO INC	NORTHAMIConsDiscretion	4,488.0		1	1	1	BB	BBB	BB
2840549	STANLEY WORKS	NORTHAMIConsDiscretion	4,965.5		1	1	4	A	BBB	AAA
2903550	TRIBUNE CO	NORTHAMIConsDiscretion	2,369.2		1	4	4	B	BB	CCC
2105505	BLOCK H & R INC	NORTHAMIConsDiscretion	7,194.3		1	4	4	B	BB	CCC
2550707	MCDONALDS CORP	NORTHAMIConsDiscretion	60,792.7		1	3	1	AA	BBB	AA
2300601	EASTMAN KODAK CO	NORTHAMIConsDiscretion	7,547.2		1	5	1	AAA	AAA	AAA
2572303	MATTEL INC	NORTHAMIConsDiscretion	10,150.2		1	3	1	BB	AA	BB
2136475	SERVICEMASTER CO	NORTHAMIConsDiscretion	4,473.0		2	5	3	BBB	CCC	BBB
B018V87	LIBERTY GLOBAL INC	NORTHAMIConsDiscretion	6,661.3		2	5	3	BB	CCC	B
2511920	LENNAR CORP	NORTHAMIConsDiscretion	4,688.2		2	3	2	B	B	CCC
2193544	BRINKER INTL INC	NORTHAMIConsDiscretion	3,485.0		2	2	2	CCC	CCC	CCC
2754907	ROYAL CARIBBEAN CRUISE	NORTHAMIConsDiscretion	7,195.3		2	1	4	BBB	BB	A
B198391	WYNDHAM WORLDWIDE	NORTHAMIConsDiscretion	6,644.8		2	4	4	NA	NA	NA
2523044	CARNIVAL CORP/PLC (US)	NORTHAMIConsDiscretion	30,191.1		2	1	2	BB	CCC	BBB
2149309	BRUNSWICK CORP	NORTHAMIConsDiscretion	3,033.0		2	2	2	BB	B	BB
2708841	PULTE HOMES INC	NORTHAMIConsDiscretion	5,390.3		2	5	5	BB	BB	BB
2365804	GENERAL MOTORS CORP	NORTHAMIConsDiscretion	17,794.3		2	1	3	BB	BB	BB
B0SRLF4	VIACOM INC	NORTHAMIConsDiscretion	24,238.0		2	1	2	B	B	CCC
2632003	NEW YORK TIMES CO	NORTHAMIConsDiscretion	3,539.7		2	5	5	AA	A	B
2293819	EBAY INC	NORTHAMIConsDiscretion	36,216.6		2	1	3	A	BB	A
2289874	DARDEN RESTAURANTS INC	NORTHAMIConsDiscretion	5,877.3		2	2	1	BBB	BBB	A
2510682	LEGGET & PLATT INC	NORTHAMIConsDiscretion	4,007.7		2	2	2	BB	BB	BB

FIGURE 11.6 Climate risk factors. Source: Innovest Strategic Value Advisors

So now what? Well, first of all, it is important to recognize that there are no "right" or "wrong" answers to this question. Second, the appropriate *balancing* among those factors is, and ought to be, entirely the province of investors and/or their advisors. Indeed, in the latter case, that is precisely what they are getting *paid* for.

Clearly, though, one important determining factor will be the time horizon of invesstors. If they intend to hold the stock for only a short period of time they might be inclined to downplay the importance of the climate risk factor, since it will likely be relatively slow to manifest itself in Black and Decker's share price. If, on the other hand, they intend to own the stock for 5 years or more, they may very well decide that the risk may be material, and possibly a red flag for concerns about the company's long-term strategic management capabilities in other areas as well. Either way, the important thing is that *at least now investors have the information.* They are no longer forced to confront twenty-first century investment challenges with twentieth century analytical tools.

As we noted earlier, there is absolutely *no* "one size fits all" approach to the integration of sustainability research into the investment process. The examples provided here are illustrative of only one approach. The important thing for readers to note is that it *can* indeed be done. Precisely *how* to do it, however, is best left to the discretion and talent of individual money managers—let a thousand flowers bloom!

Indeed, that's what you should be paying your money managers and advisors to do. *Your* job, as investors, is simply to ensure that the integration is actually being done and that both the managers and the process are of top quality. Fortunately, with each passing month, both the variety and the quality of choices available to investors are improving markedly.

So there you have it! No further excuses remain. Throughout this book we have endeavored to provide the reader with the logic, the evidence, some practical examples, and the analytical tools with which to pursue sustainable investment with conviction and confidence. The rest is up to you; what are you waiting for?

Chapter 12

Some Final Thoughts

In the same way that the discovery of gravity and the theory of relativity revolutionized physics, sustainability issues and climate change have revolutionized the way business and financial institutions conduct their activities and interact.

—PAUL WATCHMAN, PARTNER, LE BOEUF, LAMB, GREENE & MACRAE[1]

Reengineering the very "DNA" of the global capital markets actually turns out to be *very* hard work *and* enormously time consuming! But make no mistake—it *is* happening. All over the world mainstream investors are beginning to awaken from their multidecade dogmatic slumber. It must be said that they are awakening at very different rates and, once awake, their epiphanies are taking very different forms, from the timorous to the bold. But one way or another, the Sustainable Investment Revolution is well underway. It is admittedly *not* yet in full swing, but that day is coming soon. It absolutely *has* to; the tectonic sustainability forces and imperatives that are currently reshaping the basis of global companies' competitive advantage are simply too powerful to resist. And where successful companies go, successful investors are bound to follow.

Three Cheers for the "Lemming Instinct"!

One of the defining characteristics of most large institutional investors is that they are cautious and conservative—to a fault. They also tend to have a pronounced disinclination to accept "maverick risk"—the risk of being different from their peers. In short, they travel in packs or herds. Like lemmings, they often follow one another blindly, even if it means plunging over a metaphorical cliff—such as was the case with subprime mortgages.

For several decades now this "lemming instinct" has served as a powerful *impediment* to the Sustainable Investment Revolution; no one wanted to break ranks and step out of line. Today, however, that same lemming instinct is about to come in very handy; now that the first few dozen institutions have begun to take the plunge, we can expect to see the next 30,000 soon join in. Conformity will now become our *friend*—and the planet's friend as well. That investors will inevitably join the Revolution is no longer at issue; the only real question is the *speed* at which they will do so. I would wager that 10 years from now every laggard profiled in Chapter 3 will have joined the Revolution.

Over the past two decades I have heard just about every critique and reason imaginable for the dismissal of the sustainable investment thesis. Ninety-nine percent of them are of the ideologically blinkered sort that we examined in Chapter 2; they involve one of two alternative postulates: either sustainability factors are simply *not* germane to companies' and therefore investors' financial performance and are thus a waste of time and money or, alternatively, they *could* conceivably be material, but only in a *negative* way: by arbitrarily restricting the range of investment choices, sustainability considerations actually tend to *harm* financial returns and are therefore incompatible with fiduciary responsibilities. We have argued throughout this book that both of these propositions are manifestly false and reflect either total ignorance of what sustainable investing is really all about, a complete confusion with traditional "socially responsible" investing, or both. I fervently hope that by this point in the book no further convincing will be required.

A More Thoughtful Critique

There *is,* however, a more insightful critique of sustainable investing that, although far more rare than the others, merits a serious response. The objection goes something like this: "the sustainable investment thesis is essentially an 'information arbitrage' play. That is, advocates of this approach (such as the author of this book) argue that they have *material* information that more conventional investors lack, and that this information advantage can be translated into superior returns. So far, so good. But what happens when *everybody* has the same sustainability research and that information advantage disappears?"

That is a good and an entirely fair question. The honest answer is that *like any other* information-based investment strategy (and, at the end of the day, which ones *aren't?*), the widespread availability of the same information *does* indeed undercut its value. Having said that, however, there are at least three valid, countervailing retorts:

1. Not every investor has the same skill level, investment objectives, time horizon, and approach when they *use* sustainability or any other investment research. For that reason, even if 10 out of 10 investors are given the same sustainability data and analysis with which to work, it is almost certain that some would make more effective use of it than others. We need only contemplate the traditional investment scene, where 95 percent of the players have access to the same historical performance data, securities filings, analyst research reports, and consensus earnings forecasts. Despite this, there is still a huge dispersion of investment returns.

2. The second rebuttal may be even more persuasive. The simple fact is that *we are still a long, long, long way from a situation in which anything close to a majority of investors have sustainability research sitting on their Bloomberg terminals and use it religiously.* So, far from the complete information transparency that would be required to undermine the practical efficacy and advantage of the sustainable investment thesis, for the majority of investors there is still massive information *opacity.*

    A simple example should suffice to demonstrate this point. As we have seen, climate change is by consensus *the* sustainability issue of our generation. Indeed, we know from the Carbon Disclosure Project that over 55 *trillion* dollars worth of institutional investors *say* that they are terribly concerned about it. Yet we also know from our own research at Innovest that even within the same industry sectors, the net exposure of companies to climate risk can vary by *30* times or more. Moreover, as we have already seen, there appears to be a "Carbon Beta™" premium for investors in companies with superior "carbon management" capabilities. Despite all this, however, I ask you: how many chief investment officers or their staffs or advisors today could even *begin* to tell you which companies are which? And how many are making a concerted effort to *find out?* Most important of all, how many of their trustees or boards of directors are *demanding* that they do so? I would be enormously surprised—and delighted—if more than 1 percent could honestly answer in the affirmative.

So if that is the level of research availability and use with regard to the *number one* sustainability issue, what can we presume to conclude about other sustainability issues such as human capital management, human rights, water availability, supply chain management, and income disparity? I think it is safe to say that both longtime and new converts to the sustainable investment thesis can rest easy; even assuming a quintupling of the current rate of diffusion and utilization of sustainability research, their information advantage should be quite secure for at least a decade or more. And that brings us to the third rebuttal point.

3. It should be abundantly clear by now that "sustainability" is a moving target; the bar is being raised continually. To differentiate themselves companies need better performance on the well-established sustainability issues and metrics today than they did even 2 years ago. What was cutting-edge performance several years ago has today become commonplace, being nothing more than the basic "price of admission" or "entry ticket" to even enter markets and be competitive. And it is not even just a question of raising the bar on the "traditional" sustainability issues; *new* ones are emerging every year if not more frequently. Remember that as recently as 5 years ago climate change was not yet part of the public or investor discourse; today it is difficult to pick up a general newspaper or magazine without being confronted with it. "Traditional" sustainability issues such as the environment, human capital, and human rights are likely to follow a similar trajectory into becoming common intellectual currency. The key will be anticipating the next major sustainability issues.

And this raises an important point for investors from a pure financial performance perspective. We have argued throughout this book that, quite apart from its environmental and social merits, sustainability investing gives investors a crucial *information* edge. It provides potentially useful insight about companies' management quality and capacity for innovation. At some (distant) point in the future, though, it *is* conceivable that knowledge of, say, Royal Dutch Shell's sustainability performance will be as common among investors as its price/earnings ratio and last year's profit figures are today.

Let us then make the even more outrageous assumption that Royal Dutch Shell's competitors have all raised their games and have become Royal Dutch's sustainability equals. At that point, sustainability performance would cease to become a competitive advantage for Royal Dutch Shell and any of its competitors *and* sustainability analysis would also cease to be an advantage for *investors* as well.

So sustainability investing will, at that point, have outlived its usefulness, or at least its outperformance advantage, right? No, wrong! Remember that sustainability is a moving target. *New* sustainability issues will have emerged such as access to affordable medicines in emerging markets, access to water, and opportunities for the majority at the "base of the pyramid." *These,* and other issues like them, will become the *new* indicators for superior company management and responsiveness, agility, and competitive advantage. And information and analysis about them will become the source of a new information and outperformance edge for *investors* as well.

One final point needs to be made. The scenario sketched out above—complete sustainability information transparency, and widespread company equality on sustainability performance—will take at least a decade to materialize, if it *ever* does. So newly convinced sustainability investors (and existing practitioners) have little to fear!

The Tao of Chicken Soup

The Tao is an ancient Chinese Confucian concept. The written Chinese character translates directly (apparently; I'm no Chinese scholar) as "the path" or "the way." There is also a second venerable concept, although quite a bit younger and perhaps somewhat less mystical: the Jewish concept of using a bowl of chicken soup as an elixir and cure-all for colds and other minor health afflictions. The basic logic attributed to many a Jewish mother over the years has been this: "go on, *have* a bowl of chicken soup; it will probably help your cold and it couldn't possibly *hurt.*"

And thus it is with sustainable investment. Although, as we have seen, there is every reason to be highly optimistic that sustainable investment strategies will *add* value, at the *very* least we can always fall back on the logic and the Tao of chicken soup: it might help, and there is no way on God's earth that it could possibly *hurt*. After all, since when is having additional information, analysis, and perspective about a company being considered for investment a *bad* thing?

The only conceivable remaining argument against sustainability investing is the cost in time and money required to undertake and/or pay for the additional research. I would make two quick counterarguments. First, in the twenty-first century, sustainability research should now simply be an automatic part of the thorough job an analyst does in looking at a company; it should have become a basic part of the job description. Second, as we hope has been amply demonstrated throughout this book, the benefits of acquiring and using sustainability research generally *far* outweigh the costs. And the cost of *not* using it is increasing with each passing day.

Looking Over the Horizon

But what will the *next* generation of sustainability challenges and issues look like? Only a rash person would attempt a prediction with a high level of confidence. But one thing is certain: those companies that have shown themselves to be sufficiently strategic, farsighted, and nimble to cope with the *current* sustainability issues better than their competitors are by far the most promising candidates to be able to manage the *next* set effectively as well. As we have argued repeatedly throughout this book, *those* will be the best-managed companies of the early twenty-first century. They are precisely the types of companies that sustainable investors, their advisors, and their money managers should seek. And if they do so, they can expect to be rewarded. If not, well don't say you weren't warned! Sustainability investors, unite!

Sovereign Wealth Funds to the Rescue?

At present an enormous amount of business and general media attention is being directed at the so-called "sovereign wealth funds" (SWFs). One good reason for all this attention is that the SWFs have collectively invested some $80 billion recently for strategic stakes in such iconic but troubled U.S. commercial and investment banks as Citigroup, Morgan Stanley, and Merrill Lynch. The SWFs are huge blocks of investment capital controlled at the national level by public or quasipublic agencies.

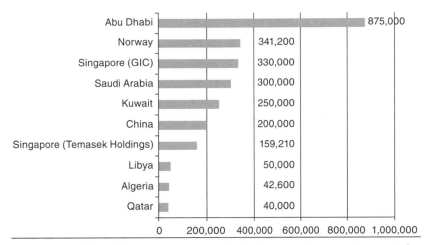

FIGURE 12.1 The 10 largest sovereign wealth funds. Source: Innovest Strategic Value Advisors

In total, the SWFs currently control some $3.5 trillion in investable assets, much of it fueled by unprecedented oil prices. The largest of them all is the fund controlled by the Emirate of Abu Dhabi on the Persian Gulf, which is believed to have nearly a trillion dollars in investable assets, an amount equal to roughly 500% of the emirate's entire gross domestic product (GDP)! Other large funds are held by Norway, Singapore, Kuwait, Dubai, Saudi Arabia, Qatar, Russia, and, mostly recently, China (Figure 12.1).

The SWFs have grown dramatically over the past 3 years, largely propelled by exponential increases in world oil prices. Collectively, the SWFs are expected to control some $12 trillion by 2015. While that is not a dominant share of the $60+ trillion in total global investable assets, it is hardly inconsequential. (By way of comparison, $12 trillion would be roughly the size of the entire U.S. economy.)

Moreover, unlike other huge blocks of investment capital, SWF assets can usually be mobilized very rapidly, coherently, and without the delay-causing niceties of multiple committee meetings, public discussions and debates, or pesky shareholder activism. The decision-making chain is short and efficient. This speed and agility, coupled with the sheer volume and growth rates of the assets involved, make SWFs potentially major, strategic players in the Sustainable Investment Revolution in the decade ahead. In the Persian Gulf region alone the sovereign funds together earned an estimated $180 *billion* in investment income in 2007. That's a tidy little supplement to the $315 billion they earned from their oil and gas production. As a result, in the Gulf today, one of the most pressing and difficult challenges they have—quite literally—is figuring out how to *spend* and invest it! Fortunately, we just happen to have a few suggestions in that regard, just to be helpful.

Numerous critics in the West have accused many of the SWFs of having a lack of transparency and of having motives that are driven more by (allegedly malign) national policy interests than by "pure" commercial considerations. The Western critics argue that this creates unfair advantages in the increasingly competitive world of international investment. Whatever the substantive merits of these criticisms, there can be no doubt that the SWFs see this Western backlash as a serious and growing problem. It has already caused at least two major, high-profile transactions to be blocked in the United States. The first was the attempt in 2005 by the China National Offshore Oil Company (CNOOC) to take over U.S. oil major Chevron. CNOOC is essentially a state entity, and the proposed $16.5 billion takeover aroused precisely the same sort of strategic angst and animosities that would have been generated by CIC, China's new SWF. Several United States senators and congressmen (plus James Woolsey, a former Central Intelligence Agency head) described the bid as "a threat to national security." Political and popular uproar ultimately caused CNOOC to withdraw its bid and walk away.

The second example occurred in 2006. Dubai Ports (DP) World, one of the world's largest and most successful port operators, made a bid to acquire the management companies of six major U.S. ports, including New York, New Jersey, and Miami. DP World was—and is—wholly owned by the government of Dubai and is controlled by the emirate's ruler, Sheikh Mohammed bin Rashid Al Maktoum. The sale had been agreed to by the owners (interestingly, another foreign firm, but in this case British) and was strongly supported by U.S. President George W. Bush. Notwithstanding all of that, DP World evidently decided that discretion would be the better part of valor and withdrew in the face of howls of objection. The port operations were subsequently sold to an American investment company, AIG's Global Investment Group. The episode continues to rankle in Dubai to this day and has affected the wealthy emirate's strategy for dealing with the West. (Indeed, *one* of its strategies now appears to be dealing with the *East* instead, where similar problems are much less likely to arise.)

The sovereign funds represent a potentially powerful accelerant for the Sustainable Investment Revolution. Their size, growth rates, decision-making mechanisms, and high visibility all give them the ability to make an enormous difference. Imagine what introducing sustainability considerations into the heart of 12 *trillion* worth of investment strategies could do! To date, however, the majority of that potential has yet to be realized. The only sovereign fund that has so far devoted any real intellectual or financial resources to environmentally and socially enhanced investing is Norway's well-regarded Government Pension Fund—Global. Organizations such as the OECD and the International Monetary Fund (IMF) frequently identify the Norwegian Fund as the "poster child" for transparency and good governance that other SWFs should follow. And that is not unfair; the Norwegian Fund *is* indeed a model of transparency and good governance. But even Norway's efforts in this area have so far been confined to traditional, negatively screened socially responsible investment approaches, *not* the third-generation, returns-seeking sustainability strategies recommended in this book.[2] Perhaps they soon will; we certainly hope so. But until they do, there is an excellent opportunity for one of the other SWFs to "leapfrog" them and take a global leadership position.

I have a suggestion to make. The SWFs are all universal owners *par excellence.* They are investing for the long term and for the overall economic and social health of their entire countries. They thus have all of the usual reasons for adopting sustainable investment strategies—although to date only Norway has done so.

They also have, in our opinion, one powerful and *additional* motivation for joining the Sustainable Investment Revolution—creating invaluable reputational capital in the West. If, for example, the recently created $200 billion Chinese Investment Corporation or the $875 billion Abu Dhabi Investment Authority were to announce publicly that all of their investments would henceforth be carefully reviewed for their environmental and social impact and that best-in-class companies would likely be favored as investment candidates, the degree of suspicion that several of the SWFs currently evoke in the West could be significantly reduced.

It is still too early to tell just how quickly the sovereign funds (and, for that matter, other large investors) will grasp the full implications and potential of the global transformation which is now underway. But they could certainly do a lot worse than to wrap themselves in the protective cloak and aura (not to mention superior *returns*) of sustainable investment! And with sovereign wealth funds expected to grow by some 700 percent over the next decade, there are no better vehicles to accelerate the Sustainable Investment Revolution.

Whether or not the sovereign funds actually rise to that challenge remains to be seen. But we can predict one thing with complete confidence: twenty-first century investors who understand, embrace, and harness the power of that Revolution will outperform those who do not.

Appendices:
How It's Actually Done

The first two appendices are intended to provide the reader with some concrete examples of what company-specific sustainability research actually looks like.

Appendix 1 contains a broad-based sustainability profile of Petro-China, one of the most important companies in Asia. That analysis, which is based on the "Four-Piller" concept of sustainability advanced in this book, addresses: Environment, Human Capital, Stakeholder Capital, and Strategic Governance. The company profile is called an "Intangible Value Assessment."

Appendix 2 provides an example of "drilling" down more deeply within the Environmental pillar to focus on one company's (Arcelor's) specific exposure to climate risk. We use the term "Carbon Beta™" to describe a company's *net* risk exposure, which, in addition to downside risk, also includes an assessment of both risk management capability and a company's capacity to seize commercial opportunities on the upside. The resulting company profile is, accordingly, called a Carbon Beta™ profile.

Appendix 3 contains a list of the Global 100—the "100 most sustainable large companies in the world," as presented at the World Economic Forum in Davos, Switzerland in January 2008.

Appendix 4 contains a list of independent, specialist sustainability research providers. The list includes the top 20 firms as determined in the 2007 Thomson Extel survey of over 180 institutional asset owners and managers, with combined asset owners and managers, that have combined assets under management of over $2 trillion. The percentage figures on the right reflect the relative level of support each firm received.

Appendix 1: "Intangible Value Assessment" of Petro China

Innovest
STRATEGIC VALUE ADVISORS

www.innovestgroup.com
New York: +1 212 421-2000
London: +44 (0) 20 7073 0470
Toronto: +1 905 707-0876
Paris: +33 (0)1 44 54 04 89

Intangible Value Assessment

Aug-07

PetroChina Company

Country:	China
Ticker Symbol:	857-HK
Industrial Sector:	Integrated Oil & Gas
Combined IVA Rating:	CCC
Sub-Factors:	
Strategic Governance:	1.8
Human Capital:	1.3
Environment:	2.9
Stakeholder Capital:	3.3
Analyst:	Dana Sasarean 905-707-0876 dsasarean@innovestgroup.com

Intangible value comprises a growing percentage of companies' market capitalization. Innovest's IVA™ ratings analyze relative corporate performance on intangible value drivers related to the strength and sustainability of companies' competitive advantage. By assessing differentials typically not identified by traditional securities analysis, IVA™ ratings uncover hidden risks and value potential for investors. Ratings range from AAA (best) to CCC (worst). Scores on subfactors range from 10 (best) to 0 (worst).

PERFORMANCE / ALPHA INTENSITY MATRIX

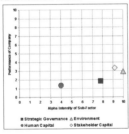

■ Strategic Governance △ Environment
● Human Capital ◇ Stakeholder Capital

This matrix situates the four key intangible value drivers along 2 dimensions: 1. How well or poorly the company performs on each of the 4 key factors. 2. How much impact that particular factor has on financial performance in that industry sector; its "alpha intensity".

RATING OUTLOOK: Negative

PetroChina does not have a comprehensive strategy to address environmental, social and governance (ESG) issues. The performance in key areas continues to be low with little prospects for improvement. Recent initiatives into clean technologies should provide good proxy for improvement in the future.

AREAS OF POTENTIAL RISK

Governmental Control and Restricted Governance Capability: PetroChina is a majority state owned company in an emerging market governed by a totalitarian regime. The sustainability ESG is merely compliance driven and lacks building blocks such clear commitments, disclosure and transparency, stakeholder feedback and engagement lags the sector with respect to standard governance mechanisms. Issues of concern include weak disclosure of corporate governance practices, majority non-independent board, majority of senior management and directors' involvement with the parent company (CNPC). CNPC is China's state-owned oil and gas company and holds 88.2% of PetroChina's share capital (see Strategic Governance section).

Ongoing Poor Health and Safety Performance: The company's series of explosions and fires resulting in injuries and deaths remains a serious issue of concern. In 2005 compared to 2004, the accident rate has decreased but the number of fatalities increased from 29 to 33. In a 2003 blast, 243 people died and thousands of others were injured and evacuated. Petro China has one of the worst fatality records in the sector, and that does not include any contractor data, usually a higher risk workforce. While the risk for financial consequences is somewhat limited, given the lack of adequate regulatory framework safeguarding health and safety practices, the impact on production, and productivity expands through low employee morale and poor work-conditions (see Human Capital section)

Human Rights Concerns Prompt Divestment: CNPC (PetroChina's parent company) presence in Sudan is fueling human rights atrocities there. For instance, in 2006, a number of high profile institutional investors in the US receded holdings in PetroChina. following pressure by human rights groups over the Chinese oil firm's links to Sudan. Such development reflects the reputation factor implication, despite the fact that PetroChina inherited the Chinese assets and has not know direct involvement in Sudan.

AREAS OF COMPETITIVE ADVANTAGE

Regulatory Focus on Clean Energy Opportunity Strategic developments: PetroChina, with recent initiative to set up a renewable energies department enters new business. While its emerging interest in renewable energies has strong links to the governmental policy for cleaner fuels PetroChina has also reportedly set-up a joint-venture with India's state company exploring a clean coal gasification technology with clear intellectual capacity and profit opportunity building (see below)..

STRATEGIC PROFIT OPPORTUNITIES

Leading firms in the sector are engaged in the development of alternative energy technologies. Initiatives include; higher-efficiency, lower-carbon fuels and energy systems, focus on natural gas, liquefaction and gasification technologies (coal-to-gas, gas-to-liquids), renewable power generation (wind, solar, biomass, geothermal) and biofuels, as well as hydrogen and carbon capture and storage technologies. Such activities will in our view create significant environmental and social benefits over the long term, in addition to being attractive investment opportunities.

PetroChina had taken specific steps to develop biofuels. In 2007, the company started work at its first biodiesel plant with a 10,000 million ton annual capacity. While its emerging interest in renewable energies has strong links to the governmental policy for cleaner fuels and securing a diverse energy base, PetroChina will benefit from its recent initiative to set up a renewable energies department. Unlike best practices, there is no disclosure of concrete commitments or targets.

PetroChina has also reportedly set-up a joint-venture with India's state company exploring a clean coal gasification technology with clear intellectual capacity and profit opportunity building. There is no follow up information detailing any concrete developments. Industry leaders in developed countries and in emerging markets are currently pursuing projects in this area acknowledging that the industry is experiencing the effects of national and international regulations and public pressure in this respect. China's government is also increasingly acknowledging the environmental implication of its economic boom and the need for long-term strategies and environmental protection.

Innovest
STRATEGIC VALUE ADVISORS

Intangible Value Assessment

COMPANY OVERVIEW

PetroChina Company Limited (Petro-China), one of China's largest companies, was established in 1999 as a subsidiary of the restructured state-owned China National Petroleum Corporation (CNPC). Petro-China produces close to two-thirds of China's oil and gas. The company inherited most of the domestic exploration and production (E&P), refining and marketing (R&M), chemicals, and natural gas assets of CNPC. In 2005, the company had proved reserves of 11.5 billion barrels of oil and 48 trillion cubic feet of natural gas. The company owns more than 8,500 miles of natural gas pipeline in China, operates 25 refineries and 12 chemical plants, and owns or operates more than 15,900 gas stations. Total revenue for 2006 was USD 88,237.41 million (CNY 668,978 million), a 21.5% increase from USD 68,432.22 million in 2005, of which Exploration and Production accounted for 12.5%, Refining and Marketing 71.5%, Natural Gas 4%, and Chemicals 12%. Other activities include pipelines construction and consulting services. Revenue broken down geographically for 2006 was Asia, 96.2%; and other, 3.8%. The company employed 446,290 at year-end 2006, up from 439,220 at the year-end 2005 (2004: 424,175 employees).

INDUSTRY DRIVING FORCES

Climate Change: Oil and gas companies are sizeable emitters of greenhouse gases. In the EU, production facilities are subject to emissions allocation under the EU trading scheme following Kyoto implementation. Other countries around the world are taking steps to address the carbon emissions challenge: in the US on a state-by-state basis, and in Canada federal regulation is on the way. Non-conventional oil exploration and refining, as well as heavier crude availability will result in higher energy intensity associated with bringing products to market. The carbon embedded within fuel products may also become a strategic management issue. Of strategic concern are the first generation biofuels development and potential global economic implications. Research and development of carbon capture and storage, fuel-cell, renewable energy, biofuels, as well as high efficient energy systems both for fuel engines and power generation are shaping the intellectual capital arena providing a highly competitive edge to companies embracing a proactive approach.

Global Energy Trends: The supply/demand equation remains tight and largely dominated by the supply side.

Global demand for crude oil is forecasted to grow an average of 2.2 % annually by 2012, while supply from non-OPEC countries is forecasted at a modest 1% annual growth. Global energy demand is expected to increase by 50-60% by 2030, fuelled by China and India's economic growth. Fossil fuels will remain the dominant energy source for decades to come, accounting in average for 83% of the overall increase in demand. The stress on the supply/demand equation is exacerbated by political instability, such as is found in the Middle East and Latin America, and has resulted in sustained record high oil prices. Such trends help the feasibility of non-conventional oil exploration such as oil sands, deep water, and arctic exploration and production. While the pressure on consumers increases, companies continue the trend in reporting large profits. One major challenge facing oil and gas companies is providing an adequate supply in a sustainable and socially acceptable manner.

Emerging Market Risk: Companies are increasingly searching for oil and gas reserves in volatile non-OECD regions. Companies operating in many emerging market countries are exposed to armed, civil and interethnic conflict, corruption, and human rights violation risks. Security remains an issue of concern as previous years reflect a surge in the attacks on installations and hostage-taking, especially in Nigeria. Staff evacuations and production stoppages affect output and returns; environmental impact in such regions has also increasingly emerged and resulted in lawsuits, such as the cases of Ecuador and Peru, or the widespread environmental pollution in Niger Delta. Mass poverty despite substantial oil revenues in the context of corrupt governments prompted calls from foreign governments and humanitarian organizations for revenue transparency and accountability. This is particularly pertinent to the situation in post-war Iraq. Other countries of concern include Angola, Nigeria, Sudan, Chad, and Azerbaijan.

Changing Regulatory Environment: Regulations are affecting all facets of operations in the oil and gas industry. Compliance with changes in fuel content standards as well as operational emissions has large cost impact on refining activities. Across the US and Canada, oil refineries were required to limit their sulfur content for vehicle emission requirements. Petrochemical and chemical regulations in the EU have been recently reinforced with the launch of REACH regulation in June 2007. MTBE (a gasoline additive) legislation has

also impacted producers of gasoline and led to significant environmental liabilities, especially across the US.

Mergers and Acquisitions/Privatization and Nationalization: Industry consolidation is still evident through two mergers and acquisitions over the past year; Royal Dutch Shell acquired Shell Canada and there is an upcoming merger between Statoil and part of Norsk Hydro. In Venezuela, Bolivia and Ecuador indigenous peoples' demands for better oil wealth distribution has led to civil unrest, protests and strikes, and pressure on governments to nationalize the oil and gas resources. For example, Venezuela has forced foreign companies to render control to the state, failure to reach asset ownership and production agreements have resulted in state seizing assets and companies stopping production, such is the case of ConocoPhillips. Some OPEC countries (Iran, Saudi Arabia) that were once closed to foreign investment are now opening; other markets, including Libya, are re-opening, changing the industry's competitive landscape.

STRATEGIC GOVERNANCE: **1.8**
Trend: **Down**

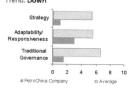

0   2   4   6   8   10

■ PetroChina Company   □ Average

PetroChina does not have a comprehensive strategy to address environmental, social and governance (ESG) issues. It lacks some of the building blocs of a good approach while it faces significant environmental and social challenges.

Best practice for the sector includes formal policies, implementation of management systems and setting up improvement targets, monitoring, disclosure, and independent verification mechanisms.

The company is slowly moving from a focus on safety and pollution management, into developing a renewable energy strategy. In 2007, the company started work at its first biodiesel plant with a 10,000 million tons annual capacity. In 2006, it launched a new division for renewable energy under the exploration and development department.

Innovest
STRATEGIC VALUE ADVISORS

Intangible Value Assessment

However, unlike most of the companies in the sector, PetroChina's take on climate change lacks the building blocks in addressing GHG emissions or energy efficiency.

PetroChina does not have corporate governance guidelines but has adopted codes of business conduct and ethics for senior management and employees. PetroChina now have a health, safety and environment (HSE) committee on the board, additional to its Quality, Safety and Environmental Protection Department reporting directly to the CEO.

Superior to some of the emerging market companies in the sector, PetroChina publishes and annual HSE report, which includes some qualitative information and limited key environmental performance data.

Despite some good developments, such as the HSE management system implementation, the company's approach to sustainability remains largely compliance driven. Regulatory framework in China remains lower compared to the EU, the US and some other Western countries, and enforcement is much weaker or non-existent in comparison.

Governance Metrics International, the corporate governance ratings firm and our research partner, gives the company an overall global rating of 1.5 for its corporate governance attributes. All companies rated by GMI are scored on a scale of 1.0 (lowest) to 10.0 (highest). All company ratings are calculated relative to the other 3800 companies rated by GMI worldwide. A GMI rating of 9 or higher is considered to be well above average. A rating of 7.5 to 8.5 is considered to be above average, 6.0 to 7.0 is considered average, 3.5 to 5.5 is considered to be below average and 3.0 or less is considered to be well below average.

Issues of concern include weak disclosure of corporate governance practices, majority non-independent board, majority of senior management and directors' involvement with the parent company (CNPC). CNPC is China's state-owned oil and gas company and holds 88.2% of PetroChina's share capital.

PRODUCTS & SERVICES

Product innovation and intellectual capital is pursued in this industry by involvement in a range of diversified energy and technology initiatives.

PetroChina has a corporate R&D department that includes the Science, Technology and Information Management Department.

PetroChina as well has an Exploration and Development Research Institute. It is not clear however; how much the company is investing into areas with substantial upside potential. The company is stating interest in R&D for reducing the operational environmental impact. There is also evidence that the company is serious about investing in renewable energy and biofuel.

The company is lagging behind the sector in terms of initiating strategic partnerships for developing and researching cleaner and more efficient energy systems, GHG emissions management, and CO_2 capture and storage.

Media reports point out some developments, such as the joint PetroChina-ONGC (India's state-owned company) testing of a new underground coal gasification project, with a significantly smaller environmental footprint. Such developments are significant given the high reliance on coal-generated energy in the region. Similar to other competitors in the sector, PetroChina manufactures and distributes a range of products considered to be hazardous and which would represent a general product safety concern if improperly handled. For instance, PetroChina produces ethylene, synthetic resins and rubber, and polymers.

Unlike the case of other companies in the sector, it is not clear how the company is handling the H&S management of its products. Best practice includes integrated product safety management and extensive product information venues. There is no evidence of the availability of material safety data sheets online.

HUMAN CAPITAL: 1.3

Trend: **Steady**

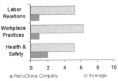

PetroChina's number of employees has steadily increased over the past years. The company employed 439,220 at the year-end 2005 (2004: 424,175 employees), a 3.5% increase compared to previous year.. According to numerous NGOs and labor activist groups, freedom of association is still denied in the communist China. The regulatory framework in China is also highly

criticized for lacking basic provisions for protecting labor and human rights, such as freedom of association, collective bargaining, and the right to strike, except in situations that threatens personal safety and which violate health and safety rules. The government exclusively allows the centrally controlled All-China Federation of Trade Unions (ACFTU), criticized as highly ineffective in protecting workers' rights.

PetroChina fails to disclose any specific information with regards to human resources policies and programs. It however states that safeguarding health and safety (H&S) is a priority. H&S is apparently included in an integrated management system that theoretically includes improvement targets. In the light of poor performance in the past, PetroChina is building a stronger H&S training platform in an effort to build a safety culture. In 2005, more than 207, 000 employees participated in various safety training.

The H&S performance disclosure includes good quantitative indicators that show wide fluctuations, and with some exceptions, unstable improvement trends, especially on a business department basis. Unlike many peers, the company leaves out contractors' performance from performance reporting, a material aspect of H&S for the sector.

PetroChina has one of the worst fatality records in the sector, and that does not include any contractor data. In a 2003 blast, 243 people died and thousands of others were injured and evacuated.

In 2005 compared to 2004, the total accident rate has decreased but the number of fatalities increased from 29 to 33. In 2005, PetroChina experienced 108 accidents, of which there were 20 fatal accidents, causing 33 fatalities (including 11 production accidents involving 20 deaths and 13 fatalities in road accidents). The company states that direct economic losses were RMB 81.26 million yuan. Compared to 2004, the accidents decreased 28 percent in 2005 but the death toll rose 14 percent. In 2006, PetroChina experienced at least 21 fatalities. The company's series of explosions and fires resulting in injuries and deaths remains a serious issue of concern.

The company's exposure to human rights, health and safety, and work practices related risk remains high while the strategy is at best regulatory compliance oriented.

Innovest
STRATEGIC VALUE ADVISORS

Intangible Value Assessment

ENVIRONMENTAL PERFORMANCE: 2.9
Trend: **Steady**

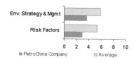

PetroChina's approach to environmental management is far from proactive, lacking clear commitment towards key environmental issues facing the industry such as climate change, and water contamination and water use.

The company states that HSE criteria are included into the decision-making process. However, the approach is compliance-based, at best oriented towards issuance of internal rules and regulations.

According to company's 2005 HSE report, in 2005 it had audited its HSE Management System at 21 regional companies, established at 54 such companies.

The HSE management system implementation was completed in 2005. Unlike best practices the company does not seek external validation trough internationally recognized certification of such system such as the ISO14001.

PetroChina's environmental performance disclosure is minimal compared to other companies in the sector; however, it does include some performance indicators. Key indicators missing include spills, GHG emissions, energy efficiency, and water use. The company reports water discharges, down 23% in 2005 compared to 2004, and SO_2 and NOx, both increased by 10% and 3.4% respectively. In 2005, PetroChina was below median for SOx intensity compared to peers (tons/million USD sales).

PetroChina's exposure to accidents with high environmental impact risk remains high. In 2005, an explosion, that killed 5 and injured 23, at the Jilin company's benzene plant contaminated the Songhua river with a 100 ton spill that traveled hundreds of km, reaching Russia and possibly the coasts of Japan. Millions of people in two cities had water cut for days. Wildlife has also been drastically affected by the highly carcinogenic benzene. The company and the government have been heavily criticized for delays and cover-ups in informing the public and the neighboring Russia about the spill. In 2006, in relation to this spill and related water contamination, PetroChina was handed the maximum

fine of 1 million yuan (USD 125,000), the largest to date in China.

PetroChina's environmental performance lags behind the sector given the evident lack of disclosure and transparency coupled with many challenges and ineffectiveness in implementation of the HSE management system.

STAKEHOLDER CAPITAL: 3.3
Trend: **Steady**

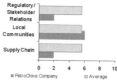

Similar to the other sustainability aspects, PetroChina lags behind the sector with respect to stakeholder strategy. This puts the company at a disadvantage in terms of anticipating stakeholder expectations and managing risks associated with these demands. While such demands are drastically undermined given China's authoritarian government, the public and civil society have reportedly become, in recent years, more vocal on pollution and poorly design industrial projects. Private environmental organizations have reportedly persuaded authorities to block development or revise development plans. Given an up-trend in the strengthening of environmental regulations in China, the company may also face liabilities in connection with its past and current emissions and ground and water contamination levels.

In the US, shareholder activism repeatedly targets large investment and pension funds persuading them to divest PetroChina shares on the grounds that the company's parent CNPC presence in Sudan is fueling human rights atrocities there. For instance, in 2006, a number of high profile universities in the US, including Yale and Harvard, pursued by students' activism have receded holdings in PetroChina. Fidelity Investments, the world's largest mutual fund company, divested 91% of its holdings in PetroChina following pressure by human rights groups over the Chinese oil firm's links to Sudan.

Despite its proclaimed 'people-oriented' and 'society-benefited' concepts, there is no indication of any initiative to contribute

to local communities. Average strategies for the sector include: basic mechanisms for stakeholder communication and engagement, reporting and collaboration with the local communities on key issues, such as emissions and contamination impact on health, and contribution to local development. Lacking such orientation and given past environmental challenges, PetroChina is rated below average for the sector.

EMERGING MARKETS:

As previously mentioned, PetroChina was established as a subsidiary of the state-owned China National Petroleum Corporation (CNPC) when it inherited most of the domestic assets and liabilities of CNPC relating to E&P, R&M, chemicals and natural gas businesses. CNPC still controls about 90% of shareholding capital and many of the corporate leaders are simultaneously on the board of CNPC. Thus, due to ties to the CNPC and the government, many of the human rights violations allegations are often targeting PetroChina too. China is the second most populous country in the world with an impressive economic growth linked to an estimated doubling of its energy demand by 2030. China's authoritarian communist government's quest for natural resources, specifically oil and gas, have been allegedly supporting corrupt and repressive regimes in Africa, Latin America, and Asia, to the disadvantage of the people of these regions. Prominent international human-rights watchdogs criticize the Chinese oil purchasing and massive oil-backed loans as well as donations without the pledge to respect human rights that, at least theoretically, accompanies Western enterprises. Examples include involvement in Sudan, Zimbabwe, Angola, as well as Myanmar (former Burma). China is notorious for human and labor rights violations, lack of freedom of expression and poor working and living conditions.

Innovest

Intangible Value Assessment

SRI NEGATIVE SCREENING INFORMATION

The following information is provided for investors who for various ethical or social reasons may wish to avoid investments in companies involved in the following business areas. Innovest's IVA product uses a positive screening approach to identify superior management. Beyond assessing potential market risks, involvement in the following businesses does not impact IVA ratings.

SCREEN

Weapons Production: No known involvement.
Tobacco: No known involvement.
Nuclear Power: No known involvement.
GMO: No known involvement.
Animal Testing: No known involvement.
Alcohol: No known involvement.
Pornography: No known involvement.
Gambling: No known involvement.
Burma: No known involvement.
Other: No known involvement.

COMPETITIVE SET

Integrated Oil & Gas
BG Group PLC
BP PLC
Chevron Corp.
ConocoPhillips
ENI S.p.A.
Exxon Mobil Corp.
Gazprom Inc
Hess Corp.
Husky Energy Inc
Imperial Oil
Lukoil OAO
Marathon Oil Corp.
MOL Magyar Olaj Gazipari
Murphy Oil Corp.
Norsk Hydro AS
Novatek
Occidental Petroleum Corp.
Oil & Gas Development Company
Oil & Natural Gas Corp. Limited
OMV AG
Origin Energy Limited
Petro-Canada
PetroChina Company
Petroleo Brasileiro S.A. - Petrobras
Petroleos (CEPSA)
PTT Public Company Limited
Repsol YPF
Royal Dutch Shell Plc
Sasol Limited
Sinopec Corporation
Statoil
Suncor Energy Inc
Surgutneftegas Oao
Tatneft
Total SA

Appendix 2: Carbon Beta Profile of Arcelor SA

Innovest
STRATEGIC VALUE ADVISORS

Carbon Beta™ Profile
ARCELOR SA
February 2008

Generated by Innovest Strategic Value Advisors
www.innovestgroup.com

ARCELOR SA

Carbon Beta™

Company Rating	AA
Carbon Improvement Vector:	▲

Carbon Scores

Carbon Management Strategy:	9
Carbon Risk Exposure:	2
Carbon Strategic Opportunities:	6
Carbon Performance Improvement:	8

Industry Carbon Combined Intensity

Carbon Combined Intensity [a]	4
Carbon Direct Intensity:	5
Carbon Indirect Intensity:	5
Carbon Market Sensitivity:	3
2006 Sales (USD millions):	$61,336
Market Cap. (USD Million):	$99,411

Carbon Sector Snapshot

SUMITOMO METAL INDUSTRIES LIMITED	
KOBE STEEL LIMITED	
ARCELOR SA	AA
RAUTARUUKKI OYJ	
OUTOKUMPU OYJ	
THYSSENKRUPP AG	
NIPPON STEEL CORPORATION	
JFE HOLDINGS	
VOESTALPINE AG	
NISSHIN STEEL COMPANY LIMITED	
DAIDO STEEL COMPANY LIMITED	
SSAB AB	
NUCOR CORP.	
TOKYO STEEL MANUFACTURING LIMITED	
BLUESCOPE STEEL LIMITED	
BOEHLER-UDDEHOLM AG	
ACERINOX SA	
UNITED STATES STEEL CORP.	
ALLEGHENY TECHNOLOGIES INC	

Compliance Costs

WACCRT™[c]	-5.8%
Industry Discount Rate [d]	10.2%

	Exp. Case	Min.Case	Max. Case
Carbon Price ($/t CO2e)	$28	$18	$45
Annual Cost of Compliance ($1000)	$256,262	$156,216	$411,263
Exposure (% of EBITDA)	4.6%	2.8%	7.4%
NPV of Abatement Costs ($1000)	$1,064,882	$676,054	$1,709,760
Exposure (% of Mkt. Cap.)	1.1%	0.7%	1.7%

Company Carbon Positioning

Scope 1: Direct Carbon Emissions (t CO2e):	54,900,000 r
Scope 2: Electricity Indirect Carbon Emissions (t CO2e):	4,400,000
Scope 3: Other Indirect Carbon Emissions (t CO2e):	NR
Industry Average Direct Carbon Emissions (t CO2e):	29,646,556
Direct Carbon Emissions Ratio: [e]	1.85
Carbon Intensity (t CO2e /USD sales in millions):	895
Industry Average Carbon Intensity (t CO2e /USD sales in millions):	1,458
Direct Carbon Intensity Ratio: [f]	0.61

Company Overview

Arcelor was established in February 2001 following the merger of Luxembourg" s Arbed, France" s Usinor and Spain" s Aceralia. The group" s principal activities are the production, processing and distribution of a wide range of steel products, which are then used in the automobile, construction, mechanical engineering, packaging and domestic appliance industries. Main product areas are flat and long carbon steel, stainless steel and distribution, processing and trading. The merger significantly increased the group" s geographic coverage and product diversity, and Arcelor now employs 95,000 individuals in over 60 countries. Employees are based in the EU (82%); South America (16%); the US (1%); and the rest of the world (0.3%). Arcelor made shipments of 51 million tons of steel in 2004 (2003: 40.2 million).

Arcelor plans to channel resources into its most profitable European operations and develop businesses in Brazil, Argentina and China, where high automobile sales are generating a growing demand for steel. While Arcelor is restructuring its European operations, it is building its presence overseas, including a joint venture with Nippon Steel and Baoshan Iron & Steel Company. In 2004, turnover was EUR 30.2 billion (USD 36.8 billion), (2003: EUR 25.9 billion [USD 31.6 billion]). The majority of revenues in 2004 were generated in the EU (80%) followed by the US (8%); South America (7%) and other (5%).

The group has recently acquired Canadian competitor, Dofasco Inc., for USD 1.5 billion (EUR 1.2 billion), and Arcelor, itself, is the object of a hostile takeover bid by Mittal Steel Company. (See Industry Driving Forces.)

Carbon Management Strategy

Arcelor has developed one of the most advanced carbon management strategies in this sector, although investors should be aware that the company's recent merger with Mittal could have detrimental affects on its long-term strategy. In relation to climate change, Arcelor collaborates with other International Iron and Steel Institute (IISI) members to develop new technologies to reduce CO2

Carbon Beta[TM] Profile
ARCELOR SA
February 2008

Generated by Innovest Strategic Value Advisors
www.innovestgroup.com

emissions from blast furnaces. Policy at Arcelor is made at Management Board level. The company's EVP R&D is in charge of innovation and research projects related to climate change, while the company's EVP Finance is in charge of the financial aspects of the CO_2 management. Arcelor reports a wide range of environmental KPIs, including CO_2, sulfur oxide and nitrogen oxide emissions.

Carbon Risk Exposure

The company faces generally high carbon risk exposure as a result of its expansive international presence, high absolute emission levels and operational focus in Europe, where environmental regulations are tightening. As a result of developments such as the EU ETS, Arcelor is under increasing pressure to reduce energy use and GHG emissions. Arcelor has voiced concerns over the allocation and trading of GHG emission allowances in the EU ETS, claiming the allowances distort competition among steel producers. Arcelor has set a clear objective of reducing its CO_2 missions in Europe by 25% by 2012 compared with 1990.

Carbon Strategic Opportunities

Arcelor's high strength steels are lighter and when used in a car they allow less fuel consumption thus meaning less CO_2 emission per vehicle. Arcelor Body Concept (ABC) allows a reduction of 20% of the total weight of a car body in white. For automotive, packaging, construction and domestic appliances, the indefinitely recyclability of steel is a clear competitive advantage. In Europe, Arcelor heads the ULCOS (Ultra Low CO_2 Steel-making) project, which brings together 48 partners consisting of companies, research centres and universities. It is evaluating all feasible techniques such as gas recycling in blast furnaces, the use of hydrogen and biomass, and techniques for separating and storing CO_2 in suitable geological structures. In the meantime, Arcelor is also exploring alternative ways to cut down its CO_2 emissions by means of using renewables energies. Through its Brazilian subsidiaries, the Arcelor Group is a major player in the field of renewable energies.

Carbon Performance Improvement

Arcelor is at the leading edge of addressing climate change-related risks and opportunities for this sector, and we anticipate continued developments in this area.

[a] Carbon Combined Intensity. In order to identify industry sectors that are the most exposed to climate change risks and opportunities, Innovest has developed a three pronged approach to rate the specific risks of sectors along their entire value chain: upstream, internal and downstream. This composite Carbon Intensity factor (0-lowest exposure, 5-highest exposure) is derived from the three categories of carbon intensities: Direct, Indirect, and Market Sensitivity. The index reflects the relative carbon risk exposure of the sectors along the entire value chain.

[b] Compliance costs are calculated as the cost of mitigating emissions above the limit established by a target applied to a baseline level. In the model, it is assumed that permits are being grandfathered up to the baseline level minus the abatement target. Additionally, the permits corresponding to the exceeding emissions above the target imposed to the baseline are being purchased in the market.

[c] Weighted Average Country Carbon Reduction Target (WACCRT™). The WACCRT™ refers to the expected emissions reduction targets according to applicable legislations where a company has relevant assets, domestically and internationally. In this sense, the metric shows a weighted average for the restrictions that a firm faces in the countries and regions it operates during the mandated compliance period.

[d] Industry Discount Rate. The industry discount rate is calculated from the Weighed Average Cost of Capital (WACC) from each specific industry as of January, 2007. For calculating it, we used the weighted average of the cost of equity and after-tax cost of debt, weighted by the market values of equity and debt. For the weights, there were used cumulated market values for the entire sector.

[e] Direct Carbon Emissions Ratio. The ratio between the direct CO_2 emissions (tonnes of CO_2e) of the company and the industry average direct carbon emissions. It is a measure of the company's current or potential emissions abatement requirement that the company faces in its sector. If the Direct Carbon Emissions Ratio is greater than 1, the company is considered to have a relatively high risk exposure in its sector.

[f] When specific industry output is available (e.g., MWh in the Electric Utilities sector), it is used instead of revenues to calculate the firm and sector's Carbon Intensity. However, CI in monetary terms is a practical measure to compare carbon efficiencies across sectors.

Appendix 3: The "Global 100" Most Sustainable Companies*

Company Name	Country	GICS© Sector
3I Group PLC	United Kingdom	Financials
Acciona SA	Spain	Industrials
Accor	France	Consumer Discretionary
Adidas Salomon Agency	Germany	Consumer Discretionary
Advanced Micro Devices	United States	Information Technology
Agilent Technologies Inc	United States	Information Technology
Air France-KLM	France	Industrials
Alcoa Inc	United States	Materials
American International Group Inc	United States	Financials
Atlantia	Italy	Industrials
Atlas Copco AB	Sweden	Industrials
Australia And New Zealand Banking Group	Australia	Financials
Babcock & Brown	Australia	Financials
BASF AG	Germany	Materials
Baxter International Inc	United States	Health Care
British Land Company PLC	United Kingdom	Financials
British Sky Broadcasting Group PLC	United Kingdom	Consumer Discretionary
BT Group PLC	United Kingdom	Telecommunication Services
Cable & Wireless PLC	United Kingdom	Telecommunication Services
Cattles PLC	United Kingdom	Financials
Centrica PLC	United Kingdom	Utilities
Coca Cola Company	United States	Consumer Staples
Credit Agricole SA	France	Financials
Daikin Industries Limited	Japan	Industrials
Denso Corp.	Japan	Consumer Discretionary
Deutsche Boerse AG	Germany	Financials
Deutsche Post AG	Germany	Industrials
Dexia	Belgium	Financials
Diageo PLC	United Kingdom	Consumer Staples
Eastman Kodak Company	United States	Consumer Discretionary
Electrocomponents PLC	United Kingdom	Information Technology
Fabege AB	Sweden	Financials
Fortum Corp.	Finland	Utilities
FPL Group Inc	United States	Utilities
Fresenius Medical Care AG	Germany	Health Care
General Electric Company	United States	Industrials
Genzyme Corp.	United States	Health Care
H & M Hennes & Mauritz AB	Sweden	Consumer Discretionary

*This list, updated annually, is created for the World Economic Forum in Davas, Switzerland. The project is a collaboration between Innovest Strategic Value Advisors and the publisher, Corporate Knights.

Company Name	Country	GICS© Sector
Hbos PLC	United Kingdom	Financials
Hewlett-Packard Company	United States	Information Technology
Honda Motor Company Limited	Japan	Consumer Discretionary
Iberdrola SA	Spain	Utilities
Inditex SA	Spain	Consumer Discretionary
ING Groep NV	Netherlands	Financials
Insurance Australia Group	Australia	Financials
Intel Corp.	United States	Information Technology
Johnson Matthey PLC	United Kingdom	Materials
Kesko Corp.	Finland	Consumer Staples
Kuraray Company Limited	Japan	Materials
Lafarge	France	Materials
Land Securities PLC	United Kingdom	Financials
Liberty International PLC	United Kingdom	Financials
L'Oreal	France	Consumer Staples
Marks & Spencer Group PLC	United Kingdom	Consumer Discretionary
Matsushita Electric Industrial Company	Japan	Consumer Discretionary
Mayr-Melnhof Karton AG	Austria	Materials
Mitchells & Butlers PLC	United Kingdom	Consumer Discretionary
Mitsubishi Heavy Industries Limited	Japan	Industrials
MTR Corporation Limited	China	Industrials
Neste Oil Corporation	Finland	Energy
Nestle	Switzerland	Consumer Staples
Nexen Inc	Canada	Energy
Nike Inc	United States	Consumer Discretionary
Nippon Yusen KK	Japan	Industrials
Nokia Corporation	Finland	Information Technology
Novo Nordisk A/S	Denmark	Health Care
Novozymes A/S	Denmark	Materials
NSK Limited	Japan	Industrials
NTT Docomo Inc	Japan	Telecommunication Services
OMV AG	Austria	Energy
Pinnacle West Capital Corp.	United States	Utilities
Reed Elsevier PLC	UK/Netherlands	Consumer Discretionary
Ricoh Company Limited	Japan	Information Technology
Rio Tinto PLC	UK/Australia	Materials
Roche Holdings Limited	Switzerland	Health Care
Royal Bank Of Canada	Canada	Financials
Royal Bank of Scotland	United Kingdom	Financials
Royal Dutch Shell PLC	United Kingdom	Energy
Sainsbury (J) PLC	United Kingdom	Consumer Staples
Saipem	Italy	Energy
SAP AG	Germany	Information Technology
SCA AB	Sweden	Materials
Scania AB	Sweden	Industrials

Company Name	Country	GICS© Sector
Sekisui Chemical Company Limited	Japan	Consumer Discretionary
Serco Group PLC	United Kingdom	Industrials
Smith & Nephew PLC	United Kingdom	Health Care
Societe Generale	France	Financials
State Street Corp.	United States	Financials
Swiss Reinsurance Company	Switzerland	Financials
The Capita Group PLC	United Kingdom	Industrials
Tietoenator OYJ	Finland	Information Technology
Toppan Printing Company Limited	Japan	Industrials
Toyota Motor Corp.	Japan	Consumer Discretionary
Transcanada Corp.	Canada	Energy
Unilever PLC	United Kingdom	Consumer Staples
United Technologies Corp.	United States	Industrials
Vestas Windsystems A/S	Denmark	Industrials
Walt Disney Company	United States	Consumer Discretionary
Westpac Banking Corp.	Australia	Financials
Yell Group PLC	United Kingdom	Consumer Discretionary

Appendix 4: Top 20 Independent Sustainability Research Providers (Thomson Extel)*

THOMSON EXTEL & UKSIF SRI & SUSTAINABILITY SURVEY 2007

JUNE 28, 2007

POSITION	RANK THE INDEPENDENT RESEARCH PROVIDERS YOU USE:	2007%
1	INNOVEST	21.05
2	Vigeo	17.07
3	Trucost	11.22
4	EIRIS Services	10.77
5	Governance Metrics (GMI)	8.56
6	ISS	5.33
7	Glass Lewis	4.28
8	Manifest Information Services	4.27
9	Oekom Research	3.72
10	Proxinvest SARL	2.74
11	SIRI Company	2.36
12	KLD Research and Analytics	1.91
13	Jantzi Research	1.35
14	RREV	1.05
15	Stoxx Limited	1.03
16	World Resources Institute	0.94
17	FTSE	0.79
18	Independent Minds	0.56
19	European Corporate Governance Services (ECGS)	0.45
20	New Energy Finance	0.19

*List derived from 2007 Thomson Extel survey of global institutional investors. Percentages indicate the level of investor support.

Notes

Changing Finance and Financing Change: The Genesis of This Book

1. Innovest research is referenced several times throughout this book. This is not an effort to create an "advertorial" for the firm, but rather for two very pragmatic reasons: first, for the most part, similar research is simply not available elsewhere, and second, I am obviously far more familiar with it. I beg the reader's indulgence.

2. Much of the contemporary literature uses the acronym "ESG," with the "G" standing for "governance." I break with this convention throughout this book and content myself with only *two* letters—ES. I do so because I believe that corporate governance, at least as it has traditionally been defined, has entirely different philosophical origins, concerns, and adherents. The "ESG" moniker is, to me, an alphabetical marriage of convenience, and a somewhat forced one at that. The "E" and the "S" seem to me to be qualitatively different from the "G," and are the prime focus of this book.

3. Thomas Friedman, *The World is Flat—and Hot!;* Peter Senge *et al. The Necessary Revolution* (New York: Doubleday, 2008).

Chapter 1. Welcome to the Sustainable Investment Revolution!

1. For a convincing litany of concrete examples, see, for example, Daniel Esty and Andrew Winston, *Green to Gold: How Smart Companies Use Environmental Strategy to Innovate, Create Value, and Build Competitive Advantage* (New Haven: Yale University Press, 2006). We shall provide a number of additional examples ourselves in Chapter 7.

2. The unofficial starting gun for the revolution was arguably sounded with the publication in 1987 of the seminal Brundtland Commission report *Our Common Future* to the United Nations. It was followed up in 1992 by the "Earth Summit" in Rio de Janeiro, Brazil, which attracted more than 100 heads of state.

3. See Robert Monks and Nell Minow, *Watching the Watchers: Corporate Governance in the 21ˢᵗ Century* (Cambridge, MA: Blackwell Publishers, 1996); James Hawley and Andrew Williams, *The Rise of Fiduciary Capitalism* (Philadelphia: University of Pennsylvania Press, 2000); and "Universal Owners: Challenges and Opportunities," *Corporate Governance: An International Review* 15 (May 2007): 415–20.

4. Hawley and Williams, *op. cit.*

5. *Pensions & Investments*, September 3, 2007.

6. In 1968, Garrett Hardin wrote an influential article by that name, pointing out the folly of maximizing what *appears* to be individual self-interest, while simultaneously impoverishing the collective welfare. In the article, he used the effective metaphor of individually owned cattle overgrazing a collective pasture or commons. See Garrett Hardin, "The Tragedy of the Commons," *Science,* 162 (1968): 1243–48.

7. World Commission on Environment and Development, *Our Common Future* (Oxford: Oxford University Press, 1987).

8. Peter Wallison and Robert Litan, *The GAAP Gap: Corporate Disclosure in the Internet Age* (Washington D.C.: American Enterprise Institute/Brookings Joint Center for Regulatory Studies, 2000).

9. Baruch Lev, *Intangibles: Measurement, Management, and Reporting* (Washington, D.C.: The Brookings Institution Press, 2001).

10. Wallison and Litan, *op. cit.*, p. 74.

11. To the best of my knowledge, the metaphor and concept of the "Iceberg Balance Sheet" were first introduced in my previous book, *The 11 Commandments of 21ˢᵗ Century Management* (Englewood Cliffs, NJ: Prentice Hall, 1996).

12. Baruch Lev, *op. cit.*

13. See, for example, Bauer *et al.*, "The Eco-Efficiency Premium Puzzle in the U.S. Equity Market," *Financial Analysts Journal* 61 (2005); K. Gluck and Y. Becker, "The Impact of Eco-Efficiency Alphas," *Journal of Asset Management* 5 (2005); West LB Panmure Bank, *More Gain Than Pain: Sustainability Pays Off* (2002) and *From Economics to Sustainomics: SRI—Investment Style with a Future* (2002); UBS Warburg, *Sustainability Investment: The Merits of Socially Responsible Investment* (2001); Bank Sarasin, *Sustainable Investments: and Analysis of Returns in Relation to Environmental and Social Criteria* (1999); and *Environmental Shareholder Value* (1998). It is to be hoped that a group of recent breakthrough reports, such as those from the UN Environment Program's Finance Initiative and from Mercer Investment Consulting and the Freshfields law firm, will go some distance toward putting these shibboleths to rest. We shall discuss them in Chapter 8.

Chapter 2. What's *Taken* Us So Long? The Power of Intellectual and Organizational Inertia

1. Having said that, however, there is a slight irony here to which I must confess. While the quotation itself is quite accurate (and one with which I heartily concur), it actually represents something of a somewhat belated, Damascene conversion by this particular firm in 2008, after a decade or more of consistent denial and resistance. At the end of the day, however, we can only say: "much better late than never; welcome to the party!" With the conspicuous exception of Mercer Investment Consulting, however, which we will examine in Chapter 10, this unfortunately remains a fairly *atypical* view in the investment consulting world today.

2. We shall return to modern portfolio theory in Chapter 5.

3. Lars Hassel and Henrik Nilsson, "An Empirical Study of the Actual Use of Environmental Information by Financial Analysts" (MISTRA; Umea School of Business, 2006).

4. European Centre for Corporate Engagement, "Use of Extra-Financial Information by Research Analysts and Investment Managers" (March 2007).

5. Innovest Strategic Value Advisors, Risk Management Institute, University of Toronto, *Finance and the Environment in North America* (2005).

6. We shall explore this body of evidence in depth in Chapter 4.

7. See Burton Malkiel, "Reflections on the Efficient Markets Hypothesis: 30 Years Later," *Financial Review* 40 (February 2005): 1–9.

8. See, for example, Innovest Strategic Value Advisors, *Carbon Beta and Equity Price Performance* (2008).

9. There is often a second, equally vacuous basis for declaring a company well managed: the CEO is a "good guy."

10. Michael Mauboussin, *More Than You Know: Finding Financial Wisdom in Unconventional Places* (New York: Columbia University Press, 2006), p. 136.

11. *Wall Street Journal,* "Best on the Street Analyst Survey" (March 18, 2008).

Chapter 3. Perverse Outcomes and Lost Opportunities

1. UNJSPF, *Sustainable Development Agenda 21,* p. 4.

2. https://pengval.unjspf.org/UNJSPF_web/page.jsp?role=invest_comm&page =Documents&lang=eng

3. In fairness, it should be acknowledged that this situation may actually be about to change—eventually. The Fund has just issued a request for proposals for advisors to assist it in this regard. It is to be hoped that the organization will indeed follow through with this initiative. At the earliest, however, this would come more than *2 years* after the fund's adoption of the UN Principles for Responsible Investment and at least 10 years after the "oversight" was first publicly brought to its attention—at one of the UN's *own* conferences on sustainable investing!

4. The Global Compact's Principles include two concerning human rights, four for labor standards, three for environment, and one addressing corruption. See www.unglobalcompact.org. Several independent research houses provide research on the level of compliance of companies with the Global Compact Principles.

5. See Appendix 4 for a list of the top 20 independent sustainability research providers, as ranked by the 2007 Thomson Extel survey of institutional investors.

6. http://treasury.worldbank.org/web/worldbanksociallyresponsibleinvestments brief.pdf

7. World Bank, *Sustainability Report,* 2005–2006 (2007).

8. IFC CEO and World Bank Group Executive Vice President Lars Thunell, quoted in *IFC Annual Report 2007,* p. 5.

9. http://pip.worldbank.org

10. Mellon Analytical Solutions. U.S. Public Fund Universe (2008).

11. Stephen Viederman, "Foundations: $600 Billion of Assets That Need to Get Active," *Responsible Investor* (March 14, 2008).

12. Warren Buffet has also stipulated that the proceeds from Berkshire Hathaway shares he still owns at death are to be used for philanthropic purposes within 10 years after his estate has been settled.

13. http://www.latimes.com/news/nationworld/nation/la-na-gatesx07jan07,0, 6827615.story?coll=la-home-headlines

14. Stephen Viederman, *op. cit.*

15. Mellon Analytical Solutions, U.S. Foundation/Endowment Fund Universe (2008).

16. http://www.socialfunds.com/news/article.cgi/article774.html

17. Boston *Globe,* November 22, 2007.

18. One of the curiosities of U.S. corporate law is that most shareholder resolutions are *not* binding upon companies. Examples are legion of resolutions endorsed by a strong

19. *Failed Fiduciaries: Mutual Fund Proxy Voting on CEO Compensation.* Produced by the American Federation of State, County and Municipal Employees (AFSCME), the Corporate Library, and the Shareowner Education Group (2007). AFSCME is the largest union in AFL-CIO; AFL-CIO (2006) *Enablers of Excess: Mutual Funds and the Overpaid American CEO.* Produced by American Federation of State, County and Municipal Employees (AFSCME), AFL-CIO, and the Corporate Library.

20. See, for example, Innovest Strategic Value Advisors, *Carbon Beta and Equity Performance: An Empirical Analysis* (2007).

Chapter 4. But What Does the Evidence *Really* Say?

1. See, for example, Christopher Luck and Nancy Pilotte, "Domini Social Index Performance," *Journal of Investing* (Fall 1993); S. Hamilton and Meyer Statman, "Doing Well by Doing Good: The Investment Performance of Socially Responsible Mutual Funds," *Financial Analysts Journal* (Spring 1993); Lloyd Kurtz and Dan DiBartolomeo, "Socially Screened Portfolios: An Attribution Analysis of Relative Performance," *Journal of Investing* (Fall 1996); and John Guckard, "Is there a Cost to Being Socially Responsible in Investing?," *Journal of Investing* (Summer 1997).

2. See Rob Bauer *et al.,* "The Eco-Efficiency Premium Puzzle in the U.S. Equity Market," *Financial Analysts Journal* 61 (Issue 2, 2005).

3. U.K. Environmental Agency and Innovest Strategic Value Advisors, *Corporate Environmental Governance* (2004).

4. In the interest of full disclosure, SSgA is, along with APG from the Netherlands, a strategic, minority investor in the firm the author leads, Innovest Strategic Value Advisors.

5. K. Gluck and Y. Becker, "Can Environmental Factors Improve Stock Selection," *Journal of Asset Management* 5 (2004): 220. The environmental ratings used to tilt the SSgA portfolio came from Innovest Strategic Value Advisors.

6. J. Derwall, N. Guenster, R. Bauer, and K. Koedijk, "The Eco-efficiency Premium Puzzle," *Financial Analysts Journal* 16 (2005): 51.

7. Bauer Derwall *et al., op. cit.,* p. 61.

8. Alex Edmans, "Does the Stock Market Fully Value Intangibles? Employee Satisfaction and Equity Prices," Wharton School, University of Pennsylvania (January 2008).

9. UNEP FI, *Demystifying Responsible Investment Performance: A Review of Key Academic and Broker Research on ES Factors.* A joint report by the Asset Management Working Group of the United Nations Environmental Program Finance Initiative and Mercer (October 2007).

10. I have heard this statement made, verbatim and at a high-profile public conference, by a senior member of one of Wall Street's leading investment banks. Similar comments by fellow financiers and investment consultants abound.

Chapter 5. Toward a New *Post*modern, Sustainable Portfolio Theory

1. For the financial newcomer, CDOs contain a myriad of individual loan obligations, such as residential mortgages or credit card debt. These individual obligations are then bundled together, "sliced and diced" into new packages of differing risk levels, turned into securities, and then sold to (supposedly) sophisticated investors such as pension funds, insurance companies, and other investment banks. One particularly dangerous subspecies of CDOs that has been featured in the press is the CMBSs—collateralized, mortgage-backed securities. Credit derivatives are simply a rather complex form of insurance against the possible default by companies on the bonds they have sold to investors.

2. In the interests of post-Sarbanes-Oxley transparency and full disclosure, I must confess a shameful secret: in a much earlier life, I was a senior partner of a "Big 4" accounting firm, albeit on the strategy consulting side of the house.

3. Today, the expensing of options is commonplace, with corporate stalwarts such as Coca Cola and General Motors having led the way; this particular accounting assumption will therefore be less problematic going forward. Still, the example does illustrate the profound difference that such assumptions can make.

4. B. Halsey and G. Soybel, "All About Pro Forma Accounting," *The CPA Journal* (April 2002). The numbers cited were from 2001.

5. U.S. Securities and Exchange Commission, "Cautionary Advice Regarding the Use of 'Pro Forma' Financial Information in Earnings Releases" (December 4, 2001).

6. The relevant section of Sarbanes-Oxley was Section 401 (B).

7. See Baruch Lev *et al.*, "Rewriting Earnings History," *Science and Business Media* (2007). For a persuasive examination of the impact of widespread earnings restatements, see W. B. Elliott, "Are Investors Influenced by Pro Forma Emphasis and Reconciliations in Earnings Announcements?," *The Accounting Review* 81 (2007): 113–33. For an analysis of the abuses of pro forma earnings statements, see Kevin James and Franklin Michello, "The Dangers of Pro Forma Reporting," *The CPA Journal* (February 2003) and Fabrice Taylor, "Earnings by Any Other Name," globeinvestor.com 5 (January 2008).

8. Harry Markowitz, "Portfolio Selection," *Journal of Finance* 7 (March 1952): 77–91.

9. Eugene Fama, "The Behaviour of Stock Prices," *Journal of Business* 37 (January 1965): 34–105.

10. J. Stiglitz and S. Grossman, "On the Impossibility of Informationally Efficient Markets," *American Economic Review* 70 (1980): 393–408.

11. "Shorting" is effectively betting that a particular stock or basket of them will go down.

12. See, for example, Daniel Kahneman, Amos Tversky, and Paul Slovic, "Judgment Under Uncertainty," *Science* 185 (1974): 1124–31; Daniel Kahneman and Amos Tversky, "Prospect Theory," *Econometrica* 47 (March 1979); and "Loss Aversion in Riskless Choice," *Quarterly Journal of Economics* 106 (November 1991).

13. Peter Bernstein, quoted in Advisor Perspectives, *Advisor Perspectives* (January 29, 2008).

14. Andrew Lo, "The Adaptive Markets Hypothesis: Market Efficiency from an Evolutionary Perspective," *Journal of Portfolio Management* 30 (2004): 15–29.

15. Baruch Lev, quoted in Alan Webber, "New Math for a New Economy," *Fast Company* (January/February 2000).

16. William H. Donaldson, Remarks to the CFA Institute Annual Conference Philadelphia Pennsylvania (2005).

17. See, for example, T. Stewart, "Brainpower: How Intellectual Capital Is Becoming America's Most Valuable Asset," *FORTUNE* June 3 (1991): 44–60 and *Intellectual Capital: The New Wealth of Organizations* (New York: Doubleday/Currency, 1997); L. Edvinsson and M. Malone, *Intellectual Capital: Realizing Your Company's True Value by Finding Its Hidden Brainpower* (New York: HarperBusiness, 1997); and K.-E. Sveiby, *The New Organizational Wealth: Managing and Measuring Knowledge-Based Assets* (San Francisco: Barrett-Kohler Publishers, 1997).

18. Lev, *op cit.* See also B. Lev and S. Radhakrishan, "The Valuation of Organizational Capital," Working Paper, New York University, Stern School of Business (June 2004). See also J. Low and P. Kalahut, *Invisible Advantage: How Intangibles Are Driving Business Performance* (Cambridge, MA: Perseus Publishing, 2002). Two of the major accounting firms (one since disappeared) also published major reports on the importance of addressing intangible factors. See PricewaterhouseCoopers, *The Value Reporting Revolution: Moving Beyond the Earnings Game* (New York: Wiley, 2000) and Arthur Andersen, *Cracking the Value Code* (New York: Harper Business, 2000).

19. Another popular synonym for these "nontraditional" factors is "extrafinancial." That is, for example, the terminology used by the Enhanced Analytics Initiative, which we shall discuss in Chapter 8. In our view, such terminology is not only inaccurate but actually counterproductive: the entire point of the sustainable investment thesis is that ES factors *are* indeed financially material.

20. Lev, *op. cit.*

21. See A. Rappaport and M. Mauboussin, *Expectations Investing* (Cambridge, MA: Harvard University Press, 2001).

22. I am indebted to Columbia Business School professor (and Legg Mason chief strategist) Michael Mauboussin for insights shared at a presentation to the International Centre for Pension Management, University of Toronto, June 6, 2006.

23. This view has been publicly supported by at least one major, European-based asset manager, Axa Investment Management. See R. Thamotheram, "Money Saver?," *Pensions World* (February 2008): 23–24.

24. Net risk exposures are determined by a complex combination of factors, including the companies' energy source fuel mix, the geographic locations of their production facilities and local regulatory environments, the robustness of their risk management systems, and their company-specific marginal costs of abating CO_2 emissions. Assumptions on the cost/price of carbon have been based on the average of the daily price for the futures contracts for carbon allowances from actual trading in the EU Emissions Trading System over the past 3 years+. In this case, the average expected price was $28 per ton.

25. The relevant accounting regulation is Rule FIN 46R.

26. "Shorting" a security is essentially betting against it.

27. See Innovest Strategic Value Advisors, *Global Banking Report: Retail Lending* (October 2006).

28. See Innovest Strategic Value Advisors, *Global Banking Report: Retail Lending* (October 2006). Emphasis added.

Chapter 6. Why Does It All *Matter* Anyway?
The State of the World

1. Jeffrey Sachs, *Common Wealth: Economics for a Crowded Planet* (New York: Penguin Press, 2008).

2. *Millennium Ecosystem Assessment, Ecosystems and Human Well-Being: Current State and Trends* (Washington, DC: Island Press, 2005).

3. United Nations Environment Program, *Global Environmental Outlook— GEO 4: Environment for Development* (2007).

4. Sachs, *op. cit.*

5. Sachs, *op. cit.*

6. P. Senge *et al., The Necessary Revolution* (New York: Doubleday, 2008).

7. United Nations Development Programme, *Human Development Report 2000* (New York: Oxford University Press, 2000).

8. ILO, *Every Child Counts: New Global Estimates of Child Labour 6,20* (Geneva: ILO, 2001).

9. *Ibid.*

10. United Nations, *The World's Women 2000: Trends and Statistics* (New York: United Nations, 2000).

11. The Coalition to Stop the Use of Child Soldiers. Child Soldiers, Global Report 2008. (London, 2008).

12. World Meteorological Organization. Generally, for this section, JP Morgan, *Watching Water* (April 2008).

13. ITT Industries. Quoted in the *Wall Street Journal* (April 20, 2008).

14. World Bank, *World Development Indicators 2003* (Washington, DC: 2003).

15. Worldwatch calculation based on data. *Ibid.,* pp. 168–69.

16. *Ibid.*

17. *Ibid.*

18. UNEP and the Center for Clouds, Chemistry, and Climate, *The Asian Brown Cloud: Climate and Other Environmental Impacts* (Klong Luang, Thailand: Regional Resource Centre for Asia and the Pacific, UNEP, August 2002), 44.

19. World Bank, *Fuel for Thought: An Environmental Strategy for the Energy Sector* (Washington, DC: June 2000), 98.

20. American Lung Association, *State of the Air,* 2003 (May 2003).

21. B. Ostro and L. Chestnut, *Assessing the Health Benefits of Reducing Particulate Matter Air Pollution in the United States.* Office of Environmental Health Hazard Assessment, California Environmental Protection Agency, Berkeley, California (March 1997).

22. World Resource Institute, *Health Effects of Air Pollution,* 1998–1999. (2000).

23. Earth Policy Institute, *Air Pollution Fatalities Now Exceed Traffic Deaths by 3 to 1* (September 2002).

24. World Health Organization, *WHO Strategy on Air Quality and Health* (revised May 2001).

25. J. M. Holland, M. A. S. Hutchison, B. Smith, and N. J. Aebischer, "A Review of Invertebrates and Seed-Bearing Plants as Food for Farmland Birds in Europe," *Annals of Applied Biology* 148 (2006): 49–71.

26. Mike Holland *et al., Economic Assessment of Crop Yield Losses from Ozone Exposure* (UK: Centre for Ecology and Hydrology, April 2002), 1–2.

27. Fred Pearce, "Smog Crop Damage Costs Billions," *New Scientist* (11 June 2002).

28. *Morbidity and Mortality Weekly Report,* "Surveillance for Asthma," U.S. CDC (2002).

29. Worldwatch Institute, Green Jobs (UN Office in Nairobi, Publishing Services Section: December 21, 2007).

30. The McIlvaine Company, *Houston/Beaumont Air Pollution Control Market and Sales Leads, April 2006.*

31. The Freedonia Group, *Air Pollution Control in China to 2010* (Cleveland 2003).

32. World Health Organization, *World Health Statistics 2008* (WHO Library Cataloguing-in-Publication Data, Geneva, 2008).

33. UNAIDS, *AIDS Epidemic Update 2007* (WHO Library Cataloguing-in-Publication Data, Geneva, December 2007).

34. Cashing in on Climate Change, March 2008 *IBISWorld.*

35. BBC, *The Guide to Life, The Universe and Everything—Waste* (October 2005). http://www.bbc.co.uk/dna/h2g2/A4643787.

36. *Ibid.*

37. Frost & Sullivan, *North American Biomass and Waste to Energy Markets, April* 2007.

38. The Bureau of International Recycling.

39. The International Food Policy Research Institute (2000).

40. G. Fischer, M. Shah, H. van Velthuizen, and F. O. Nachtergaele, *Global Agroecological Assessment for Agriculture in the 21st Century* (Laxenburg, Austria: IIASA, 2001).

41. Sara J. Scherr, "Soil Degradation: A Threat to Developing-Country Food Security by 2020?" 2020 Brief No. 58 (Washington, D.C.: International Food Policy Research Institute, 1999).

42. International Food Policy Research Institute, "Global Study Reveals New Warning Signals:? Degraded Agricultural Lands Threaten World's Food Production Capacity" (Press release, 21 May 2000). http:/ /www.ifpri.org/pressrel/2000/052500.htm.

43. N. W. Arnell *et al.,* "The Consequences of CO2 Stabilisation for the Impacts of Climate Change." *Climate Change.* Volume 53, Number 4/June, 2002 Springer Netherlands; and M. L. Parry *et al.* "Effects of climate change on global food production under SRES emissions and socio-economic scenarios." *Global Environmental Change* 14 (2004): 53–67 Elsevier UK.

44. Sara J. Scherr and Satya Yadav, "Land Degradation in the Developing World: Issues and Policy Options for 2020," 2020 Brief No. 44 (Washington, D.C.: International Food Policy Research Institute, 1997); and Sara J. Scherr, *op. cit.,* 1999.

45. H. E. Dregne, and N. T. Chou, Global desertification dimensions and costs. In *Degradation and Restoration of Arid Lands* (Lubbock: Texas Tech. University, 1992).

46. R. Lal, "Soil Degradation by Erosion," *Land Degradation & Development* 12(6) (2001): 520–39.

47. OECD, OECD Environmental Outlook to 2030 (2008).

48. The World Conservation Union, *Confirming the Global Extinction Crisis* (London, Washington, Geneva, Ottawa, Thursday, 28 September 2000).

49. WWF, *Living Planet Index* (2008).

50. Sachs, *op. cit.*

51. Zeeya Merali, article in *New Scientist* (April 2006).

52. UNEP, *Global Environment Outlook 4 (GEO-4): Environment for Development* (Stevenage, England: Earthprint, 2007).

53. Ecotourism, also known as ecological tourism, is a form of tourism that appeals to ecologically and socially conscious individuals. It typically involves travel to destinations where flora, fauna, and cultural heritage are the primary attractions.

54. Wetland Credits are generated by parcels of land with functional wetland value that serve as ecological capital. This capital may be used in offsetting unavoidable wetland impacts. Wetland banking is the process of tracking and managing these credits. Wetland mitigation banking is used to ensure no net loss of wetland area. Basically, mitigation banking allows developers who damage or destroy wetlands to buy off-site wetlands as compensation.

55. J. Bishop *et al., Building Biodiversity Business: Report of a Scoping Study* (Shell International Limited and the World Conservation Union: London, UK and Gland, Switzerland, 2006: Discussion Draft—September), 58.

Chapter 7. Sustainability and Competitive Advantage: The New Corporate Imperative—and Some Success Stories

1. See, *inter alia,* Chris Laszlo, *Sustainable Value: How the World's Leading Companies Are Doing Well by Doing Good* (Stanford: Stanford University Press, 2008); Peter Senge et al., *The Necessary Revolution* (New York: Doubleday, 2008); Jonathan Lash and Fred Wellington, "Competitive Advantage on a Warming Planet," *Harvard Business Review* (March 2007); Daniel Esty and Andrew Winston, *Green to Gold* (New Haven: Yale University Press, 2007); and J. Keeble et al., *How Leading Companies Are Using Sustainability-Driven Innovation to Win Tomorrow's Customers* (Boston: Arthur D. Little, 2005).

2. New Energy Finance, *Clean Energy League Tables 2007* (February 2008). For two engaging accounts of some of the leading clean technologies and the entrepreneurs behind them, see Fred Krupp and Miriam Horn, *Earth: The Sequel* (New York: Norton & Co., 2008) and Ron Pernick and Clint Wilder, *The Clean Tech Revolution* (New York: Collins Business, 2007).

3. For an excellent overview of the emerging field of carbon finance, consult Sonia Labatt and Rodney White, *Carbon Finance: The Financial Implications of Climate Change* (New York: Wiley, 2007).

4. Point Carbon, March 11, 2008. "Largest Survey Ever Conducted into the World's Carbon Markets." Press release. At the time of writing, Europe had the only legally regulated carbon market in the world, although there are smaller "voluntary" markets elsewhere. As U.S. federal climate policy is expected to become more aggressive regardless of who is president, it can be expected that a more global regulated carbon market will emerge.

5. Two previously high-flying "carbon companies," Agcert and Eco Securities, have hit some extremely rough patches recently. Irish-based Agcert lost over 75 percent of its value and filed for bankruptcy protection in the first quarter of 2008. It has since been bought by U.S. electric utility AES. At its peak, its shares traded in London at over 270 pence per share. When the company was forced to delist in February 2008, its shares had dropped to 68 pence each. Eco Securities' problems, while less severe, have nonetheless been significant. Its share price dropped nearly 50 percent in late 2007 when the company announced that a number of expected project approvals from the UN had not been forthcoming.

6. Carbon funds are sufficiently new that they have not yet really become part of any recognized asset class. However, at least one major and sophisticated institutional investor funded its participation in a carbon fund from its "commodities" asset allocation, so we will categorize them similarly here.

7. Those countries include Poland, the United States, Germany, France, Estonia, China, Greece, Portugal, Spain, Mexico, Brazil, Italy, and the U.K.

8. CSR report, p. 69.

9. For an insightful discussion of fat-tail risk from a former financial trader on Wall Street, see Nassum Nicholas Taleb, *The Black Swan: The Impact of the Highly Improbable* (New York: Random House, 2007).

10. Swiss Re's partner in creating that product was RNK Capital LLC.

11. Access to Medicine Foundation, website.

12. C. K. Prahalad and Stuart Hart, "The Fortune at the Bottom of the Pyramid," *Strategy + Business* 26 (2002): 54–67; C. K. Prahalad, *The Fortune at the Bottom of the Pyramid* (Upper Saddle River, NJ: Wharton School Publishing, 2005).

13. Eric Simanis and Stuart Hart, "Beyond Selling to the Poor: Building Business Intimacy Through Embedded Innovation" (Cornell University, unpublished manuscript, 2008).

Chapter 8. The Game-Changers
Part I: Collective Initiatives

1. See, for example, UNEP-FI Asset Management Working Group, *The Materiality of Social, Environmental, and Corporate Governance Issues to Equity Pricing,* and *Show Me The Money: Linking ES Issues to Company Value* (2004).

2. Freshfields Bruckhouse Deringer, *A Legal Framework for the Integration of ES Issues into Institutional Investment* (2005).

3. UNEP-FI Asset Management Working Group, *Demystifying Responsible Investment Performance* (2007).

4. *Ibid., Responsible Investment in Focus: How Leading Pension Funds Are Meeting the Challenge* (2007).

5. We shall learn more about Climate Change Capital in Chapter 10.

6. *Fortune* 157(4) (March 3, 2008): 52.

7. In the interest of full disclosure, the firm I lead, Innovest Strategic Value Advisors, has been appointed by the CDP Secretariat to write the project's global report in each of the first 5 years of the project's existence.

8. www.cdproject.net/

9. Founding members were AGF Asset Management (France), BNP Paribas Asset Management (FR), MISTRA (Swedish Foundation), PGGM (NL), RCM (U.K.), Deutscher Investment Trust and Dresdner bank investment management (Germany), and Universities Superannuation Scheme (USS) (U.K.).

10. http://www.onvalues.ch/

11. The author was a participant in the "expert group" despite his questionable credentials as an "expert!"

12. Indeed, in a private conversation with the Chief Investment Officer of one major asset owner signatory, I was told flatly that he and his institution had no

intention of actually implementing the Principles, although they were *very* supportive and enthusiastic about them in principle!

Chapter 9. The Game-Changers
Part II: The *Individual* Owners of Capital

1. In the spirit of transparency and full disclosure, I would like to make the following acknowledgment: APG is both a client and a strategic investor in Innovest Strategic Value Advisors, the firm founded and currently led by me. I do not believe, however, that this should in any way invalidate the considerable achievements of this company in this field or disqualify it from inclusion in this chapter on "Game-Changers."

2. Two of the investment professionals who played a catalytic role in putting APG on the path toward sustainability investing were Dr. Rob Bauer and Fred Nieuwland. Both have since left the organization.

3. Quoted in an interview with Hugh Whelan in *Responsible Investor* (October 1, 2007).

4. Personal interview, December 2007.

5. *Ibid.*

6. Andrew Junkin and Thomas Toth, *The "CalPERS Effect" on Targeted Company Share Prices* (Wilshire Associates, 2007).

7. B. M. Barber, "Monitoring the Monitor: Evaluating CalPERS' Activism," Working Paper, Graduate School of Management, University of California at Davis (2006).

8. Unless otherwise noted, details regarding CalSTRS' statement of investment principles are sourced from http://www.calstrs.com/Investments/cginvestresponse .aspx.

9. http://www.calstrs.com/Investments/calstrs_risk_factors.pdf

10. Pg 4, http://www.calstrs.com/Newsroom/What's%20New/GreenInitiative _Exhibits.pdf, pg. 4.

11. Interview, *Business Wire* (September 10, 2007).

12. PGGM website. Emphasis added.

13. http://www.fondsdereserve.fr/IMG/pdf/05_5_SRI_principles_FRR.pdf

14. We shall learn more about SAM in the next chapter.

15. *Institutions and Pensions* (November 13, 2007).

Chapter 10. The Game-Changers
Part III: The Service Providers

1. Islamic screens are increasingly popular today, as a growing number of Muslims seek to align their investment strategies with their religious values. So-called "Shariah-compliant" funds are not unlike the negatively screened socially responsible investing (SRI) funds in avoiding alcohol and gambling; however, in addition, they do not invest in pork-related businesses and financial institutions charging interest (i.e., 99 percent of conventional Western banks). The Islamic investment market is already at $400 billion and has an annual growth rate of 20 percent.

2. In the interests of full disclosure and transparency, the author was a member of the CCC's initial external advisory board.

3. This occurs through one of the most important mechanisms of the Kyoto Protocol—the Clean Development Mechanism (CDM). Under the CDM, companies in developed countries can earn "carbon credits" by financing and participating in projects in emerging markets that achieve greenhouse gas reductions that are judged to be incremental—that is, over and above those that would have occurred under a "business-as-usual" scenario.

4. Interview in *Environmental Finance* (March 2008), p. 10.

5. Once again, in the interests of full disclosure and transparency for the reader, the author was also a contributor to this group.

6. In 2005 a review of over 30 sustainability research providers prepared for the Swedish environmental foundation MISTRA judged that Innovest had the "best research methodology" and "highest quality analysis." In both 2006 and 2007 Innovest was rated first in the Thomson Extel survey of over 180 institutional investors with combined assets of over $2 trillion. The firm won a special award in 2007 from the UN Environment Program's Finance Initiative for "innovation and contributions to the emerging field of carbon finance."

Chapter 11. Making It Happen

1. Appendix 4 contains a list of the top 20 independent research providers according to the 2007 Thomson Extel survey of over 180 major institutional investors.

2. Indeed, in the case of price/earnings ratios, as we saw in Chapter 5, the historical evidence suggests that they are actually much *less* useful than high-quality sustainability research.

3. Readers may have noted that we have deliberately dropped the "G" (corporate governance) from the commonly used acronym ESG. "Strategic governance," as we use the term here, refers to company executives' and boards' governance *of sustainability issues* and to how the company is organized to deal with them.

4. Figures 11.2 and 11.3 were both constructed by David Reynard, a former head of quantitative analysis at Deutsche Asset Management. I would like to acknowledge and thank him for this contribution.

5. See R. Bauer et al., "The Eco-Efficiency Premium Puzzle in the U.S. Equity Market," *Financial Analysts Journal* 61(2) (2005): 51–63; K. Gluck and Y. Becker, "The Impact of Eco-Efficiency Alphas," *Journal of Asset Management* 5(4) (2005).

6. The period selected was chosen because the first significant carbon-restricting regulation took place in Europe only in 2005. Therefore it is most likely that the market started capturing the climate change effects on the perceived value and risk of a company and sector at this time. For the purposes of this study, "top carbon performers" were defined as those achieving an Innovest Carbon Beta™ rating of BBB "investment grade" or better.

Chapter 12. Some Final Thoughts

1. When at his previous law firm, Watchman was the lead author of the influential "Freshfields report" on the evolution of the concept of fiduciary responsibility, which we discussed in Chapter 8.

2. However, the Norwegian Government I now, to its credit, having an active and thoughtful debate about whether to take this next step forward.

References

Ambachtsheer, Keith (2007) *Pension Revolution: A Solution for the Pensions Crisis.* New York: John Wiley & Sons.

_____ (2005) "Reflections: Beyond Portfolio Theory—the Next Frontier." *Financial Analysts Journal,* 61(1), 29–33.

_____ and D. Ezra (1998) *Pension Fund Excellence: Creating Value for Stakeholders.* New York: John Wiley & Sons.

Bauer, Rob et al. (2005) "The Eco-Efficiency Premium Puzzle in the U.S. Equity Market." *Financial Analysts Journal,* 61(2), 51–62.

Bernstein, Peter L. (2007) *Capital Ideas Evolving.* Hoboken, NJ: John Wiley & Sons.

Bogle, Jack (2005) *The Battle for the Soul of Capitalism.* New Haven: Yale Univ. Press.

CERES (2006) *Corporate Governance and Climate Change: Making the Connection.* Boston: CERES.

Christensen, Clayton et al. (2004) *Seeing What's Next.* Boston: Harvard School Press.

Daum, Juergen H. (2003) *Intangible Assets and Value Creation.* Chichester, UK: John Wiley & Sons.

D'Aveni, Richard A. (1994) *Hyper-Competition: Managing the Dynamics of Strategic Maneuvering.* New York: Macmillan.

Davis, Stephen, J. Lukomnik, and D. Pitt-Wilson (2006) *The New Capitalists: How Citizen Investors are Reshaping the Corporate Agenda.* Boston: Harvard Business School Press.

Drucker, Peter (1993) *Post-Capitalist Society.* New York: HarperCollins.

Edmans, A. (2007) "Does the Market Fully Value Intangibles? Employee Satisfaction and Equity Prices." Working Paper, Wharton School of Business, Univ. of Pennsylvania.

Edvinsson, Leif and Michael S. Malone (1997) *Intellectual Capital.* New York: HarperCollins.

Esty, Daniel and Andrew Winston (2006) *Green to Gold: How Smart Companies Use Environmental Strategy to Innovate, Create Value, and Build Competitive Advantage.* New Haven: Yale Univ. Press.

Freshfields Bruckhaus Deringer (2005) *A Legal Framework for the Integration of ESG Issues into Institutional Investment.* London: United Nations Environment Program Finance Initiative.

Gluck, Kim and Ying Becker (2005) "The Impact of Eco-Efficiency Alphas." *Journal of Asset Management,* 5(4), 220–222.

Hamel, Gary and C.K. Pralahad (1994) *Competing for the Future.* Boston: Harvard Business School Press.

Hamel, Gary and L. Valikangas (2003) "The Quest for Resilience." *Harvard Business Review,* September, 22–29.

Hart, Stuart (2007) *Capitalism at the Crossroads: Aligning Business, Earth, and Humanity.* Philadelphia: Wharton School Publishing.

Hawley, J., and Williams A (2006) The Universal Owner's Role in Sustainable Economic Development." In R. Sullivan and C. Mackenzie (eds.) *Responsible Investment, Greensleaf Publishing.* Sheffield, UK: Greensleaf Publishing.

_____ (2000) *The Rise of Fiduciary Capitalism.* Philadelphia: Univ. of Pennsylvania Press.

Institutional Investors Group on Climate Change et al. (2006) *A Climate for Change.* London: Institutional Investors Group.

Kiernan, Matthew (2005) "Climate Change, Investment Risk, and Fiduciary Responsibility." In K. Tang, *The Finance of Climate Change.* London. Middlesex University Press, 56-74.

_____ (2005) "A New Long-Term View." *Pensions & Investments,* January 10.

_____ (2004) "Sustainable Development." In G. Dallas (ed.) *Governance and Risk.* New York: McGraw-Hill, 216–232.

_____ (2003) "What Lies Beneath: Intangible Value and the Iceberg Balance Sheet." *Investments and Pensions Europe,* February.

_____ (1996) *The Eleven Commandments of 21st Century Management.* Englewood Cliffs, NJ: Prentice Hall.

Krupp, Fred and Miriam Horn (2008) *Earth: The Sequel.* New York: W.W. Norton.

Lev, Baruch (2001) *Intangibles: Management, Measurement and Reporting.* Washington, DC: Brookings Institute.

Lev, Baruch and John Hand (2003) *Intangible Assets: Values, Measures, and Risks.* New York: Oxford Univ. Press.

Low, Jonathan and Pam Kalafut (2002) *Invisible Advantage: How Intangibles Are Driving Business Performance.* Boston: Perseus Publishing.

Malkiel, Burton G. (2007) *A Random Walk Down Wall Street.* New York: W.W. Norton.

Mauboussin, Michael (2008) "The Sociology of Markets." *Mauboussin on Strategy.* Legg Mason Capital Management, July 15.

_____ (2006) *More Than You Know: Finding Financial Wisdom in Unconventional Places.* New York: Columbia Univ. Press.

Monks, R (2006) "Companies Run in Shareholders' Long-Term Interests Also Serve Society's Long-Term Interests." In R. Sullivan and C. Mackenzie (eds.) *Responsible Investment.* Sheffield, UK: Greensleaf Publishing, 226–241.

_____ (2002) *The New Global Investors.* Oxford, UK: Capstone Publishing.

Pfau, Bruce and I. Kay (2002) *The Human Capital Edge.* New York: McGraw-Hill.

Pralahad, C.K. (2005) *The Fortune at the Bottom of the Pyramid.* Upper Saddle River, NJ: Wharton School Publishing.

Rappaport, Alfred and Michael Mauboussin (2001) *Expectations Investing.* Boston: Harvard Univ. School Press.

Sachs, Jeffrey D. (2008) *Common Wealth.* New York: Penguin.

Sakaiya, Taichi (1991) *The Knowledge-Value Revolution.* Tokyo: Kodansha.

Senge, Peter (2008) *The Necessary Revolution: How Individuals and Organizations Are Working Together to Create a Sustainable World.* New York: Doubleday.

Siegel, Jeremy J. (2005) *The Future for Investors.* New York: Random House.

Simanis, E. and S. Hart (2008) "Beyond Selling to the Poor: Building Business Intimacy Through Embedded Innovation." Unpublished manuscript, Cornell Univ.

Index